SEXUAL DIFFERENCE, GENDER, AND AGENCY IN KARL BARTH'S *CHURCH DOGMATICS*

T&T Clark Explorations in Reformed Theology

Series Editors
Paul T. Nimmo
Paul Dafydd Jones

Editorial Board
Christophe Chalamet
David A. S. Fergusson
Angela Dienhart Hancock
Leanne Van Dyk
Matthias D. Wüthrich

Volume II

SEXUAL DIFFERENCE, GENDER, AND AGENCY IN KARL BARTH'S *CHURCH DOGMATICS*

Faye Bodley-Dangelo

LONDON • NEW YORK • OXFORD • NEW DELHI • SYDNEY

T&T CLARK

Bloomsbury Publishing Plc

50 Bedford Square, London, WC1B 3DP, UK
1385 Broadway, New York, NY 10018, USA
29 Earlsfort Terrace, Dublin 2, Ireland

BLOOMSBURY, T&T CLARK and the T&T Clark logo are
trademarks of Bloomsbury Publishing Plc

First published in Great Britain 2020
This paperback edition published in 2021

Copyright © Faye Bodley-Dangelo, 2020

Faye Bodley-Dangelo has asserted her right under the Copyright, Designs
and Patents Act, 1988, to be identified as Author of this work.

For legal purposes the Acknowledgments on p. ix constitute an
extension of this copyright page.

Cover design © Anna Berzovan

All rights reserved. No part of this publication may be reproduced
or transmitted in any form or by any means, electronic or mechanical,
including photocopying, recording, or any information storage or retrieval
system, without prior permission in writing from the publishers.

Bloomsbury Publishing Plc does not have any control over, or responsibility for,
any third-party websites referred to or in this book. All internet addresses given
in this book were correct at the time of going to press. The author and publisher
regret any inconvenience caused if addresses have changed or sites have ceased
to exist, but can accept no responsibility for any such changes.

A catalogue record for this book is available from the British Library.

Library of Congress Cataloging-in-Publication Data
Names: Bodley-Dangelo, Faye, author.
Title: Sexual difference, gender, and agency in Karl Barth's Church dogmatics /
by Faye Bodley-Dangelo.
Description: 1 [edition]. | New York : T&T Clark, 2019. | Series: T&T Clark
explorations in reformed theology | Includes bibliographical references and index.
Identifiers: LCCN 2019020060 (print) | ISBN 9780567679307 (hardback)
Subjects: LCSH: Barth, Karl, 1886-1968. Kirchliche Dogmatik. | Theology, Doctrinal. |
Sex–Religious aspects–Christianity. | Theological anthropology–Christianity.
Classification: LCC BT75.B286 B63 2019 (print) | LCC BT75.B286 (ebook) | DDC 233/.5–dc23
LC record available at https://lccn.loc.gov/2019020060
LC ebook record available at https://lccn.loc.gov/2019980124

ISBN:	HB:	978-0-5676-7930-7
	PB:	978-0-5676-9828-5
	ePDF:	978-0-5676-7931-4
	ePUB:	978-0-5676-7932-1

Typeset by Integra Software Services Pvt. Ltd.

To find out more about our authors and books visit www.bloomsbury.com
and sign up for our newsletters.

To Suzannah Gail Bodley

CONTENTS

Acknowledgments	ix
INTRODUCTION	1
Tracking ordered binaries	2
Tracking the human agent	8
Scope and outline of the argument	14
Chapter 1	
REHABILITATING THE AGENT OF THEOLOGICAL DISCOURSE	19
Introduction	19
Bad epistemic habits of the modern subject	20
The humbled and hopeful doer of theology	23
Mary and Elizabeth as model agents	32
Conclusion	34
Chapter 2	
PLAYING THE NEIGHBOR IN AN "ORDER OF PRAISE"	37
Introduction	37
The neighbor within the "orders of creation"	39
The neighbor within an "order of praise"	45
The Good Samaritan as a model neighbor	49
The Jewish Samaritan and the *völkisch* church	55
Conclusion	59
Chapter 3	
REORIENTING THE AGENT IN THE DOCTRINE OF CREATION	61
Introduction	61
Myth, maternity, and sexual difference in contemporaneous scholarship	64
Christ concealed in the first article	68
Myth-critique and matriarchal repression in Genesis 1	74
Sexual difference and divine likeness in Genesis 1	76
Conclusion	80
Chapter 4	
PLAYING ADAM AND SILENCING EVE	83
Introduction	83
Freedom, masculinity, and Genesis 2	88

Adam as a model agent	90
Constraining Eve	101
Re-animating Eve	106
Conclusion	110

Chapter 5
REORIENTING THE AGENT OF A THEOLOGICAL ANTHROPOLOGY — 113

Introduction	113
A christocentric method	118
The love of God	120
The love of neighbor	123
The sexually differentiated neighbor	137
Conclusion	144

Chapter 6
AN ETHIC FOR THE SEXUALLY DIFFERENTIATED SELF — 149

Introduction	149
The agent in a divine command ethic	150
Ethical guidelines for securing sexual difference	155
Ethical guidelines for ordering the sexual relationship	165
Conclusion	173

CONCLUSION — 175

Disentangling the agent from a sexist order	175
Disentangling the agent from a heteronormative framework	177
Interrogating gender norms	180

Bibliography	182
Index	191

ACKNOWLEDGMENTS

This book is a revision of my ThD dissertation at Harvard Divinity School, which began under the guidance of Ronald F. Thiemann. Ron died before the first chapter was written, but his guidance through the first stages of my research left an indelible mark upon the project. I would like to give a special word of thanks to my dissertation committee. Amy Hollywood, my dissertation director, introduced me to the trajectory of gender theory that has deeply shaped my work. Offering critical feedback and editing on multiple drafts, she patiently guided the project from its earliest stages. Francis X. Clooney, S. J. gently and persistently nudged me toward a more charitable and constructive reading of Barth. Paul Dafydd Jones joined my committee after Ron's death. Without his enthusiasm, support, and indispensable guidance, I would not have stayed the course. He has given generously of his time to reading, editing, and providing critical feedback from the first chapter of the dissertation to the book's final manuscript.

This project has been deeply enriched and shaped by the intellectual life and community at Harvard Divinity School. I must give a special word of thanks to Emily Click, for the encouragement, friendship, and pastoral care she has given me and my family over these past years. Sarah Coakley was a theological mentor in the nascent stages of this project and profoundly shaped my critical engagement with theological texts. I am grateful to Jon Levenson, Kevin Madigan, and Ahmed Ragab for their support of my theological and professional development. A number of colleagues have been a source of encouragement and comradery along the way, among them, Brad Bannon, Philip Francis, Nan Hutton, Piotr Malysz, Mark McInroy, Mark Scott, Jen Wade, and Bryan Wagoner.

Beyond Harvard's community, I recall with gratitude the influence of several teachers whose courses, mentoring, and guidance directed me on the path of study that has culminated in this project. The late Donald Bowdle of Lee University first introduced me to reformed systematic theology and to the writings of Karl Barth. Kurt Richardson further supported this interest and guided my first foray into the topic of gender in Barth's theology, in the form of a master's thesis at Gordon-Conwell Theological Seminary, where I was first introduced to feminist hermeneutics by the late Catherine Kroeger. Khaled Anatolios guided my research into the late antiquity trinitarian and christological texts that have provided the theological framework for this project.

I have deeply benefitted from conversations with members of a community of Barth scholars whom I have met at many conferences and meetings over the past decade, among them George Hunsinger, Bruce McCormack, David Congdon, and Travis McMaken, and especially Kaitlyn Dugan, Gillian Breckenridge, and Kendall Cox. I was given invaluable opportunities to present portions of this project at the

Karl Barth Society of North America's annual meeting at the American Academy of Religion in 2014 and 2016, and also at the Karl Barth Conference hosted by Princeton Theological Seminary in 2014 and 2018. The process of revising the dissertation into a book has been an extremely positive one thanks to the encouragement, support, careful editing, and feedback of Paul Dafydd Jones and Paul T. Nimmo, editors of T&T Clark Explorations in Reformed Theology series to which this book belongs. I am deeply grateful to both of them for the opportunity to bring this project of many years to publication.

My husband, Mike, has been an enduring source of encouragement, support, and love, and a critical dialogue partner at every stage. He never gave up on my ability to complete this work, even when I did. Our daughter, Suzannah, has provided much-needed distraction, with her persistent, sunny interruptions and joyful exuberance. The friendship, comradery, and challenging debates with my dear friend Marta Napiorkowska have sustained me through the long writing process. I also want to thank Maggie Mulqueen for continually urging me to bring this project to completion.

Finally, I want to thank my parents, Sue and Lawrence Bodley. My father, who first introduced me to theological texts as a child, deeply engrained in me the interests that set me on this theological trajectory, and he passed on to me his own set of *Church Dogmatics* before this project began. My mother's character, fortitude, and her thoughtful critical spirit are a constant inspiration, as are her optimism, patience, and love. I dedicate this book to her.

Portions of this book appear in print elsewhere. I gratefully acknowledge permission to incorporate into Chapter 2 my essay "The Jewish Samaritan: Karl Barth's Ethical Critique of the *Völkisch* Church," in *Karl Barth: Post-Holocaust Theologian?*, T&T Clark Theology, edited by George Hunsinger (London: T&T Clark, an imprint of Bloomsbury Publishing Plc, 2018) 55–66. Chapters 5 and 6 include components of my essay "Barth and Gender," in *The Oxford Handbook of Karl Barth*, edited by Paul T. Nimmo & Paul D. Jones (forthcoming 2019), ©, by permission of Oxford University Press. www.oup.com.

INTRODUCTION

In recent decades, Barth's theology has invited a variety of nonfoundational and postmodern theological readings and appropriations. It has been used as a resource for theological projects that refuse central foundational principles, that are open to multiple and contextual ways of knowing, that resist bringing multiple sites of particularity under a single, totalizing, universal framework.[1] Yet when it comes to Barth's sexist and heteronormative conception of sexual difference obstacles and limits to such readings arise, and these have yet to be carefully analyzed. For at the heart of his theological anthropology and its accompanying special ethics Barth situates a binary, hierarchically ordered, marital relationship between a man and woman as the norm for conceptualizing not only sexual difference but all inter-subjective relationships among human beings. Human beings find in the opposite sex their paradigmatic human "other," and marriage to someone of the opposite sex provides the occasion in which one is able most fully to realize the sort of being-in-encounter that conforms to the self-giving, self-revealing, covenantal relationship that Christ has established with the Christian community. The asymmetry of the relationship between Christ and his community likewise finds an analogy in an ordering between the sexes wherein men lead, direct, and inspire women, and this ordering applies not only in marriage but across all interactions between the sexes and thus has significant political and domestic implications. In Barth's special ethics this ordering underlies his

1. The result has been comparative analyses with figures like Derrida, Levinas, and Wittgenstein, among them: Steven G. Smith, *The Argument to the Other: Reason beyond Reason in the Thought of Karl Barth and Emmanuel Levinas* (Chico, CA: Scholars Press, 1983); Stephen H. Webb, *Re-Figuring Theology: The Rhetoric of Karl Barth* (Albany: State University of New York Press, 1991); Walter Lowe, *Theology and Difference: The Wound of Reason* (Bloomington: University Press, 1993); Graham Ward, *Barth, Derrida and the Language of Theology* (Cambridge: Cambridge University Press, 1995); Isolde Andrews, *Deconstructing Barth: A Study of the Complementary Methods in Karl Barth and Jacques Derrida* (New York: Lang, 1996); William Stacy Johnson, *The Mystery of God: Karl Barth and the Postmodern Foundations of Theology* (Louisville: Westminster John Knox Press, 1997).

recommendation that women in abusive relationships should inspire men to better behavior through quiet self-restraint. This ordering manifests also in his depiction of the feminist movement as an envious grasping after the God-given agential prerogative of men. It is not surprising, then, that Barth has often been viewed as a poster-child for modern patriarchal theologies and, more recently, for heterosexist and complementarian theologies.

Tracking ordered binaries

These features of Barth's theological anthropology have evoked a great deal of criticism and been subjected to a number of reconstructive interventions, which, until relatively recently, have focused on Barth's ordering of the sexes but not the heteronormativity of his theological anthropology. Many critics appreciate the central place that Barth's theological anthropology gives to the relationships between the sexes and direct their critical and reconstructive energies to his subordination of women to men. They examine the ways in which Barth grounds the ordering between the sexes in a recurring pattern of asymmetrical ordered relationships and his selection and interpretation of biblical texts to support this ordering. This dominant approach takes its cue from Barth's references to an "analogy of relations," in which he speaks of a correspondence in a series of relationships: Father and Son *ad intra*, Father and Son *ad extra*, Christ's divinity and Christ's humanity, God and humanity, Yahweh and Israel, Christ and Church, heaven and earth, soul and body, and so forth. The driving question from this vantage point is whether the hierarchical ordering of the male–female relationship is the unavoidable symptom of a pervasive pattern of asymmetrical ordering that favors one party over the other, or whether some of these relationships offer alternative resources for re-imagining an egalitarian mutual interaction between the sexes. This question has given rise to two trajectories of critique, one that locates internal resources for a constructive reconfiguration of Barth's ordering of the sexes, and another that argues that even such resources are too deeply distorted by his systemic ordering.

The first trajectory finds in one or more of the binary, asymmetrical dyads of Barth's "analogy of relations," a reciprocity and mutuality, a shared give-and-take, between partners that could correct Barth's rigid hierarchical sexual binary. The immanent trinitarian relationship (the eternal relational movement and fellowship between the persons of the Trinity) is seen by many as the most fruitful site for serving this reconstructive end. Barth develops his doctrine of the Trinity in the first volume of *Church Dogmatics*. Although Barth says very little in the third volume's theological anthropology about the correspondence between this inter-trinitarian relationship and inter-human relationships, the very fact that he draws an analogy between them, and that he even links the *imago dei* of Genesis 1 to the relationship between the sexes, is considered warrant enough for the trinitarian relationship to serve as *the* corrective for reconfiguring Barth's ordering of the sexes.

These critics privilege the relationship between Father and Son as articulated in *Church Dogmatics* I for a number of reasons: the inter-trinitarian relationship is seen to occupy the highest rung on the ontological ladder of Barth's "analogy of relations"; the relational partners inhabit the same ontological plane; Barth maintains an orthodox rejection of any subordination in being or activity in the immanent economy of Father, Son, and Holy Spirit; and Barth speaks of a perichoretic exchange among the triune "persons," entailing a mutual interpenetration and exchange of functions, wherein each participates fully in the electing, creating, saving activity of the others.

The claim is that this equality in being and exchange of function could be used to reconfigure Barth's rigid distinction and hierarchy in the roles, characteristics, and functions distinguishing the sexes. Leading and following, however these may play out in everyday life, cannot be assigned strictly to any one sex, if the perichoretic participation of each triune person in the activity of the other is the primary analogue. If Barth can recognize the full humanity of both men and women, and if he can speak of a mutuality and reciprocity between the sexes (and he does both), then the immanent trinitarian relation provides a corrective that secures an egalitarian relationship between the sexes.[2]

---

2. Most book-length projects and dissertations on the topic of sexual difference in Barth's theology come to the conclusion that the immanent Trinitarian relation offers a corrective to an otherwise pervasive problematic ordering. Cynthia M. Campbell ("*Imago Trinitatis*: An Appraisal of Karl Barth's Doctrine of the *Imago dei* in Light of His Doctrine of the Trinity" [PhD diss., Southern Methodist University, 1981]) wants to retrieve the perichoretic reciprocity between Father and Son in *CD* I to correct the problematic sequence of first and second actors that follows Barth's revamping of the doctrine of election in *CD* II, where he incorporates the ordering between God and creature into the immanent trinitarian life (see esp. 95–138). Yet she suspects Barth's problematic ordering pervades his entire *Dogmatics*, embedded in a doctrine of revelation driven by a commanding divine actor and an obedient human responder. Elizabeth Frykberg (*Karl Barth's Theological Anthropology: An Analogical Critique regarding Gender Relations* [Princeton: Princeton Theological Seminary, 1993]) recognizes that Christ is the primary analogue for the ordering of the sexes. Christ (qua Son) participates in two different relational orderings: the unilateral perichoretic relationship between Father and Son and the hierarchal relationship between God and humankind. Barth wants both patterns of order to play out in the relationship between the sexes, and so he subordinates women to men while at the same time insisting that this entails no diminishment of the dignity of women in an otherwise reciprocal relationship of interpersonal exchange. Her corrective is to retain both types of orderings within inter-human relationships by assigning the hierarchical order to the relationship between parent and child alone, while the sexes follow the trinitarian order of mutual exchange (51–2). A number of article-length assessments agree that the trinitarian perichoretic relationships of *CD* I can correct Barth's rigid, undialectical ordering of the sexes, by allowing a dialectical reconfiguration wherein male and female identity interpenetrate, and attributes and functions—including authority and leadership—are shared (Alexander J. McKelway,

In this interpretive trajectory, critics often link the immanent trinitarian relationship, laid out in the first volume of *Church Dogmatics*, with Barth's detailed discussion of inter-human fellowship between an "I" and a "Thou" found in his third volume's theological anthropology. There Barth employs the phenomenology of dialogical personalism to describe human fellowship as an interaction of mutual seeing, hearing, speaking, and aid-lending, and he makes no mention of a hierarchical ordering when he describes the reciprocity of the shared give-and-take between "I" and "Thou." Some find this mutuality and fluidity to be analogous to the perichoretic relation between Father and Son. Only thereafter does Barth name the relationship between the sexes as the site in which such an exchange is most fully realized, in all its reciprocity and mutuality, but critics find that he goes on to compromise this insight when he imposes upon this mutual relationship an order in which men lead, initiate, and inspire.

Many suspect that this compromise results because Barth wants the relationship between the sexes to correspond not only to the mutuality and reciprocity of the immanent trinitarian fellowship but also to relationships that embed the ontological distinction between God and humankind, with its unavoidable hierarchical order. Barth wants to secure in human fellowships not only an analogy of the relation between Father and Son, but also (and with a greater emphasis in his account) an analogy between Yahweh's relationship to Israel and, above all, Christ's relationship to the Church. The proposed corrective therefore requires both an emphasis on the role of the immanent Trinity in shaping and correcting Barth's theological anthropology, and a corresponding de-emphasis of the christological shape that his anthropology takes.[3]

"Perichoretic Possibilities in Barth's Doctrine of Male and Female," *Princeton Seminary Bulletin* 7, no. 3 [January 1986]: 231–43; Paul S. Fiddes, "The Status of Woman in the Thought of Karl Barth," in *After Eve: Women, Theology and the Christian Tradition*, ed. Janet Martin Soskice [London: Marshal Pickering, 1990], 138–53, 150–3, esp. 148–9; Timothy J. Gorringe, *Karl Barth: Against Hegemony* [Oxford: Oxford University Press, 1999], 197–207; Jason Springs, "Following at a Distance (Again): Gender, Equality, and Freedom in Karl Barth's Theological Anthropology," *Modern Theology* 28, no. 3 [July 2012]: 447–77).

3. Not all who seek internal resources to reconfigure the relationship between the sexes agree that the doctrine of the Trinity provides the corrective, for some argue that the ordering of the analogy of relations corrupts even his doctrine of the Trinity in *CD* I. Lisa P. Stephenson ("Directed, Ordered and Related: The Male and Female Interpersonal Relation in Karl Barth's *Church Dogmatics*," *SJT* 61, no. 4 [2008]: 435–49) argues that Barth's doctrine of the Trinity in *CD* I provides the analogical grounding for Barth's later ordering of the sexes, in its ordering of origin and sequence, which Barth later uses to subordinate women in his reading of Eve's creation. Barth's reformulation of the doctrine of election serves to further support the trinitarian basis for his ordering of the sexes when it all but collapses the economic Trinity into the immanent Trinity, embedding the ontological distinction between Creator and creature (and its order of origins) in the eternal electing will and

This proposed corrective, however, has some significant limitations. If it intends to correct Barth on his own terms and within his own methodological framework, the trinitarian corrective is a tricky intervention, for Barth's christocentric methodological commitments keep the distinction between God and humankind at the center of his theological anthropology. Barth constructs his theological anthropology from a christology that embeds the ontological distinction between God and humankind in the being and existence of Christ. Christ's human existence is directed and governed by the activity and identity of the triune Son, and so the ordering that critics problematize is embedded in the christology that shapes his theological anthropology. Barth depicts human agency as a response to, and imitation of, Christ's existence. He correspondingly makes very limited references to the analogy between inter-human relations and immanent trinitarian relations as he develops his anthropology. Furthermore, this approach fails adequately to recognize that the analogical connection Barth draws between the *imago dei* and the Trinity does not forge a direct connection between inter-human relations and inter-divine relations (uncomplicated by the incarnation), for Barth identifies the *imago dei* specifically with the humanity of Christ, which is bound from eternity to the electing Son. Barth's connection of the *imago dei* with the relationship between the sexes is thus a christological connection. Because Barth builds his theological anthropology upon this christology, the incarnation keeps the relationship

---

communion of Father and Son. Thus Stephenson locates the problem in the Trinity itself when its ordering and sequence are analogically imposed onto sexual difference. But she sees hope in the reciprocal exchange between "I" and "Thou" in Barth's account of inter-human fellowship, found in *CD* §45.2. Elouise Renich Fraser ("Karl Barth's Doctrine of Humanity: A Reconstructive Exercise in Feminist Narrative Theology," PhD diss., Vanderbilt University, 1986; Fraser, "Jesus' Humanity and Ours in the Theology of Karl Barth," in *Perspectives on Christology: Essays in Honor of Paul K. Jewett*, ed. Marguerite Shuster, et al. [Grand Rapids: Zondervan, 1991], 179–96) goes a step further than Stephenson, arguing that not only the ordering of the immanent Trinity but even the ordering of "I" to "Thou" in §45.2 is distorted by an asymmetrical power differential that corrupts Barth's entire doctrine of creation and its hierarchically arranged dyadic relationships. The irreversible priority of Father over Son, God over creature, and man over woman, is reiterated in the priority of "I" over "Thou" in §45.2: Barth depicts the "I" as first to act upon the "Thou," rather than as one who is acted upon or imposed upon by the "Thou." Her corrective is an alternate pattern of order, one that prioritizes the "other," which she finds in Barth's ethical configuration of the neighbor in *CD* I/2, §18 and in his depiction of Christ's relationship to his community (§45.1). Here the human agent is imposed upon by the needs and activity of the other and obligated to respond accordingly. While I too will find in §18 and §45.1 an agential corrective to Barth's ordering of the sexes, I will show that this reconfigured pattern of agency is far more widespread than Fraser recognizes: from *CD* I onward, it is embedded in multiple images of the subject's relationship to divine and creaturely alterity, and it can be seen in the relationship of "I" to "Thou" in §45.2 as well.

between Creator and human creature at the center of his theological anthropology, and with it the subordination of human agency to divine agency. Consequently, a trinitarian corrective would seem to require a complete revamping of Barth's theological anthropology and the doctrine of election upon which it is built—if it is to rebuild his theological anthropology from his doctrine of the Trinity. Not all critics seem to realize the full extent to which his theological anthropology would need to be reworked if the immanent trinitarian relations were to provide the central frame of reference for his theological anthropology.

With this qualification we come to the second trajectory, which argues that the ordering of the relationship between men and women reveals a pervasive systemic pattern of domination and submission that arises from Barth's commitment to an absolute qualitative distinction between Creator and creature, one in which the divine actor overwhelms and eviscerates the human actor. These critics find this hierarchy embedded at the center of Barth's christocentric theological anthropology in the very ontological constitution of the incarnate Christ, and some recognize that Barth's innovative revamping of the doctrine of election in the second volume of *Church Dogmatics* limits the usability of his first volume's doctrine of the Trinity as a corrective to his third volume's theological anthropology. The immanent Trinity (who God is in Godself) and the economic Trinity (who God is in God's relationship to creation) converge in Barth's doctrine of election, when Barth projects the eternal decision of God to elect and sustain a relationship with humankind back into the eternal immanent relationship between Father and Son: from eternity the electing Father and the elected Son have resolved to establish the unity of the Son with an individual human being—Jesus Christ. These critics suspect that because this eternal intimate union of the Son with Jesus Christ pushes the distinction between the Creator and creature back into the immanent trinitarian relations, it secures the immanent trinitarian ground for an ordering of will and activity in which one leads and the other follows, one commands and the other obeys. This order is then replicated in the relationship of Christ to the Church and men to women. Still others note that even the first volume's doctrine of the Trinity lends support to Barth's problematic ordering of the sexes, for the eternal generation of Son from Father has an order of origin that is analogous to the order of origin to which Barth appeals in the scene of Eve's creation (Gen. 2). In his exegesis of this text, Barth argues that the sequential origin of Eve from Adam reflects the divinely ordained sequential ordering of their activity, wherein men initiate and women respond. For this interpretive trajectory, there is no corrective—Barth's theology is hopelessly compromised from the very beginning.[4]

---

4. In this trajectory of critique, some attribute Barth's recurring pattern of ordering to a problematic use of analogy that compares the incomparable. Scholars argue that Barth seeks analogies where there can be no analogies, for the relationship between the trinitarian persons and the relationship between God and creation defy any analogy whatsoever between human beings (JoAnn Ford Watson, *A Study of Karl Barth's Doctrine of Man and Woman* [New York: Vantage Press, 1995]; Yolanda Dreyer, "Karl Barth's Male-Female Order

We arrive, then, at an impasse. Either critics turn their backs on the systemic patriarchalism of Barth's entire dogmatic project, which compromises even the most traditionally egalitarian of relations—that between the persons of the Trinity. Or they secure a corrective that would require a daunting project of reconstruction from the top-down: an overhaul of his christocentric doctrine of election that must carefully distinguish immanent from economic trinities, and a reconstruction of his theological anthropology from a trinitarian rather than a christological center.

as Asymmetrical Theoethics," *Hervormde Teologiese Studies* 63, no. 4 [November 2007]: 1493-521; Emma J. Justes, "Theological Reflections on the Role of Women in Church and Society," *The Journal of Pastoral Care* 32, no. 1 [March 1978]: 42-54). Others find that Barth's pervasive hierarchical ordering derives from his emphases on divine enabling activity and utter creaturely incapacity, which enshrines an active/passive dichotomy at the heart of his theological project, that is then replicated in every part of his analogy of relations. Along these lines, Rosemary Radford Ruether (*Sexism and God-Talk: Toward a Feminist Theology* [Boston: Beacon Press, 1983], 94-9) includes Barth among the exemplars of a patriarchal anthropology that situates female subordination within a pervasive ordering of leaders and followers. Jacquelyn Grant (*White Women's Christ and Black Women's Jesus: Feminist Christology and Womanist Response* [Atlanta: Scholars Press, 1989], 68-74) finds in Barth's theology a representative of the theological and social dualisms that feminists have faulted for funding a patriarchy in which active, strong, independent traits are associated with men and passive, weak, dependent traits are associated with women. Joan Arnold Romero ("Karl Barth's Theology of the Word of God: Or, How to Keep Women Silent and in Their Place," in *Women and Religion*, ed. Judith Plaskow Goldenberg [Missoula, MT: University of Montana, 1973], 35-48) finds in Barth a theology of domination and oppression that preserves at its heart a master-servant relation in which God commands and humans obey. Thus the subservience of a passive, incapacitated human to the divine actor finds its human analogy in the domination of women by men. Such a theology leads to destructive relations of domination within church and society. Some *defenders* of Barth's account of sexual difference offer similar observations to these critics insofar as they draw attention to a pervasive pattern of order, which they embrace rather than oppose. They trace an order of sequence and origin through multiple relations all the way up the ontological ladder to the eternal trinitarian relation between the begetting Father and the begotten Son, although—as will be seen in the later chapters of this book—they on occasion try to find ways to soften (if not completely ignore) the implications this ordering has for the interactions between the sexes. See Robert Osborn, "Man and/or Woman According to Karl Barth," in *Theology and Corporate Conscience: Essays in Honor of Frederick Herzog*, ed. Douglas Meeks, et al. (Minneapolis: Kirk House, 1999); Gary W. Deddo, *Karl Barth's Theology of Relations: Trinitarian, Christological, and Human: Towards an Ethic of the Family* (New York: Peter Lang, 1999); Christopher Chenault Roberts, *Creation and Covenant: The Significance of Sexual Difference in the Moral Theology of Marriage* (London: T&T Clark, 2007).

Tracking the human agent

It is my contention that this impasse is reached through a distorting emphasis upon the *ordering* of central relationships in Barth's *Dogmatics*. In the literature I have discussed, the examination of the ordering is undertaken at the expense of an adequate grasp of Barth's understanding of human *agency* that is operative in these relationships. With their sights set on "order" as it is instantiated in these many relationships, critics tend to approach Barth's dogmatic project as a network of analogous, asymmetrical dyads consisting of first and second actors (leaders and followers): they assume that (rather than question whether) Barth has more than one account of human agency, and they question the ways in which he grounds these different types of actors (leaders and followers) by means of his analogy of relations.

Instead of tracking an analogous pattern of ordering through the various relationships of *Dogmatics*, I look at the ways in which Barth depicts human agency as a response to a pattern of relationship-constituting activity that calls human beings into existence as responsive and responsible actors—a divinely initiated activity that sets them on the path toward finding aid in, and lending aid to, their human neighbors. We will see that because of his christocentric commitments Barth's theological anthropology offers only one, christologically informed, account of what the human agent is and does. I will argue that Barth's privileging of male actors is not the symptom of a pervasive asymmetrical ordering but rather the consequence of his refusal to allow women fully to appropriate the only model of human agency he has: a pattern of activity that he carefully crafts as an imitative response to Christ's activity for and on behalf of humankind. Thus while Barth claims that women are fully functioning human agents, his efforts to subordinate their activity to male activity contradicts this claim by setting ambiguous and ultimately unlivable constraints upon the female agent.

By attending carefully to Barth's christologically funded construal of human agency, I argue that the critical corrective to Barth's gender trouble is far closer to home than his more generous critics realize, and it does not demand an extensive trinitarian overhaul of his anthropology from the top-down. I shall show that the human agent at the heart of his christocentric theological anthropology cannot support his efforts to restrain women in a subordinate relation to men. My claim is that, far from being symptomatic of a pervasive hierarchical power-differential, Barth's ordering of the sexes does not cohere with his account of human agency and ethical responsibility carefully patterned after the gracious, aid-lending, self-revelatory activity of the incarnate Christ. Thus Barth's understanding of human agency itself provides a corrective, which, I will suggest, lends itself to critical and performative accounts of sexual difference that resonate with some contemporary currents in gender theory.

Over the last three decades, several developments in scholarship on Barth have opened space for a fresh inquiry into Barth's account of sexual difference—one that focuses on the human agent. However, most of the literature on sexual difference surveyed above either precedes or does not engage these developments.

In a first development, a growing line of scholarship has turned attention to Barth's understanding of human agency and has refuted the suspicion (echoed in much of the literature on his account of sexual difference) that Barth's divine actor overwhelms and eviscerates a passive human agent in every locus of Barth's *Church Dogmatics*: revelation, christology, theological anthropology, and ethics. Barth's career-long emphasis upon the human being's utter incapacity for the saving knowledge and redemptive work of God, along with his depiction of that divine work as a miraculous activity that makes possible the humanly impossible, has evoked the criticism that his human agent is the passive object of divine manipulation. Over the past few decades, however, a series of monographs has examined the space that Barth's christocentric account of divine activity clears for human agency, while some have read *Church Dogmatics* as a moral theology exhibiting a robust and multifaceted concern with the human agent.[5]

5. These monographs on human agency, ethics, and its relationship to dogmatics have shown that Barth's understanding of divine being and activity clear space for a particular account of ethical agency. John Webster has famously argued that the failure to accept and investigate Barth's claim that dogmatics is necessarily ethical has resulted in inadequate readings that fail to appreciate Barth's work as, among other things, a moral ontology, "an extensive account of the situation in which human agents act." Barth decenters human activity, pushing aside focus on moral selfhood in order to give an account of the moral life as genuine action. The agent is enclosed and governed by the creative, redemptive, and sanctifying work of God in Christ, and good action is action that conforms to prior divine action. Since the human being is characterized by good action, if dogmatics is to witness to the action of God and its goodness, it will have the problem of ethics in view from the beginning (*Barth's Ethics of Reconciliation* [Cambridge: Cambridge University Press, 1995], 1–4; see also Webster, *Barth's Moral Theology: Human Action in Barth's Thought* [Edinburgh: T&T Clark, 1998]). This recent literature on ethics also includes: Paul D. Matheny, *Dogmatics and Ethics: The Theological Realism and Ethics of Karl Barth's "Church Dogmatics"* (Peter Lang: Frankfurt, 1990); Timothy J. Gorringe, *Against Hegemony* (Oxford: Oxford University Press, 1999); Paul T. Nimmo, *Being in Action: The Theological Shape of Barth's Ethical Vision* (London: T&T Clark, 2007); Gerald P. McKenny, *The Analogy of Grace: Karl Barth's Moral Theology* (Oxford: Oxford University Press, 2010); David Clough, *Ethics in Crisis; Interpreting Barth's Ethics* (Aldershot: Ashgate, 2005); Archibald James Spencer, *Clearing a Space for Human Action: Ethical Ontology in the Theology of Karl Barth* (New York: Peter Lang, 2003); Frank Jehle, *Ever against the Stream*, trans. Richard and Martha Burnett (Grand Rapids: Eerdmans, 2002); Joseph L. Mangina, *Karl Barth on the Christian Life: The Practical Knowledge of God* (New York: Peter Lang, 2001); William Werpehowski, *Karl Barth and Christian Ethics: Living in Truth* (Burlington, VT: Ashgate, 2014). This literature has refuted the once widely held view that Barth's preoccupation with the divine actor leaves no place for human action. For a discussion of the earlier negative readings of Barth's ethics and the common misperceptions, see Nimmo, *Being in Action*, 2–4; Nigel Biggar, *The Hastening That Waits: Karl Barth's Ethics* (Oxford: Clarendon, 1993), 19–25; Webster, *Ethics of Reconciliation* (Cambridge: Cambridge University Press, 1995), 5–8; and McKenny, *Analogy of Grace*, 292–4.

This trajectory of scholarship exposes the need for a reading of Barth's account of sexual difference that is especially attentive to his depiction of human agency, its christological shape, and the intimate relationship he maintains between dogmatics and ethics. While much of this literature acknowledges the central site the relationship between the sexes occupies in his ethics, none undertakes a substantial critique of its heterosexist and heteronormative features. My project thus contributes to this literature by exposing the problems in his account of sexual difference and locating resources in his construal of agency that resist his sexism and heterosexism.

In a second development, a lively ongoing debate over the trinitarian implications of Barth's reformulation of the doctrine of election in *Church Dogmatics* II has produced a consensus among Barth scholars that after *Church Dogmatics* II/2 Barth's references to the immanent Trinity serve a more limited methodological function, while some argue that these references serve no material function at all. Scholars disagree over the extent to which this limited function obviates Barth's earlier depiction of the immanent Trinity in the *Church Dogmatics* I. Some prominent interpreters have argued that after *Church Dogmatics* II/2, the ontological identity of the Son is always already complicated by the eternal decree that unites the Son to the human nature of Jesus Christ. As a consequence, after *Church Dogmatics* II/2 it becomes very difficult to talk about the immanent relationship between Father and Son apart from any consideration of God's eternal decision to establish a relationship with the creature.[6]

---

6. For a synopsis of this debate (which I address in Chapter 5) and a selection of key contributions (including essays by Bruce McCormack, Paul Molnar, George Hunsinger, Paul Dafydd Jones, and Paul Nimmo), see *Trinity and Election in Contemporary Theology*, ed. Michael T. Dempsey (Grand Rapids: Eerdmans, 2011). See also Bruce McCormack, "Grace & Being: The Role of God's Gracious Election in Karl Barth's Theological Ontology," in *Orthodox and Modern: Studies in the Theology of Karl Barth* (Grand Rapids: Baker, 2008); McCormack, "The Ontological Presuppositions of Barth's Doctrine of the Atonement," in *The Glory of the Atonement: Biblical, Historical and Practical Perspectives: Essays in Honor of Roger R. Nicole*, ed. Charles E. Hall and Frank A James III (Downers Grove, IL: IVP, 2004), 346-66; McCormack, "Seek God Where He May Be Found: A Response to Edwin Chr. van Driel," *SJT* 60, no.1 (2007): 62-79; Nimmo, *Being in Action*, 4-12; Matthias Gockel, *Barth and Schleiermacher on the Doctrine of Election: A Systematic-Theological Comparison* (Oxford: Oxford University Press, 2006), 158-97; Paul Dafydd Jones, *The Humanity of Christ: Christology in Karl Barth's Church Dogmatics* (London: T&T Clark, 2008), 60-116; George Hunsinger, *Reading Barth with Charity: A Hermeneutical Proposal* (Grand Rapids: Baker, 2015); Paul Molnar, *Divine Freedom and the Doctrine of the Immanent Trinity: In Dialogue with Karl Barth and Contemporary Theology* (London: T&T Clark, 2005), 60-4. The monographs of Nimmo (*Being in Action*) and Jones (*The Humanity of Christ*) show the significance of Barth's reformulation of the doctrine of election for human agency, a point I will address in Chapter 5.

This scholarship requires the recognition that Barth's appeals to an analogy between inter-human fellowship and inter-divine fellowship is deeply shaped by what Bruce McCormack has described as the solidification of Barth's "christocentric concertation," which begins in *Church Dogmatics* II/1 and drives the modification of his doctrine of election to center on the election of Christ rather than the election of individuals. Barth's reformulation of the doctrine of election in *Church Dogmatics* II/2 functions, henceforth, as a "regulative principle" that secures Christ (both the subject and object of God's election) as the controlling center of all Barth's subsequent work.[7]

This scholarship exposes the restricted methodological function of the immanent Trinity in Barth's later volumes. It problematizes the assumption of an ontological homogeneity in the immanent Trinity, an assumption which underlies much of the literature that proposes a trinitarian "fix" to Barth's ordering of sexual difference. This christocentric concentration and the regulative impact of Barth's reformulation of the doctrine of election will support my claim that Barth offers only one pattern of human agency for all humans to appropriate, enacted by Jesus Christ who is eternally bound by election to the second person of the Trinity. The problem with Barth's ordering of the sexes is not, then, that he directs men to imitate the humanward activity of God and women to imitate the Godward activity of humans (rendering men commanding leaders and women obedient followers), as many suspect. Rather the problem is that, whenever Barth attempts to order the relation between the sexes, he turns his singular account of human agency, together with its ethical impulse, into a male prerogative, and consequently eviscerates the would-be female agent.

In a third development, Barth's heteronormative framing of inter-human fellowship has only recently come under scrutiny. Most of the critics of gender in Barth's work, noted above, praise Barth for giving the relationship between the sexes so central a role for human existence—understood as a being-in-relationship. They appreciate his affiliation of this particular relationship with the *imago dei*, in that he includes women within the *imago dei* and fosters a constructive and positive approach to sexual identity and desire, all the while resisting a tradition that depicts woman as a lesser version of man. However, several critics have now problematized Barth's heteronormative framing of inter-human fellowship. His complementarian account of sexual difference and the central place it occupies in his theological anthropology underlie his depiction of homosexual relationships as the pathological, isolated, self-loving rejection of the human "other." This newer trajectory of critique draws attention to the need for an analysis of Barth's elevation of sexual difference itself to the primary site of inter-human alterity.[8]

---

7. Bruce McCormack, *Karl Barth's Critically Realistic Dialectical Theology: Its Genesis and Development, 1909–1936* (Oxford: Oxford University Press, 1995), 20–3, 453–8.

8. Several publications have worked to unsettle the heteronormativity of Barth's theological anthropology and ethics on his own terms. Eugene Rogers (*Sexuality and the Christian Body: Their Way into the Triune Life* [Oxford: Blackwell, 1999]) conducts

Barth's christocentric account of human agency will aid my critique of this move, and I will expose the trouble that the biblical figure of the unmarried Christ causes for Barth's account. Because Christ is, for Barth, the central paradigm for human agency and thus for inter-human fellowship, he must also serve as the central

a book-length interrogation of Barth's heteronormative depiction of human existence, which he finds to be the strongest theological account there is of the complementarity of the sexes. He wants to preserve Barth's use of the Pauline symbology that finds in the love of Christ for the church a model of marriage, while freeing Barth's depiction of co-humanity from compulsory complementarity (141–7). Like many of the other critics I note above, he is especially critical of Barth's use of dyadic relational structures, and he worries that Barth exhibits a preference for binary relations that distorts his reading of biblical narratives by effacing the role that third parties play. He argues that because of this compulsory complementarity Barth's account of human fellowship loses its christological (and narratival) moorings to a binary relationship, and suggests that more must be made of Christ's celibate state than Barth is willing to make. He questions Barth's selection of biblical narratives for exemplars of co-humanity, the Adam and Eve scene in Gen. 2 above all. He finds resources in other narratives that show co-humanity in relationships between the same sex. Rogers argues that had Barth not been so fixed on establishing a basis for compulsory heterosexuality, he might have configured the I/Thou relation not as a binary but as the condition for the variety of relationships that Christ enacted (180–91).

Graham Ward ("The Erotics of Redemption: After Karl Barth," *Theology & Sexuality* 8 [March 1998]: 52–72) likewise faults Barth for reifying naturalistic observations and premises in his account of sexual difference. Ward argues that sexual difference remains a highly unstable site in Barth's analogy of relations. Barth does not succeed in providing an account of sexual difference but instead produces an economy of the same in which woman serves the narcissistic project of reflecting man's image, and the Adam–Eve scene of recognition enacts this economy. Ward, like others, locates a critical corrective in Barth's immanent trinitarian relations. There he finds an alternate economy of desire where encounter with alterity is expressed in a kenotic outpouring of self-giving love that exposes the problematic character of the economy of desire enacted by Adam: an economy based on lack, demand, and possession. Ward wants a single erotic economy that is not plagued by notions of complementarity and hierarchy and one that is open to same-sex erotic partnerships. While I share these aims with Ward, I find that the erotic economy that Ward appreciates does not drive the trinitarian relations alone but fuels his "analogy of relations" for it drives the movement of the incarnate Son toward creation. I will show in my third chapter that this economy drives Barth's reading of Genesis 2, but seizes up with the arrival of Eve; it also drives Barth's depiction of human agency in III/2, but again seizes up with the introduction of sexual difference and its order.

Jaime Ronaldo Balboa ("'Church Dogmatics,' Natural Theology, and the Slippery Slope of '*Geschlecht*': A Constructivist-Gay Liberationist Reading of Barth," *JAAR* 66, no. 4 [Winter 1998]: 771–89) focuses on Barth's brief discussion of homosexuality in his special ethics. Balboa argues that Barth's construal of sexual difference rests upon natural categories (i.e., the naturally sexed body desiring in a specific direction), and that in this respect he resorts to the sort of natural theology he persistently rejected.

paradigm for the sexually differentiated self, and thus Christ's unmarried status and his close relationship to a circle of twelve men is at odds with Barth's efforts to depict human existence as fully actualized in a relationship with one person of the opposite sex. I will draw on some of the images Barth uses for Christ's relationship to others (when sexual difference is not on his mind) that can both aid in decentering the heterosexual marital relationship and support a diverse range of relationships and social organizations—images that might even suggest that sexual difference does not, after all, occupy the central place in Barth's *Dogmatics* that it acquires on the few occasions that he speaks of the relationship between the sexes.[9]

9. Barth's account of sexual difference and the central place he gives to the monogamous marital relationship has also been critiqued and interrogated within the context of Barth's personal life, in particular his relationship with Charlotte von Kirschbaum, the secretary and research assistant who lived with Barth, his wife Nellie, and their children in a long-term living arrangement that was viewed as scandalous by their closest friends and beyond. See especially Suzanne Selinger, *Charlotte von Kirschbaum and Karl Barth: A Study in Biography and the History of Theology* (University Park, PA: Pennsylvania State University Press, 1998), for a careful account of the personal and collaborative relationship between von Kirschbaum and Barth, their mutual love, the life she lived among Barth's family, her indispensable role in his research and writing, and her own research and publications on the status of women in the church. Selinger compares Barth's account of sexual difference with von Kirschbaum's published essays and letters on the subject, which occupied her interests more extensively than it did his. Selinger finds much agreement and little divergence between the two, and she attempts to locate von Kirschbaum's contribution to Barth's account while recognizing the difficulty of this undertaking, given the interwoven character of their collaboration. See also: Eberhard Busch's *Karl Barth: His Life from Letters and Autobiographical Texts*; Renate Köbler, *In the Shadow of Karl Barth: Charlotte von Kirschbaum*, trans. Keith Crim (Louisville: John Knox, 1989). Von Kirschbaum's lectures are published in *Die wirkliche Frau* (Zollikon-Zürich: Evangelischer Verlag, 1949), and translated into English in *The Question of Woman: The Collected Writings of Charlotte von Kirschbaum*, trans. John Shepherd, ed. with an introduction by Eleanor Jackson (Grand Rapids: Eerdmans, 199). English translations of her two additional lectures—"Address for the Movement 'Free Germany'" (1945) and "The Role of Women in the Proclamation of the Word" (1951)— are published in Köbler, *In the Shadow of Karl Barth*. The 2008 publication of the personal letters from Barth to von Kirschbaum, between 1925 and 1935, opens avenues for a further study of the ways in which Barth and von Kirschbaum collaborated in the production of an account of sexual difference and its ethics, an account that reflects both the constraints and tensions of their domestic life, while at the same time creating an ethical space for it in the face of criticism. See Christiane Tietz's "Karl Barth and Charlotte von Kirschbaum" (*Theology Today* 74 [July 2017]: 86–111) for a study of these letters that gives a glimpse into the tensions with which they grappled and their efforts to wrestle theologically with their relationship. Unfortunately, far less attention has been given to the place and experience of Nellie Barth.

Scope and outline of the argument

In this book I look at Barth's depiction of the self's orientation to the human other as a grateful and imitative response to the gratuitous saving work of Christ. The human agent emerges in Barth's *Church Dogmatics* as the recipient of an unrepayable gift from the divine benefactor, and this gift imposes the obligation of a modest imitative activity that lends aid to the human other and to a wider sphere of creaturely others. In its orientation toward the human other, the agent not only imitates the divine, gracious aid, actualized in Jesus Christ, but also recognizes its own need for that same gratuitous aid from its fellow humans. This recognition of a shared dependency with the other and shared responsibility for the needs of the other, and above all the shared obligation to act on behalf of the other, will be key to understanding the ethical dimensions of inter-human fellowship and the corresponding problems that arise in Barth's depiction of sexual difference. In the chapters that follow, we shall see that, at specific points in his *Dogmatics*, Barth's account of the ethically oriented relation of self to other becomes deeply entangled with his efforts to elevate sexual difference above every other difference and to secure an ethical prerogative to male agents.

In the chapters that follow I aim to harness the critical and performative dimensions of Barth's account of human agency for the purpose of pushing Barth further than he was willing to go—that is, toward the destabilization and decentering of his male–female binary and toward a more open-ended construal of the sexed self. In this respect my project is particularly indebted to Judith Butler's performative account of gender.[10] There are some suggestive affinities between Barth's sexually differentiated agent and Butler's performative account of gender that will aid my analysis and constructive aims.

Butler speaks of gender as a stylized sustained practice of repeated acts (including bodily gestures, postures, movements, dress, and styles) that do not *express* but rather *constitute* an intelligible sexed identity within a regulatory framework of social norms and constraints. Our rigid two-sex framework constrains and delimits the ways in which gender is performed, and in which norms and constraints are appropriated, inhabited, and contested.[11]

In her debate with structuralist accounts of sexual difference Butler interrogates the idea that sexual difference is a quasi-transcendental division, one that conditions and makes possible human subjectivity—a difference of an order unlike any other difference. Butler objects that such a view abstracts sexual difference from the gender binary and declares it an unassailable, pre-social law, immune to critical intervention or contestation. It situates the masculine and feminine

---

10. See especially Judith Butler, *Gender Trouble: Feminism and the Subversion of Identity* (New York: Routledge, 1999); Butler, *Bodies That Matter: On the Discursive Limits of Sex* (New York: Routledge, 1993), esp. 1–81; Butler, *The Psychic Life of Power: Theories in Subjection* (Stanford, CA: Stanford University Press, 1997).

11. Butler, *Gender Trouble*, esp. 178–9.

positions beyond all contestation, setting them as the limits to contestation as such. In criticizing this view, Butler invites us to consider the seemingly indisputable givenness of sexual difference as itself a sedimentation of social practices, one that has come to exhaust the semantic field of intelligible gendered identities. She argues that the performance of gender is the apparatus by which the coherent binary of masculine and feminine is produced, normalized, and naturalized, and its coherence is secured at the cost of those permutations of gender which do not fit the binary, even as these are as much a part of gender as its most normative instances. She suggests that if the performance of gender, in its multiple iterations, is the mechanism or apparatus by which the binaries of man and woman, male and female, masculine and feminine are constructed and naturalized, it might then also be the mechanism by which they are deconstructed and denaturalized. The very apparatus that seeks to install the norm might also work to undermine that very installation.[12]

While space constraints do not allow for an explicit engagement with Butler's theory in the chapters that follow, Butler's challenge to a structuralist account of the heterosexualizing norm informs and shapes my critique of Barth's construal of sexual difference. As we shall see, Barth will depict the sexually differentiated self as a "doing," a persistent activity to be conducted in obedience to the divine command and in constant negotiation of culturally contingent conventions. Butler's work will help to expose the contingency of Barth's appeal to a pre-given, oppositional sexual binary. It will help me show how the self's relation to gender conventions might then entail performances that subvert and contest the seeming givenness of the two-sex oppositional binary and its ordering of identity and desire. In this respect, my intent is to show that Barth's account of agency contains the critical and reflective mechanisms that we might readily turn upon the constraints of the two-sex regulatory framework that he imposes.

My analysis of the normative dimensions of Barth's human agent will require careful attention not only to the ways in which Barth describes and presents the human agent but also to the ways in which he rhetorically models for his reader the openness and vulnerability of the agent toward redirection by the other. I thus approach *Church Dogmatics* as a pedagogical exercise, in which Barth describes, prescribes, and attempts to model for his readers the orientation and dispositions proper for responding to divine and creaturely "others" encountered within and beyond Christian discourse. Barth's pattern of human agency comes into view as he locates agential models within Scripture (and the confessions and theologies reflecting on it) for his readers to imitate—models that locate the epistemic vantage points the dogmatician and his readers must endeavor to occupy. By exposing the performative dimensions of Barth's dogmatic practice—that is, the work it does on the reader by modeling a pattern of responsive and responsible agency—I will be in a better position to foreground the role that biblical figures such as Adam

---

12. Butler, *Undoing Gender* (New York: Routledge, 2004), 40–56, 174–203, esp. 42–5.

and Eve can serve in modeling for readers a pattern of activity Barth commends.[13] Barth's instructions on sexual difference and the relationship between the sexes will be better understood as part of this pedagogical practice.

Chapter 1 sets the interpretive framework and interests of the book as it casts a light on these pedagogical and performative dimensions of Barth's *Church Dogmatics*, particularly as they emerge in *Church Dogmatics* I/1, his prolegomenon. I foreground that part-volume's labor as a formative textual practice that functions to assist writer and readers together in the unlearning of modern intellectual habits that Barth finds problematic, reorienting them on a perpetual search for a fresh hearing of the divine Word in the human words of Christian discourse. Barth describes, prescribes, and rhetorically enacts the stance, orientation, and attitude he perceives in biblical figures and authorial voices. As he does so, a nascent account of human agency comes into view, introducing both the agent in need of redirection and the normative model against which it should measure itself. Mary the mother of Jesus and her cousin Elizabeth provide models of this agent in its ecclesial setting. We will see these female models saying and doing what Eve later fails to do—a failing that provides Barth with a biblical figure of proper female subordination.

Chapter 2 turns to the ethical dimensions of Barth's agent and the practice of dogmatics itself. Here we find the human agent redirected by the love of God to a relationship of dependency and care for the neighbor. The twofold commandment to love God and neighbor provides the organizational schema for a life set in motion toward God and neighbor, while the parable of the Good Samaritan provides additional biblical characters in whom readers might recognize what they are and what they ought to be. I argue that Barth puts these figures to work in subtly subversive ways to undermine racial divisions operative in contemporaneous appeals to the orders of creation.

Chapter 3 turns to *Church Dogmatics* III/1 where Barth orients his readers in the doctrine of creation, while redirecting them from potential resources for a natural theology. He presents Christ as the doctrine's hidden key, and he lays the biblical groundwork for his subsequent theological anthropology (III/2) and accompanying special ethics (III/4). Barth's lengthy exegetical and figurative reading of the Genesis creation narratives provides the christological framework for the agent's relationship to multiple sites of creaturely alterity. This chapter examines the relation he constructs between myth and maternity in his reading of Genesis 1, where the maternal body appears as an ambivalent metaphorical

---

13. The rhetorical and performative strategies that Barth uses in *Church Dogmatics* to model for and elicit from his readers the orientation toward divine and creaturely others that is so central to his understanding of human agency remain a neglected topic. Stephen H. Webb provides a sustained treatment of the rhetorical features of the second edition of Barth's commentary on Romans which includes a discussion of the commentary's ethical sections where Barth's construal of the alterity of the neighbor in relation to divine alterity has affinities with his depiction of the neighbor in *CD* I/2, §18 (*Re-Figuring Theology*, 168–77).

site that threatens a proper reading of the creation narratives by promising a resource for creaturely capacities for God's work and thus a natural theology. The relationship between the sexes takes center stage at the climax of Genesis 1, specifically as an interpersonal encounter wherein the human being is conformed to the divine likeness through no creaturely capacity of its own.

Turning to Barth's reading of Genesis 2, Chapter 4 continues to track the occasional appearances and notable effacements of the maternal body while following Adam from his creation to his first free decision in the naming of Eve, wherein he reflects the *imago dei*, Christ himself. Adam functions as another biblical model of human agency. With the arrival of Eve, Barth installs heterosexual marriage and a patriarchal order at the center of human relationality and ethical responsibility. At the same time, he uses his figurative reading of Adam's relationship to Eve to carefully detach the theological significance of the difference and relationship between the sexes from a reproductive framework and from naturalizing discourses.

In Chapter 5, I turn to the theological anthropology of *Church Dogmatics* III/2, where Barth's figurative reading of Adam comes to fruition in the conception of a human agent set in motion by the creative and redemptive work of Christ and directed toward its human others in a relationship of shared need and obligation. Here Barth patterns his account of human agency after Christ's saving work enacted on behalf of humankind. Beneficiaries of Christ's gracious aid are called to conform themselves to Christ in a gratuitous, spontaneous movement toward the needy other, in whom they must also recognize their own need. I argue that, with the introduction of the topic of sexual difference into his theological anthropology, the Christ-imitating pattern of human agency becomes a male prerogative, while the would-be female agent is left without christological and ethical moorings.

Chapter 6 turns to Barth's discussion of sexual difference in his special ethics of creation, found in *Church Dogmatics* III/4, §54, where it becomes clearer that Barth's ordering of the sexes retains for men the task of overseeing ethical deliberation itself, for and on behalf of women. At the same time, he will construe the sexual relationship as an ethically oriented mutual interaction, which can take place only if each is a fully functioning (and unrestrained) human agent who hastens to the aid of the other. I interrogate and unsettle the place that sexual difference here occupies in the regulation and ordering of inter-human fellowship, and I show that Barth's efforts to integrate the unmarried Christ into his heteronormative framework expose the tenuous grounds upon which he connects his understanding of sexual difference to his broader christocentric project. I will argue that Barth configures sexual difference as an oppositional division that must be carefully policed and maintained, but that his call for a critical relationship to norms, customs, and social mores opens up space within Barth's heteronormative matrix for performances that unsettle, subvert, and transgress the reputedly unambiguous dividing line between the sexes that these norms instantiate.

Over the course of these chapters, we will see that Barth's human agent is necessarily self-reflective and ethically oriented. It requires that its central categories, frameworks, and assumptions be questioned, challenged, and undermined continually by God's self-revelation in an incarnate Christ who cannot be absorbed into contemporary orderings of social relations. This Christ calls the human agent into an analogous openness toward the impositions and challenges of other human beings. I shall show that Barth's sexually differentiated agent retains this sort of openness and vulnerability to the human other, and this need for critical challenge and redirection.

Chapter 1

REHABILITATING THE AGENT OF THEOLOGICAL DISCOURSE

Introduction

In the opening part-volume of *Church Dogmatics*, its prolegomenon, Barth devotes much labor, often quite subtly, to reorienting his readers on a path toward a fresh hearing of the divine address, that will encounter them if and when it chooses, and usually through the vehicle of Christian witness to Christ. Prescribing and himself enacting this proper orientation, Barth holds up biblical models for his readers to imitate as he guides them through the unlearning of self-aggrandizing epistemic habits inherited from modern Protestant theology. This pedagogical practice continues in future volumes, and in due course we will meet Barth's models in Mary and Elizabeth, the Good Samaritan, Adam, and, eventually, the ethically vested "I" in its encounter with the sexually differentiated "Thou."

Barth's project requires careful self-disciplining work on the part of both dogmatician and readers alike, all of whom Barth imagines as inheritors of theological traditions that are methodologically fixated on anthropology as the starting-point of dogmatic inquiry. For Barth, these traditions present a human agent bereft of the proper object of love and reflection, caught up in the isolation of a circular self-exploration: an agent in need of divine intervention and redirection outward, on a path toward a fresh hearing of the revelatory address of the Word. Barth's first part-volume outlines a methodology for a dogmatics that would follow this latter path.

In this chapter's first section, I draw together some themes in Barth's published lectures on eighteenth- and nineteenth-century Protestant theology and its philosophical influences. Produced around the time Barth was writing *Church Dogmatics* I/1, the published lectures are directed at the epistemic and methodological hubris that Barth finds endemic to Protestant liberal theology. Barth's criticisms of this theology propel the rehabilitative work he attempts on his readers and himself in *Church Dogmatics* I, to which the second section turns. As we shall see, Barth robs the human agent of any inherent capacity for theological speech by casting it in complete dependency upon the gracious decision of the divine Word to reveal itself to humanity and to empower human words to witness faithfully to it. Humility and hope emerge as the driving virtues of the ceaseless epistemic, discursive movement that is the dogmatic project, supplanting the hubris and self-sufficiency that propel many modern theological ventures. Biblical authors and characters in particular serve to model the proper orientation toward God and others. In the third section, correspondingly, I turn to Barth's use of the figures of Mary and Elizabeth (Luke 1) as exemplary hearers of and witnesses to the divine address, and precisely as such, models for the proclamatory work of preaching and theologizing.

Bad epistemic habits of the modern subject

Barth's critique of modern Protestant theological trajectories (arising from Schleiermacher and Hegel, in particular) provides a backdrop against which the rehabilitative dimensions of Barth's dogmatic project are more readily discernible.[1] In his lectures on nineteenth-century Protestant theology, he laments the self-aggrandizing epistemic fantasies of autonomy and self-sufficiency that drive these theological quests for knowledge of divine and creaturely others.

The concern driving much of Barth's critique relates to the divine prerogatives these theologians assume for themselves when securing in human faculties the capacity for the knowledge and experience of God. What Barth finds to be missing is an understanding of divine revelation as a confrontation from without—an encounter with an objectively given, divine Other, that humbles and limits a self all too inclined toward delusions of grandeur and mastery. When human faculties are attributed capacities that a proper Protestant theology should attribute to divine revelation alone, the human being becomes the central object of study and reflection, and theology becomes anthropology. Equipped with such capacities, these theologians thus assume an impossible vantage point from which to assess the movement of God within history, the relationship between history and the certainty of religious faith, the relationship between philosophy and theology, the relationship between Christianity and other religions, and so forth. They attempt to teach themselves, by way of their own resources, that which God alone can teach and make known: the nature of God and all that God has created.

---

1. Karl Barth, *Protestant Theology in the Nineteenth Century: Its Background and History* (London: SCM Press, 1972); pagination will appear in parentheses inline, denoted by *PT*. On Barth's early intellectual context and his early theological training in and positive engagement with neo-Kantianism and modern Protestant theologies, see Simon Fisher, *Revelatory Positivism? Barth's Earliest Theology and the Marburg School* (Oxford: Oxford University Press, 1988). For more on Barth's early intellectual context, see Mark Chapman, *Ernt Troeltsch and Liberal Theology: Religion and Cultural Synthesis in Wilhelmine Germany*, Christian Theology in Context Series (Oxford: Oxford University Press, 2002); Brent Sockness, *Against False Apologetics: Wilhelm Hermann and Ernst Troeltsch in Conflict* (Tübingen: Mohr Siebeck, 1998).

Different versions of this critique appear throughout Barth's lectures on philosophers and theologians of the eighteenth and nineteenth centuries. I am particularly interested in the general shape this critique takes in Barth's reading of the constraints that Kant's philosophy places upon the academically respectable Protestant theologies that followed.

In Kant's philosophy Barth finds the self-chastening production of an Enlightenment confidence that is both humbled and emboldened by the critical exercises wherein reason comes to an understanding of itself and of the limits within which it may justifiably operate (*PT*, 269-71). The humility of these exercises conceals conceit, for there is no place in Kant's philosophy for a construal of revelation under the terms Barth would have it: Kant provides no means of accounting for the reality and possibility of revelation and so refrains from any attempt at such an account (*PT*, 309). Theoretical reason possesses no empirical criterion by which to recognize God via sense perception, no criterion that can grant certainty that what is experienced is not illusory. Consequently, theoretical reason can admit no place for an objectively given, divine Other confronting the self from without. Practical reason assumes the role of the divine actor in the revelatory event, as it generates its own inner law and criterion by which to measure and discern right from wrong, and by which to evaluate the concrete empirical phenomena of religion in the context of the philosophy of religion (*PT*, 283, 304).

Such a philosophy of religion will peruse biblical texts for any claims that correspond to reason's own workings (*PT*, 304), while recognizing Jesus as a human ideal of moral perfection insofar as he corresponds to reason's production of an archetypal ideal of a human being who is pleasing to God (*PT*, 288). Reason thus provides its own resources by which to evaluate Scripture and religion; it needs no confrontation and reorientation from without. There is no place in this philosophy for a divine revelation that puts the human being's judgments into question, rendering them objects of *divine* judgment. So Barth writes, "The true miracle of revelation, or, at least, what is the highest degree to be wondered at in the founding of the religion of reason is—reason itself in its own eyes, as moral reason" (*PT*, 283).

Theologians in the trajectory of Schleiermacher accept the constraints Kant sets for a philosophically sophisticated construal of religion, but they negotiate for theology the basis for an immediate knowledge of God by way of a third *a priori* capacity, alongside theoretical and practical reason. In religious experience, encapsulated in the feeling of absolute dependence, they secure an innate universal human consciousness of God, the historical reference point of which is the figure of Jesus. Irreducible to knowledge and action, the "feeling of absolute dependence" becomes the proper object of theological reflection, and with it religious experience itself (*PT*, 253-4, 306, 316, 433-9, 457-73). For Schleiermacher and his followers, then, "Christian pious self-awareness contemplates and describes itself: that is in principle the be-all and end-all of this theology" (*PT*, 457).

Again Barth foregrounds the hubris he finds in theologians along this trajectory: "He is as certain of his power over himself as he is certain of himself, and he is quite extraordinarily certain of himself" (*PT*, 572). This theologian ascends to his "lofty watchtower" (*PT*, 576), as "the born surveyor of the world, who can put everything neatly in its place" (*PT*, 573). He postures as "a complete master of Christianity, in a position, as it were, to look into it from above ... able to elicit its nature and assess its value" and, with an artistic freedom, to shape and sculpt it in order to let it stand in compatible relationship to the progress of science (*PT*, 446). From this vantage point the theologian is confident that his own theology falls under the providential guidance that he discerns for himself in the development of doctrine throughout history (*PT*, 572). But such an epistemic vantage point can only be "a splendid illusion or figment of the imagination," Barth declares (*PT*, 574).

In comparison to Schleiermacher's immediacy of feeling, Barth admits his preference for Hegel's emphasis upon the relationship between thinking and truth (*PT*, 415), and Hegel's depiction of the human subject as, above all, a thinking being (*PT*, 396), a developing history, a continual reconstruction of itself anew in a dialectical movement (*PT*, 400). In this movement, Barth writes,

> reason, truth, concept, idea, mind, God himself are understood as an *event*, and, moreover, only as an event. They cease to be what they are as soon as the event, in which they are what they are, is thought of as interrupted ... God is God only in his divine action, revelation, creation, reconciliation, redemption ... He is a graven image as soon as he becomes identified with one single moment, made absolute, of this activity. And reason, likewise, is unreason as soon as the process in which it is reason is thought of at any stage as something stationary, when any of the moments of its motion is identified with reason itself. (*PT*, 398–9)

To catch sight of the object of Hegel's thought one has to move with it, for taking a snapshot would be an inadequate approach: a "moving film" is a better metaphor (*PT*, 399–400). If theology is to take anything from Hegel, Barth suggests, it will be this notion of the self and God as a history, a movement. We shall see, in due course, that in his own *Church Dogmatics* Barth imagines a model human agent always in motion, on its way toward an encounter with a God who is always in motion.

In Barth's view, Hegel and his followers share the hubris of the Kantian and Schleiermachian trajectories of theology. Reason is construed as a dynamic dialectical process in which the thinking subject is identical with that which is thought, in the very performance of the act of thinking itself, and so the movement of reason comes to be identified with the God who is thought. Confidence in human thinking is therefore confidence in God, and vice versa (*PT*, 391). In Hegel, then, "we have a man who absolutely and undeviatingly believes in himself, who can doubt everything because he does not for a moment doubt himself, and who knows everything for the simple reason that he has complete trust in his own self-knowledge" (*PT*, 391). If the theologian is to appropriate this construal of reason from Hegel, "the self-movement of truth would have to be detached from the self-movement of man ... to be justly regarded as the self-movement of God," and would need to be represented instead as the act, movement, and event that interrupts an individual's own movement of thought from without (*PT*, 419).

With these caricatures Barth secures the foil for a dogmatic project undertaken within the ecclesial sphere of would-be hearers of a revelatory Word that speaks (if and when it pleases) through the witness to Christ in Scripture and proclamation.[2] No external and neutral epistemic vantage point is permitted the theologian who must first be taught and judged by the Word. Self-certainty must be replaced with humility and hope: with the humbling awareness that the self brings no constructive resources to the revelatory event—that God can only be known if and when God freely decides to speak; yet with the hopeful assurance that God, to whom ecclesial discourse bears witness, is eager to speak and be known. As we shall see, the shadow of this arrogant, self-centered subject of modern theology haunts Barth's ongoing dogmatic efforts to humble and reorient his readers with various biblical depictions of the properly humbled and hopeful normative agent.

The humbled and hopeful doer of theology

Disentangling revelation from the human subject

Barth's first part-volume of *Church Dogmatics* prescribes a dogmatic methodology meant to undermine the epistemic vantage point and hubris of these liberal Protestant trajectories. It attempts this by disentangling the self-revelation of God (as sole criterion of theological reflection) from the resources and capacities of the theologian and thereby locating the criterion of dogmatic reflection outside the human subject (I/1, 206–7).[3] A theology benefiting from the Reformation's renewal, Barth argues, is one that begins with the Word of God (God's self-revelation) as the criterion by which it pursues the task of evaluating Christian discourse, and especially ecclesial proclamation. The proper object of theological reflection is not, then, the human subject and its operations but God in God's objectivity, as revealed from beyond the self's faculties and productions. The human subject will come into view only indirectly when the dogmatician is properly oriented.

Barth construes the source of revelation as an event detached from the operations of the human subject, a confrontation with the incarnate second

---

2. See Amy Marga, *Karl Barth's Dialogue with Catholicism in Göttingen and Münster: Its Significance for His Doctrine of God* (Tübingen: Mohr Siebeck, 2010), for a careful account of the ways in which Barth's epistemology, doctrine of revelation, and doctrine of God were shaped by his engagement with Roman Catholic theology in the 1920s, prior to the writing of *Church Dogmatics*. This dialogue aided him in clarifying his own position with respect to Protestant liberal theology and its focus on the experiencing subject.

3. In all inline parenthetical references to *Church Dogmatics* (ed. G. W. Bromiley and T. F. Torrance [Edinburgh: T&T Clark, 1956–1975]), page numbers will be preceded by volume number and, where necessary, followed by bracketed page references to *Die kirchliche Dogmatik* (Zürich: TVZ, 1938–1965).

person of the Trinity, whose life, death, and resurrection make God known and who witnesses to human beings in the present. God's immediate self-knowledge, hidden in the inter-trinitarian life, becomes only indirectly knowable, first in the existence of Jesus Christ and, today, in Scripture's witness to Christ and in the Church's proclamation of that witness. It is a knowledge acquired only if the Holy Spirit intervenes to enable a recognition of the Word concealed in the medium of human words (II/1, 15-20; 197-9). As such, revelation is a divine *address*, originating beyond the sphere of human subjectivity, imposing upon the human self, interrupting that self's epistemic operations by giving rise to a humanly impossible knowledge of a God who cannot be conflated with the knowing and experiencing self.[4]

With revelation so construed, Barth robs would-be hearers of the divine address of the capacity to control or manipulate the knowledge of God. For while the divine address comes to the hearer in the vehicle of language, it is not identical to that language. The revelatory Word retains its freedom to choose the speech through which it becomes present, and the Word is not bound by or to the wording of any such choice. Human language is not identical with the spoken Word (II/1, 139). Through the enabling of the Holy Spirit the writers of Scripture gave witness to Christ, prophetically in the Old Testament and through recollection in the New Testament. Likewise, only through the enabling of the Holy Spirit can individuals today hear the Word in this witness and themselves give witness

---

4. For Barth's concept of revelation, see especially *CD* I/1, §3, §4, §5; II/1, §25, and §27. Space constraints permit me only to highlight features relevant to my interest in Barth's work of reorienting his readers toward divine and human others. Much has been written on Barth's theological realism, its Kantian epistemological framework, and its development from a Cohen-informed neo-Kantianism to a more traditional Kantian realism. See especially, Bruce McCormack, *Karl Barth's Critically Realistic Dialectical Theology: Its Genesis and Development, 1909-1936* (Oxford: Oxford University Press, 1995); George Hunsinger, *How to Read Karl Barth: The Shape of His Theology* (Oxford: Oxford University Press, 1991), 43-8; Hunsinger, *Disruptive Grace: Studies in the Theology of Karl Barth* (Grand Rapids: Eerdmans, 2000), 210-25. Ingolf U. Dalferth ("Karl Barth's Eschatological Realism," in *Karl Barth: Centenary Essays*, ed. S. W. Sykes [Cambridge: Cambridge University Press, 1989], 14-45) gives a concise account of the ontological, semantical, and epistemological dimensions of Barth's realism, and he notes the unique shape that Barth's eschatology gives to his realism, in that, after 1919, the reality to which theology refers, for Barth, is the eschatological reality of the risen Christ and the new life it promises (21). It is this christological reference point to which Barth gestures in *CD* I/1. More recently, Amy Marga (*Karl Barth's Dialogue with Catholicism*) has shown that by *CD* II/1 (published in 1940), Barth's realism has shifted to a triune basis for the knowledge of God that secures God's objectivity in the eternal life of God. At this point God's objectivity in the revelatory event is not an action confined to God's works *ad extra*, but is reflective of God's eternal being, such that God does not acquire objectivity in the incarnation in order to be known, but already possesses it, for there is self-knowledge in the triune relations (see esp. 156-73).

(II/1, 15–20, 181). The hearer of the Word in human words cannot, then, grasp or possess the presence of this promised one, but can only respond in recollection and anticipation. Reflecting the anticipation of the Old Testament witness and the recollection of the New Testament, the would-be hearer of the Word moves ever forward, from and to a fresh hearing of the Word (I/1, 141).

In this account of revelation, we hear echoes of what Barth appreciates in Hegel:

> [Theology] could let itself be reminded by Hegel that the source of knowledge of Reformation theology, at all events, had been the Word of God, the word of truth. But this also means, the event of God, the event of truth. *An event that comes and goes, like a passing thunder-shower (Luther), like the angel at the pool of Bethesda,* an event at which the man for whom it is to be an event must be present; *an event, which by repetition, and by man's renewal of his presence, must ever become event anew.* (*PT*, 416; italics added)

Any thought or speech to which the hearing of the Word might give rise (theological discourse included) cannot, then, be confused with the speaking of the Word.

As the consequence of God's free decision to make Godself known in such discrete concrete moments of encounter, the knowledge of God will humble and reorient the hearer. It will turn the hearer from judge to the one who is judged, from self-taught to one who must be taught again and again. Revelation's content

> will always be an authentic and definitive encounter with the Lord of man, a revelation which man cannot achieve himself, the *revelation of something new which can only be told him*. It will also be the limitation of his existence by the absolute "out there" of his Creator, a limitation on the basis of which he can understand himself only as created out of nothing and upheld over nothing. It will also be a radical renewal and therewith an obviously *radical criticism of the whole of his present existence*, a renewal and a criticism on the basis of which he can understand himself only as sinner living by grace and therefore as a lost sinner closed up against God on his side. Finally it will be the presence of God as the One who comes, the Future One in the strict sense, the eternal Lord and Redeemer of man, *a presence on the basis of which he can understand himself only as hastening towards this future of the Lord and expecting him.* (I/1, 194; italics added)

Barth thus conceptualizes revelation as a mode of address that acts upon us from without, transposing hearers into "the wholly new state" of those who live within the sphere of God's Word (I/1, 152–3), reordering their relation to time, reconfiguring history around the event of hearing. The original time of the Word of God is the time of Jesus of Nazareth in whom the Word became present in human history as the promise of God's future for humankind. This time is preceded by that of prophetic anticipation of Christ's time, and it is followed by the time of Church recollection and proclamation of Christ's time, when the biblical witness to Christ is repeatedly heard and re-spoken (I/2, §14). The dogmatician locates himself and his hearers in this time of recollection. Their own movement toward a fresh hearing of the Word reflects the anticipation and recollection of a history reordered by Christ's advent.

In this way Barth refuses any external vantage point from which to survey the unfolding of religious history. For the dogmatician and his readers, there is no position outside this reordering of time by the revelatory address, no detached and neutral platform from which to evaluate the doings of God as an observer, spectator, or reporter. There is only the vantage point of witnesses to God's revelation: "they believe and therefore speak" (I/2, 817).

The hearer of the divine address

Barth begins the *Church Dogmatics* with this concept of revelation, positioning himself in the trajectory of Reformation theology, as one who must similarly be taught by the biblical witness about the nature of revelation. From this account of revelation, and its inaccessible accessibility, a nascent account of human agency comes into view as a response to this divine address. Barth presents the corresponding picture of the human agent as if it were imposed upon him from without. He signals his determination to construct this account, not from self-reflection or the experience of the religious subject, but rather from what such a doctrine of revelation necessarily presupposes—what the human agent must be, if the Word of God speaks in such a way. Barth's agent comes into view as an orientation, an openness, a hearing, a speaking, and an ongoing movement from and to a fresh hearing of the divine address.

In *Church Dogmatics* I/1 §6 ("The Knowability of the Word of God") Barth turns to the human, subjective side of the event of revelation, having already secured in the preceding pages the objectivity of the revelation of God in the person of Christ and in its dynamic mediation through Scripture and proclamation. Only now does he take up the role of religious "experience" (*Erlebnis* or *Erfahrung*) (I/1, 193 [201]), explicitly connecting it to yet carefully overhauling what Schleiermacher called "religious consciousness" (*religiöses Bewußtsein*) [I/1, 198 [207]]. In teaching this topic, he is persistent in his efforts to redirect his readers outward, away from the distractions of the self, toward a fresh hearing of the Word. He indicates that his pedagogical efforts are directed, in part, to the hubris and self-centeredness of Protestant liberal trajectories of theology, with their surplus of attention to the religious subject (I/1, 191–6).

Our dogmatician should thus position himself as one who must be taught by "the only competent witness in this matter, namely, the man who stands in the event of real knowledge of the Word of God as this man is presented to us by Holy Scripture" (I/1, 199). This biblical portrait, from which Barth will learn what it is to hear the divine address, is that of a human who, in the experience of the revelatory event, is told that he or she has a Lord, is a lost sinner blessed by this Lord, and awaits the eternal redemption of this Lord (I/1, 199–200).

1. Rehabilitating the Agent of Theological Discourse

Barth says little here in §6 of what this biblical portrait is or where he finds it. In this and the following chapters, I will show how Barth derives this portrait from the orientation of the authorial voices of Scriptures, from the vantage point from which narratives are told, and from particular biblical characters themselves, all of which provide for Barth models of the human response to the divine address. He will continually refer his readers to these models for imitation.

For now, Barth reinforces the point that the very hearing of the divine address is a miracle wherein God makes possible for the individual what is otherwise impossible.[5] He writes: "This specific content of the Word experienced by him will flatly prohibit him from ascribing the possibility of this experience to himself either wholly or in part or from dialectically equating the divine possibility actualized in this experience with a possibility of his own" (I/1, 199).

The revelatory event requires no capacity or potentiality [*Möglichkeit*], no Kantian-like faculty [*Vermögen*] that God actualizes in the revelatory event, whether innate to human nature or gifted permanently to and possessed by the human being in the revelatory event. The very capacity, the very possibility, of hearing God's Word is not possessed but must be continually re-gifted by the Holy Spirit in the very event of that hearing, always as a work of divine grace that enables human language and human cognition to do what they cannot do of themselves (I/1, 191–3, 211–12). Indeed, this is a recurring theme in Barth's portrayal of biblical narratives, as we shall see shortly.

Barth's depiction of religious experience aims, in part, to rob the dogmatician of the human being as the central object of theological reflection. The only human experience worthy of the dogmatician's consideration is the response of faith [*Glaube*]. Faith, in the New Testament, is a human act that depends completely on the action of God, and that expresses the priority of God as both enabler and object of the knowledge acquired (I/1, 227–9; see also II/1, 21). Barth describes this faithful hearing of the divine address as an "acknowledgment" [*Anerkennung*] that entails a knowing [*Erkenntnis*], and a self-determining reorientation to the divine address. I give some attention to this account here, for we will hear this terminology in Barth's later descriptions of the self's relations to divine and human others, as well as in his depiction of biblical characters.

What the hearer of the Word acknowledges is "primarily and predominantly speech, communication from person to person and reason to reason ... the Word of truth" (I/1, 205), as Jesus Christ becomes present in the biblical witness. This hearing is, therefore, an interpersonal, self-invested knowing that targets theoretical and practical reason. The divine address communicates through a vehicle that is accessible to the human being's senses but imposed upon the will. The hearer can now have no self-understanding that excludes a relationship with

---

5. See Hunsinger, *How to Read Karl Barth*, regarding the category of "miracle" at the heart of Barth's actualism: the event of God's revelation is a new act of God in time and history, and the biblical witness to revelation is always a narrative of miracles that happened (189). Barth's emphasis upon the creaturely incapacity for the work God does upon the creature belongs to the category of miracle.

this object of knowledge, and so this hearing reorients and redirects the self toward this object (I/1, 188–90, 198). Barth writes:

> Knowing, [human beings] are affected by the object known. They no longer exist without it, but with it ... Whatever else and however else they may think of it, they must begin by thinking of the truth of its reality [*des Wahrseins seiner Wirklichkeit*]. Face to face with this truth they can no longer withdraw into themselves in order to affirm, question or deny it thence ... This event, this confirmation, in contrast to mere cognizance [*Kenntnis*], we call knowledge (*Erkenntnis*). Cognizance becomes knowledge when man becomes a responsible witness to its content. (I/1, 188)

Such knowers are, in other words, transformed by their confrontation with an indisputably actual and real other.

The experience of this hearing engages the whole person, demanding, in response, the full self-determination, act, and decision of the human being. All human faculties—feeling, will, and intellect—are included. Thus while the human response is divinely enabled from without, the hearer is not in a state of partial or total receptivity or passivity. The responding human agent is fully self-determining even as she or he is determined [*bestimmen*] from without by God (I/1, 199–204). The human being's self-determining act is either "the right hearing of obedience or the wrong hearing of disobedience" (I/1, 201, 160).

That this hearing is an act of full self-determination is an important point for Barth, and another tool with which to redirect his readers away from improper objects of theological reflection. Barth allows for no co-operation between divine determination and human self-determination, since that would suggest a human capacity for, or a human co-operation with, God in this experience. Indeed, these two determinations are not two parts of one whole, nor is human self-determination eliminated or reduced in deference to divine determination. Such configurations must be rejected for they can only be arranged from the impossible vantage point, that of a spectator (not a participant) who is able to view the two determinations as operative on the same level as potential competitors (I/1, 199–200).

Like the biblical text itself, the human activity of hearing and acknowledging the divine address (or failing to do so) functions for Barth as another veil—what he here refers to as "a secular form"—that prevents direct access to the divine determination of the revelatory event (I/1, 207, see also 168, 175–6). While we can distinguish creaturely entities from one another (and in this sense acquire a certain cognitive mastery of them as knowable objects), we cannot, objectively, distinguish God's self-revelation from the secular form by which it comes to us (I/1, 165). Likewise, we cannot, subjectively, distinguish our own cognitive processes of hearing, cognizing, and interpreting the divine address from the revelatory act itself. Therefore, from a phenomenological vantage, theologians possess no criterion by which to discern when they have indeed heard the Word, and no "final human certainty [*Sicherheit*]" that their hearing, cognizing, and interpretation is indeed a response to the divine address (I/1, 215). We see only "a human process of a very characteristic and differentiated and at the same time comprehensive kind" (I/1, 216), one that can be lived, asserted, and described, but as such cannot be distinguished from other religious phenomena. As a fully human activity it belongs to the sphere of cultural history, and offers in itself no criterion by which we might distinguish it from other religious phenomena, for striking parallels of this mode of acknowledgment can be found in other kinds of human experiences (I/1, 215–17). In the miracle of the event of revelation itself, what we have, Barth says, is akin to what happened when Aaron's rod turned to a serpent in Pharaoh's court: Pharaoh's sorcerers did likewise (I/1, 218).

Robbing his readers of the certitude he finds in modern Protestant theologies, Barth leaves them with the "trembling assurance" of faith, which, considered in and of itself, "has no foundation, no hold on God, and it is empty compared with other human assurances which do not have their seat so strictly outside man" (I/1, 226). Its basis is hidden in the free decision of God and must therefore continually be revealed.

The human subject's self-determination thus conceals the answer to the question of whether God has spoken or has been rightly heard:

> The Word of God comes as a summons to him and the hearing it finds in him is the right hearing of obedience or the wrong hearing of disobedience. Whether it is finally the one or the other is not, of course, in his hands. For that, for obedience or disobedience in his action, he cannot resolve and determine himself. As he decides, as he resolves and determines, he is rather in the secret judgment of the grace or disfavour of God, to whom alone his obedience or disobedience is manifest. (I/1, 200–1)

The dogmatician will find nothing worth seeing in religious experience or in the self-awareness of the person in the very experience of the event. If would-be hearers of the Word should pause to reflect on what they think to be their experience of hearing and knowing God, they will have access only to their own activity, their own thoughts, concepts, and decisions.

The humbling effects of the elusiveness of the divine actor "trickle down" to theological reflection. The human thought and speech to which the hearing of the Word gives rise must not be confused with the divine address itself. Of the concepts and words with which we hear and give witness to the divine address, Barth writes:

> We have always to bear in mind that these materials are our own work and are not to be confused with the concrete fulness of the Word of God itself which we recall and for which we wait, but only point to it. What God said and what God will say is always quite different from what we can and must say to ourselves and others about its content. Not only the word of preaching heard as God's Word but even the word of Scripture through which God speaks to us becomes in fact quite different when it passes from God's lips to our ears and our lips. It becomes the Word of God recollected and expected by us in faith, and the Word which

was spoken and will be spoken again by God stands over against it afresh in strict sovereignty. (I/1, 141)

In this way, Barth preserves the freedom and mystery of the divine address from human control and manipulation. He redirects his readers from reflecting upon their own perceived experience of hearing the Word (religious experience as such) and robs them of confidence in their own theological reflection by construing the human response (with its knowledge and self-determination, its right hearing or wrong hearing) as a "wall of secularity" [*Welthaftigkeit*] that cannot be transgressed (I/1, 165, 207). There is no watchtower or vantage point from which the dogmatician might survey the miracle of the revelatory event, distinguishing the divine action from the human response.

With this construal of religious experience, Barth sets the human agent in motion on a journey from hearing to hearing. The human response is not a fixed attitude, but rather, "acknowledgment of the Word of God necessarily means letting oneself be continually led, always making a step, always being in movement from the experience felt at one time or the thought grasped at one time to the opposite experience and thought" (I/1, 207). The path is not a steady incline from one unveiling to another, nor the sort of gradual incline in which the veil is eventually done away with altogether. Rather it is a movement from mountain tops to valleys, from one moment of hearing the "God with us" unveiled and the next moment hearing only the veil of human words (I/1, 175, 179). The hearing of the Word requires, therefore, the human subject's submission to the preceding and enabling act of the divine subject, a forward movement, a being-led. It necessitates a stance of dependency upon the leading of the divine actor, rather than a return to self-reflection on one's own experiences in that movement (I/1, 175).

The dogmatician's orientation

Barth's outline of the task, shape, and scope of the dogmatic project takes its cues from this construal of revelation and the kind of self it calls into action. The dogmatician's task is to criticize and correct church proclamation by way of its criterion, the Word of God as attested in Scripture, but never immediately accessible; to call the hearing Church to hear again, and so to subject ecclesial teaching to a fresh hearing (of the biblical witness) (I/1, §7.2). The divine address, as Barth has thus described it, implies

> a turning around and placing ourselves in the direction in which we must look to see the point from which the Church realizes that its proclamation is perceived and judged and from which, therefore, it must make every effort to think about itself so that, fully aware of its responsibility, it may submit to the necessary self-examination in respect of its proclamation. (I/1, 248)

It requires that the dogmatician exemplify a relationship to the revelatory Word that is modelled on the voices and the stance of the biblical witnesses to revelation:

it requires "a kinship between the outlook, approach and method of the biblical writers and those of the Church preacher and therefore of the dogmatician" (I/2, 816). Specifically, it requires of the dogmatician a "listening" with the Church, which itself is to "listen in a readiness that its [the Church's] whole life should be assailed, convulsed, revolutionised and reshaped" (I/2, 804). And so, of the dogmatic project, Barth writes:

> It is not in the position to confront the teaching Church with the Word of God itself and to explain and apply its judgment upon it. It can bring to bear only a human, relative judgment. And it can do this only by itself submitting to the judgment of the Word of God, thus giving an example to the teaching Church (and in this consists *in concreto* the summons to which we have already referred) of what it demands from it: namely, a thinking and speaking about God which is controlled and determined, assailed and disquietened, delimited and confined by the norm of the Word of God. As dogmatics itself teaches by listening, it reminds the teaching Church of the listening which is so necessary. It attempts to do justice to its formal task by allowing itself to assume this form. It works at Church proclamation in accordance with the law laid upon the Church, by working upon itself in accordance with the same law. (I/2, 813; see also 804)

If he is to listen properly and, in so doing, become a witness himself (like the biblical voices which he imitates), then our dogmatician must allow himself to be put into question by the biblical witness to the divine address. He must place his own thinking and speaking in complete surrender to the controlling power of its object, the divine Word, and be ready to receive new insights from it, confident that the object is able to speak for itself (I/2, 867). As Barth puts it:

> This is the attitude of the witness. It is distinguished from the attitude of the interested spectator, or the narrating reporter, or the reflective dialectician, or the determined partisan, by the fact that when the witness speaks he is not answering a question which comes from himself, but one which the judge addresses to him. And his answer will be the more exact and reliable the more he ignores his own irrepressible questions in the shaping of his answer, and the more he allows it to be exclusively controlled by the realities which it is his duty to indicate and confirm. (I/2, 817)

A persistent theme in Barth's later depictions of interpersonal encounter will be the critical corrective that divine and human others impose upon the self, redirecting the self and putting the self into question, demanding a reconfiguration of the self's concept, categories, and assumptions. I turn next to the biblical figures of Mary, Elizabeth, and Zechariah, all of whom model for Barth the right and wrong hearing of the divine address, as they become witnesses. In later chapters I will attend to the performative dimensions of Barth's project, as he goes about modelling for his readers the proper orientation to the Word that he has here described.

Mary and Elizabeth as model agents

Barth uses Mary's response to the annunciation as a model of the hearing, response, and orientation to the divine address proper to proclamation and the doing of theology.[6] In a passing reference in *Church Dogmatics* I/2, §22, he likens her famous "be it unto me according to thy word" (Lk. 1:38) to Christ's words in Gethsemane, "Not as I will, but as thou wilt" (Mt. 26:39), indicating that such obedience is what the language of proclamation and dogmatics hopes to make manifest (I/2, 764). Mary also functions as this sort of model in I/2, §15, not only in her obedient response, but also in her bodily incapacity for the virgin conception. Barth draws analogies between the incapacity of Christ's human nature for its union with the Logos, the virgin Mary's incapacity to conceive without a male partner, and his readers' incapacity for acknowledgment [*Anerkenntnis*] and confession [*Bekenntnis*] of the knowledge [*Erkenntnis*] that God's revelation discloses regarding the creedal confession, *natus ex Maria virgine*. All require the miracle wherein God makes possible that which is humanly impossible (I/2, 172–202). Mary's part in Barth's published advent lectures (*The Great Promise*), produced during the same period in which Barth was writing this first part-volume of *Church Dogmatics*, will be my focus here, for Barth locates within the Lukan narrative models for both the obedience of right hearing and the disobedience of wrong hearing, and, in one notable scene, suggests that the right hearing will demand the subversion of gender conventions.[7]

---

6. The most extensive treatment of the Virgin Mary in Barth's work is Dustin Resch, *A Sign of Mystery: Karl Barth's Interpretation of the Virgin Birth* (Burlington, VT: Ashgate, 2012). Resch is particularly interested in Barth's efforts to retrieve the doctrine of the virgin birth from the influential theological and exegetical critiques of Schleiermacher and Strauss, and also in how Barth configures the relationship of the virgin conception to the incarnation, as he shifts from giving the virgin conception a constitutive role in the incarnation to presenting it as a sign with the purely noetic function of unveiling the identity of Christ. See also Geoffrey W. Bromiley, *An Introduction to the Theology of Karl Barth* (Grand Rapids: Eerdmans, 1979), 26–7; Paul S. Fiddes, "Mary in the Theology of Karl Barth," in *Mary in Doctrine and Devotion: Papers of the Liverpool Congress, 1989, of the Ecumenical Society of the Blessed Virgin Mary*, ed. Alberic Stacpoole (Colelgeviille: Liturgical Press, 1990), 111–27; Volker Strümke, "Die Jungfrauengeburt als Geheimnis des Glaubens—ethische Annmerkungen," *Neue Zeitschrift für systematische Theologie und Religionsphilosophie* 49, no. 4 (2007): 423–4l; and Tim Perry, "What Is Little Mary Here For?" *Pro Ecclesia* 19, no. 1 (Winter 2010): 46–68.

7. Karl Barth, *The Great Promise*, trans. Hans Freund (New York: Philosophical Library, 1963); pagination will appear in parentheses inline, denoted by *GP*. This series of Advent lectures on the opening chapters of Luke (published under the title *Die Verheissung*) was delivered to an audience of students who had attended Barth's formal lectures and seminars before they were forcibly terminated at the University of Bonn in the heat of the German Church struggle. Barth discusses the virgin birth also in *Göttingen Dogmatics: Instructions*

In Barth's advent lectures, the high priest Zechariah is a foil for Mary's right hearing and response to the divine address (*GP,* 2–34). Both hear the divine address through the medium of an angelic, Christ-oriented promise, and each responds with fear and incomprehension, as is appropriate to the mystery of divine revelation. Together Zechariah and Mary stand in a line of biblical "figures of the Advent" who hear the divine address through the speech of an angel and are among "those who have received the promise and now wait for the Lord" (*GP,* 18–19). But Zechariah's response is the hearing of disobedience, while Mary's is that of obedience.

When Zechariah is told in the Temple that his wife, Elizabeth, whose reproductive years have passed, will conceive a son and a forerunner to the Messiah, whom he must name John, Zechariah speaks his doubt to the angel, asking how such a birth can be possible, given the age of his wife (*GP,* 15–16). In the very moment that he should announce the promise he has heard to the people awaiting him outside the Temple (thereby becoming a faithful witness), he is instead struck mute: "man has failed; he disgraced himself and must keep quiet" (*GP,* 17). His speechlessness exemplifies, for Barth, the judgment and crisis under which all theological endeavors operate, for theologians might just as well be mute when their words are not the witness of faith but the speech of a disobedient doubter (*GP,* 17).

When Mary is told that she will conceive a son, the Messiah himself, she vocalizes her acknowledgment of the promise, declaring, "Let it be to me according to your word" (Lk. 1:38) (*GP,* 31–4). Like Mary, Elizabeth demonstrates faith—that faith which her husband lacks (*GP,* 17), and when the two women come together each confesses to the other her faith in the angelic promise. Barth presents the meeting between the pregnant women as a scene of reciprocal recognition and vocal acknowledgment of the promise of God (*GP,* 35–44). Each recognizes in the other a recipient and fulfillment of the divine promise. Each literally embodies the fulfillment of the promise, and each addresses the other as such. Barth portrays this scene of joyful recognition and address as a model of Christian fellowship, of the unity of hope in the hearts of those who have received and participate in the divine promise. He declares that Mary's subsequent song of gratitude and praise is a song the church and his audience of theologians should be ready at any moment to sing (*GP,* 48).

Elizabeth has more to say when Barth reaches the scene of the infant John's circumcision and naming. Because the mute Zechariah is unable to name his son, the family decides that he should be named, according to custom and law, after his father. But "strangely enough the mother interferes, and in spite of all that we might expect from her, proclaims: 'Not so; he shall be called *John*!'" (*GP,* 58). Barth notes Elizabeth's disruption of convention, her daring to speak where it was

in the Christian Religion, Vol. 1, trans. Geoffrey W. Bromiley (Grand Rapids: Eerdmans, 1991), 160–7; *Die christliche Dogmatik im Entwurf. Erster Band: Die Lehre vom Worte Gottes. Prolegomena zur christlichen Dogmatik,* ed. Gerhard Sauter (Zürich: Theologischer Verlag, 1982), 365–7; and *CD* IV/1, 207.

not her place, thereby displacing the role and name of the husband, and vocalizing her obedient acknowledgment of the angel's command that the promised child be named John. Barth notes the shock registering within the family at this departure from the ordained way of things, and the recurring shock when Zechariah writes on a tablet his agreement with his wife. With his act of proclamation and obedience to the angelic promise (parallel yet subsequent to that of his wife), Zechariah regains his voice, and then he too professes his faith, gratitude, and joy in a song. Thus Zechariah also finally becomes to Barth's audience an example of theological discourse that is obedient and faithful. A miracle makes possible this vocalized profession, just as it makes possible the pregnancies of a virgin and a post-menopausal woman (*GP*, 63).

Barth finds it noteworthy that in disrupting the authority of family order in the naming ritual, Elizabeth is the first person to proclaim the new name, and her husband follows after her, consenting to what she has already declared (*GP*, 60). This observation prompts Barth to question the very notion he comes later to support in *Church Dogmatics* III/1—the notion that, in the New Testament, silence is in some way proper to women in the relationship between the sexes. He writes:

> It is a very peculiar thing about the *woman's* role, just in the first chapter of Luke, a very notable and honorable role! And if it is under discussion whether a woman should have a part in preaching the gospel, such a discussion would have to be preceded by a very thorough exegesis of this chapter before one should be allowed to answer conclusively with reference to I Corinthians 14. Neither Mary with her song of praise nor Elizabeth with her "Not so!" have kept silence. They have *said* something very decisive in the community and with the community of all time. (*GP*, 60–1)

The significance of this passage for Barth's later construal of gender relations will become clearer in Chapter Four, where I will recall key features of this section of *The Great Promise* in discussing Barth's use of the scene of Adam's recognition and naming of Eve to subordinate women to men. For now, we see Barth putting biblical characters to work in exemplifying the orientation and response he prescribes and attempts to enact in his *Church Dogmatics*. We see women functioning as readily as men in this role. And we find Barth construing the subordinate role of women as a cultural convention that the revelatory address calls Elizabeth to disregard. In due course we will come to see that by *Church Dogmatics* III/1 Barth has conflated the male privilege ensconced in such cultural conventions (both of which he questions and rejects here) with a divinely prescribed order for the relationship between the sexes.

Conclusion

Throughout the first volume of *Church Dogmatics*, Barth gives subtle signals of his efforts to continually exemplify for his readers the sort of theological practice that he finds prescribed in the normative role and stance enacted by the apostles, the prophets, and the authors of Scripture. He plays the part of a dogmatician set in motion, humbled but hopeful in his orientation outward, on his way toward a self-disclosing subject whom he trusts is hastening to meet him. In the following chapters, I will attend to Barth's ongoing efforts to humble the human agent and set it in dependent relation to divine and creaturely others.

I have drawn attention to Barth's interest in the critical and disruptive potential of the divine address to expose the limits of the dogmatician's theological framework and categories, and to demand their reconfiguration. The disruptive role of the other's voice will reappear in Barth's later discussion of the sexually differentiated other, although Barth will want to constrain the extent to which female (and especially feminist) voices are permitted to interrogate the prerogatives that the male sex (however wrongly) has secured for itself.

Barth's use of the biblical figures of Mary and Elizabeth as model agents will be important for my project. I have drawn attention to Barth's words on how such models should function for his readers as images from which to construct an account of human agency and as patterns for dogmatician and reader alike to imitate. I have shown how Mary and Elizabeth function for Barth as models for his readers regardless of sex: they do so both in their obedience to the divine address and in their interactions with each other as fellow witnesses. These women do for Barth what Adam also does later on, only Adam will be the model for the male agent to imitate as he chooses and names Eve in obedience to the divine address. Eve will serve as a model for women precisely as she refrains from any such vocalization. We will see the eviscerating effects of Barth's later efforts to secure an agential prerogative for men over women.

In the next chapter we will explore Barth's account of another biblical model of human agency, but this time enacted in an exchange between two men. It will be seen that the orientation of self to neighbor will imitate and reflect the orientation of self to God, as the human other becomes the material occasion by which the self is disrupted and reoriented outward in response to the divine command.

Chapter 2

PLAYING THE NEIGHBOR IN AN "ORDER OF PRAISE"

Introduction

Toward the end of the opening volume of *Church Dogmatics* Barth presents his first extensive consideration of ethics (I/2, §18 "The Life of the Children of God"). He focuses on the ethical dimensions of theological practice and specifically the obligation that the human other (the "neighbor") imposes on the self. For my purposes, Barth's treatment of ethics in §18 is especially noteworthy in that it presents an ethically oriented intersubjective relational model that anticipates the interpersonal framework he uses in *Church Dogmatics* III/2 for human relationality, only he does not situate his encounter within the heteronormative marital framework that, in later volumes, becomes paradigmatic for his understanding of inter-human alterity and ethical duty. In fact, in §18 Barth explicitly rejects the sort of framework that would enable him to do so. He refuses to articulate his account within a quasi-Lutheran doctrine of the "orders of creation" of the kind that many of his contemporaries were using in their ethical projects to describe the duty that the neighbor imposes on the self. Marriage was included among these "orders of creation," understood as institutions of social life that are universally evident throughout human history and divinely ordained for the organization of human society. Refusing this framework as part of his broader opposition to natural theology, Barth instead sets the neighbor within a christological and revelatory framework that turns on a dialectic between gospel and law. The neighbor acquires ethical significance only when divinely appropriated to become a revelatory sign—a creaturely medium by which Christ is revealed—that incites the self to conform to Christ's aid lending activity.

As we shall see, Barth puts the figure of the neighbor to work in subtly subversive ways. He was working on this second part-volume of *Church Dogmatics* I during the time of his public role in the German church struggle of the early 1930s. I will argue that his configuration of the neighbor gestures to this urgent context, subverting the terms of antisemitic arguments for the exclusion of Jews from the German churches.[1]

The first section of this chapter situates Barth's ethical discussion of §18 in the polemical setting of the German Church struggle, drawing attention to the function of the "orders of creation" in arguments for the exclusion of Jews from the life of German churches. When §18 is seen within this context we can better

1. *CD* I/2, §18 remains relatively neglected in scholarship on Barth. Scholars who attend carefully to the ecclesial and political context of Barth's ethical work in the 1930s, specifically as it concerns his antisemitism, have not looked carefully at §18 (see for example, Gorringe, *Against Hegemony*, and Carys Moseley, *Nations and Nationalism in the Theology of Karl Barth* [Oxford: Oxford University Press, 2013]). To my knowledge Eric Gregory alone provides a sustained treatment of §18. Noting the overall relative neglect of Barth in modern Christian ethics, and of Barth's reading of the parable of the Good Samaritan by Barth scholars in particular, he foregrounds the significance of the parable's relevance (and Barth's reading of it) for current discussions of personhood, global ethics, and humanitarianism. He does not, however, address the context and so overlooks the veiled political implications for Barth's own time. See Eric Gregory, "The Gospel within the Commandment: Barth on the Parable of the Good Samaritan," in *Reading the Gospels with Karl Barth*, ed. Daniel L. Migliore (Grand Rapids: Eerdmans, 2017), 34–55. Apart from Gregory, the most sustained treatments of §18 are primarily concerned with the way Barth conceptualizes the relationship between the two commandments and do not consider its implications for Barth's sociopolitical and ecclesial contexts: Paul D. Molnar, "Love of God and Love of Neighbor in the Theology of Karl Rahner and Karl Barth," *Modern Theology* 20, no. 4 (October 2004): 567–99; David Clough, *Ethics in Crisis: Interpreting Barth's Ethics* (Aldershot: Ashgate, 2005), 84–8; John N. Sheveland, *Piety and Responsibility: Patterns of Unity in Karl Rahner, Karl Barth, and Vedanta Desika* (Burlington, VT: Ashgate, 2011), 59–110. Shevland, who provides the most extensive treatment of the paragraph, shares my interest in the epistemic virtues of theological practice that Barth articulates here. However, he finds the account of interpersonal relations in §18 to be excessively preoccupied with methodological issues, the nature of revelation, and the positions Barth rejects, at the expense of praxis and "the performative content" of love for neighbor (78). He concludes that §18 demonstrates "a weak appreciation of interpersonal responsibility and love," which he suspects is the consequence of Barth's annexing of neighbor-love to doxological concerns (93). He consequently prefers the more fully developed account of I/Thou interaction found in *CD* III/2, §45.2. The reading I advance in this chapter recognizes that §18 is constrained by its function within Barth's opening part-volume to prescribe the nature, task, and method of dogmatics and, therefore, is focused on the ethical responsibility of the preacher, the theological practitioner, and the dogmatic project. A survey of the immediate polemical context in which Barth was immersed at the time that he was preparing this part-volume will indicate that the ethical responsibility of his contemporary ministers, theologians, and biblical scholars, specifically in respect of the plight of the Jews in church and society, was an urgent issue for Barth, and I will note the ways in which §18 reflects this urgency. Barth's attention to the nature of revelation is crucial to his account of the ethical responsibility of Christians for the church's apparent outsiders.

detect the urgency in Barth's account of the ethical obligation of ministers and theologians, as he continues his dogmatic task of robbing his readers of any cultural or historical resources for theology, directing them away from natural theologies of all kinds.

Turning next to Barth's discussion of the two commandments, the second and third sections look at his configuration of neighbor-love as the "outer sign" of the "inner reality" that is the love of God. In this divinely enabled capacity, the neighbor is one who functions as both a mirror reflecting the self's sinful neediness and a sign pointing to the work of Christ in meeting that need. I draw attention to several features of Barth's discussion of the self's ethical obligation, which will reappear in his later reading of Adam's relation to the divine and to creaturely others. The parable of the Good Samaritan provides Barth the biblical template for his depiction of the neighbor.

The final section highlights the ways in which Barth's reading subtly subverts the antisemitic rhetoric of the early 1930s, as it beckons its German readers to see themselves reflected in the mirror of the parable of the Good Samaritan.

The neighbor within the "orders of creation"

In his depiction of the self's relation to the divine and human others in §18, Barth includes the orders of creation among several wrongheaded frameworks for understanding the ethical obligation that each human being has for others. Yet he devotes so little space to explaining the problems of such orders that readers unfamiliar with the polemical context in which he was immersed while writing this part-volume might think it was a marginal concern for Barth.

The orders of creation (or related frameworks referred to in a variety of ways: "orders of preservation," "orders of existence," etc.) gained momentum as a viable ethical framework in the 1920s and 1930s. Its various iterations enshrined Luther's dialectic of law and gospel in a dualist ethic that distinguished the will of God knowable in creation and providence from God's will as revealed in Christ. All humans were said to exist in a framework of universal orders, institutions, or ordinances operative prior to and independent of belief in Christ or membership in the church. These included orders such as nation, race, family, and vocation. God's law and commandments for all people were expressed through these orders, and, it was argued, the orders supplied stable reference points for the organization of human life and the configuration of ethical responsibility.[2]

---

2. See, for example, Deonna D. Neal, "Be Who You Are: Karl Barth's Ethics of Creation" (PhD diss., University of Notre Dame, 2010), 22–4; Jonathon David Beeke, "Martin Luther's Two Kingdoms, Law and Gospel, and the Created Order: Was There a Time When the Two Kingdoms Were Not?" *WTJ* 73 (2011): 191–214; Richard Higginson, "Bibliography: The Two Kingdoms and the Orders of Creation in 20th Century Lutheran Ethics," *Modern Churchman* 25, no. 2 (1982): 40–3; Jean-Loup Seban, "The Theology of Nationalism of Emanuel Hirsch," *Princeton Seminary Bulletin* 7, no. 2 (1986): 157–76.

Many of Barth's contemporaries and some of his closest colleagues made constructive use of this framework, as did Barth himself, but his interest in it changed drastically once it came to play a prominent role in antisemitic rhetoric.[3] Paul Althaus and Emanuel Hirsch, well-known scholars of Luther and supporters of National Socialism, espoused a theology of the orders of creation that had a nationalistic and antisemitic bent, incorporating the themes of nation, state, and race into the classical Lutheran framework. The idea of *Volk* became the primary *Ordnung* and, as such, an indispensable form of human social life. It was conceived as an organized unity and community, which shared a common blood, history, and destiny that was not reducible either to its biological or spiritual dimensions. The laws of the state were understood as the framework for the *Volk*'s moral life and, as such, the law of God.[4]

These nationalist theologies had become widely popular by the time the National Socialists rose to power in the early 1930s, and were used to buttress the widespread rhetoric of *Volk*, nation, and blood, and the configuration of Jews as the non-Aryan foreign threat to an authentically German Christian faith and family. Concomitant efforts to de-canonize the Old Testament and reject a Pauline "rabbinic" concept of redemption have been well documented.[5]

The "Faith Movement of German Christians," in support of the *Volk*-ideology of National Socialism, published its guiding principles for the reorganization of the German Protestant Church in a document that declared "race, folk, and nation" to be God-given orders of creation, the preservation of which was God's law for the German people. It identified Jews as "alien blood" constituting a grave threat to German nationality, and it opposed the granting of citizenship to Jews and interracial marriages between Jews and Germans.[6]

Barth was a widely recognized leader in the Confessing Church, the countermovement that mobilized against the rising influence of the German

---

3. Barth's 1928 Münster/1930 Bonn ethics lectures make positive use of the framework in a chapter titled "The Command of God the Creator," and his refusal to allow these lectures to be published during his lifetime has been attributed to his later embarrassment over this use of the orders of creation. John W. Hart, *Karl Barth vs. Emil Brunner: The Formation and Dissolution of a Theological Alliance, 1916–1936* (New York: Peter Lang, 2001), 117; Paul T. Nimmo, "The Orders of Creation in the Theological Ethics of Karl Barth," *SJT* 60, no. 1 (2007): 24–35.

4. Robert P. Ericksen, *Theologians under Hitler: Gerhard Kittel, Paul Althaus and Emanuel Hirsch* (New Haven: Yale University Press, 1985), 89; Seban, "Theology of Nationalism," 163–76.

5. See especially Susannah Heschel, *The Aryan Jesus: Christian Theologians and the Bible* (Princeton: Princeton University Press, 2008).

6. Shelley Baranowski, "Confessing Church and Antisemitism: Protestant Identity, German Nationhood, and the Exclusion of the Jews," in *Betrayal: German Churches and the Holocaust*, ed. Robert P. Ericksen and Susannah Heschel (Minneapolis: Augsburg Fortress Publishers, 1999), 90–109; Hart, *Karl Barth vs. Emil Brunner*, 142–3.

Christians and the latter's efforts to establish a Reich Church that would undermine the church's autonomy. While it must be acknowledged that many members of the Confessing Church shared the nationalism and antisemitism of the German Christians, tensions between the two movements came to a head over efforts within the German Christian movement to pass legislation aimed at purifying a *völkisch* church from "foreign" influence. Imitating the state's exclusion of non-Aryans from civil service positions, the Aryan Paragraph was a regulation that would have dismissed and barred from clergy and church office any Germans who were not of Aryan descent (i.e., any whose parents or grandparents were Jewish) or who were married to Jews.

Debate over the legislation, which took center stage at a national level in 1934, hinged on the efficacy of baptism and its relationship to racial and sexual differences. Arguments for the exclusion of Jews from church office relied on the distinction between the universal, invisible church and the visible church. In the visible church, it was argued, such distinctions as race and sexual difference remained intact, grounded in divine ordinances established in creation. Those in support of the legislation privileged race over sacramental efficacy, arguing that race determined one's place within any specific national church. Converted Jews belonged in separate congregations, they said, for an authentic church for the German people should be based on blood and not baptism. Since women could not be ordained, arguments in support of the Aryan Paragraph often drew an analogy between I Corinthians 14:34 (instructing women to keep silent in the churches) and contemporary efforts to exclude non-Aryans from pastoral office. It was argued that baptism no more eradicated sexual difference than it did racial difference, and that Galatians 3:28 ("There is no longer Jew or Greek, there is no longer slave or free, there is no longer male and female; for all of you are one in Christ Jesus" [NRSV]) referred to the universal, spiritual church but not to the visible church.[7]

The Aryan Paragraph was a divisive measure even within the German Christian movement, and efforts to pass the legislation failed, for it became a rallying point around which the Confessing Church was successfully able to mobilize public opposition to the more extreme efforts of the German Christians to remove all "Jewish influence" from the Church (including de-canonizing the Old Testament, the removal of "Jewish" elements from the New Testament, and the recasting of Jesus as Aryan). While the influence of the German Christians waned, they retained a stronghold in theological faculties, and efforts to put the Aryan Paragraph into practice continued at a regional level. In many parts of the country, policies required candidates for office in the church to provide proof of Aryan ancestry,

---

7. Baranowski, "Confessing Church," 101–2; Doris L. Bergen, *Twisted Cross: The German Christian Movement in the Third Reich* (Chapel Hill: University of North Carolina Press, 1996), 69, 86; Hart, *Karl Barth vs. Emil Brunner*, 145–6; Bergen, *Twisted Cross*, 68–9; Frank Jehle, *Ever against the Stream: The Politics of Karl Barth, 1906–1968* (Eugene: Wipf & Stock, 2012), 49.

but the immense amount of paperwork this entailed prevented such policies from being widely enforced.[8]

While the Confessing Church made the question of the Aryan Paragraph a focal point for rallying support against the German Christian movement, many of its members shared with their opponents an appreciation for nationalist *völkisch* theology and its inherent antisemitism. Jews and Judaism were viewed by many as degenerate moral and spiritual influences on the German churches.[9]

In the beginning Barth was embraced within the Confessing Church, as was the famous Barmen Declaration of 1934 that he helped draft, which declared the theology of the German Christians a heresy. Yet being from Switzerland he was viewed as somewhat of an outsider, and his public opposition to fascist nationalism, *völkisch* theology, and antisemitic policies placed him among the Confessing Church's more radical members. He was known to be outspoken against compromising positions over antisemitic policies, and many thought him insufficiently diplomatic on this point.[10]

Recent scholarship has mined Barth's letters and public statements for expressions of his opposition to ecclesial and political forms of antisemitism. He expressed his horror at the ill treatment of the Jews, spoke of haters of Jews as haters of Christ, opposed the alienation of Jews within the German churches as an abandonment of the Gospel of Christ, decried the antisemitic policies of National Socialism (which he saw as its very heart), and explicitly condemned the systematic extermination of the Jews and the weak.[11] His 1933 pamphlet, "Theological Existence Today!" (a copy of which he sent to Hitler), objected to German Christian efforts to make blood and race, rather than baptism, the criterion for membership in the church, and the following year he criticized the

---

8. Bergen, *Twisted Cross*, 88–93; Baranowski, "Confessing Church," 90–110. See Heschel, *Aryan Jesus*, on the continuing influence of the German Christian movement and efforts within the movement and in university faculties to remove Jewish influence from theology, liturgy, and Scripture.

9. Jehle, *Against the Stream,* 50. Many arguments of the Confessing Church members targeted the more extreme efforts of German Christians to eradicate Jewish influence from the Church by recasting the Old Testament prophets and Jesus as anti-Jewish in their condemnation of Israel (Heschel, *Aryan Jesus*, 5). Baranowski, "Confessing Church," 102.

10. Bergen, *Twisted Cross*, 90; Jehle, *Against the Stream*, 46–55, 143–9.

11. Friedrich-Wilhelm Marquardt, "Theological and Political Motivations of Karl Bath in the Church Struggle (1973)," in *Theological Audacities: Selected Essays*, ed. Andreas Pangritz and Paul S. Chung (Eugene, OR: Pickwick, 2010), 190–222; Eberhard Busch, *Unter dem Bogen des einen Bundes: Karl Barth und die Juden 1933-1945* (Neukirchen-Vluyn: Neukirchner Verlag, 1996); Jehle, *Against the Stream*, 46–70; Hart, *Karl Barth vs. Emil Brunner*, 143–9; Mark R. Lindsay, *Barth, Israel, and Jesus: Karl Barth's Theology of Israel* (Aldershot: Ashgate, 2007), 15–35. Jehle and Lindsay have gathered different statements from private correspondence, discussions, and public speeches in which Barth expresses outrage at the treatment of the Jews.

church's silence over the National Socialists' seizure of power, confiscation of properties, institution of concentration camps, and mistreatment of the Jews in a public statement that was cited repeatedly in the trial preceding his expulsion from Germany in 1935.[12] Returning to Switzerland, Barth continued his public opposition to National Socialism and its antisemitic policies, and he was involved in Charlotte von Kirschbaum's efforts to assist Jewish and Jewish-Christian refugees. He played a role in disseminating a report from an escaped Auschwitz prisoner that helped inform Allies of the plight of the Hungarian Jews, and he was involved in (ultimately unsuccessful) efforts to halt the mass deportation of Hungarian Jews in 1944.[13]

Barth's well-documented opposition (both public and private) to antisemitism and National Socialism has been both praised for its prophetic character and criticized for its inadequacy and restraint in comparison to his criticisms in respect of other contemporary issues.[14] My concern here is not to defend Barth against such criticisms, but rather to note the public, critical stance that he took in order to make explicit the contemporary valence of the subversive elements in his reading of the parable of the Good Samaritan and his construal of the neighbor as a revelatory event that undermines ethnic and religious boundaries.

---

12. Jehle, *Against the Stream*, 47–53; Lindsay, *Barth, Israel, and Jesus*, 22–3.

13. Jehle, *Against the Stream*, 31–4.

14. Barth's position toward the Jews and his doctrine of Israel continue to be topics of discussion and debate, the terms of which are summarized nicely by Katherine Sonderegger, *That Jesus Christ Was Born a Jew: Karl Barth's "Doctrine of Israel"* (University Park, PA: Pennsylvania State University Press, 1992) and, more recently by Mark Lindsay, *Barth, Israel, and Jesus* (esp. ch. 2). The two agree that Barth grants no lasting legitimacy to Judaism as an independent religious system. Sonderegger argues that Barth's interpretation of Judaism reproduces, in its own distinctive way, the language and logic of classic Christian descriptions of Israel and the Jews, thus representing, preserving and elaborating a broad tradition of Christian anti-Judaism (*That Jesus Christ Was Born a Jew*, 6–12). Lindsay focuses on the positive role that Judaism plays in *Church Dogmatics*, particularly in its dialectical relationship to the Church, in which each requires the witness of the other (*Barth, Israel, and Jesus*, 110). His book aims to defend Barth against what he finds to be the almost-universal conclusion among sympathetic and unsympathetic critics alike that Barth's theology is irrevocably damaged by a visceral antipathy toward Jews (25). Eugene Rogers argues that Barth reintroduces natural theology in key points of his treatment of the history of the Jews insofar as he offers their history as an empirically observable representation of the predicament of humanity and attributes their survival as an empirical proof of God's existence and human pride. Here Barth is said to depart from his familiar refusal to accept the empirical reality of history and the self-understanding of groups as proper objects for theological reflection (*Sexuality and the Christian Body: Their Way into the Triune Life* [Oxford: Blackwell, 1999], 154–7). Gary Dorrien, *The Barthian Revolt in Modern Theology: Theology without Weapons* (Louisville: Westminster, 2000), 131–45, gives a brief account of related postwar criticisms of Barth's relation to politics, advanced by Brunner, Bultmann, and Tillich.

Some of Barth's closest theological colleagues—Emil Brunner, Friedrich Gogarten, and Rudolf Bultmann—incorporated the orders of creation into their ethical works, finding in such institutions as marriage, family, and state expressions of concrete, divinely instituted arrangements through which God's will for human social life could be discerned. Barth's relationship with these allies had been unraveling for some time, and Barth's objection to their constructive interests in the orders of creation contributed to the disintegration. Barth saw here a recourse to natural theology with disturbing affiliations with the nationalist theologies of the German Christians.[15]

Barth's disagreement with his colleagues on the orders of creation played out in a well-known public debate with Brunner, which came to a head in a heated exchange in 1934 at the height of the Aryan Clause crisis.[16] Barth argued that to find God's ethical mandates for human life in socio-historical constants that are in any sense perceivable apart from Scripture's witness to God's revelation is to allow for a creaturely human capacity to know God's will and to act in accord with it. Furthermore, to identify constant patterns of social life and then elevate these to the status of binding and authoritative divine commands is to universalize a private *Weltanschauung*. Finally,

---

15. Gogarten briefly joined the German Christian movement in 1933 and criticized Barth and the Confessing Church for opposing the Nazi state, although he soon broke from the German Christians over their antisemitic policies. While Brunner did not himself join the German Christians, his *Divine Imperative* (1932) was well received by them, a strike against it in Barth's view (Neal, "Be Who You Are," 27–42; Hart, *Karl Barth vs. Emil Brunner*, 146–8; Emil Brunner, "Nature and Grace," in *Natural Theology*, 25–50; Brunner, *The Divine Imperative*, trans. Olive Wyon [Philadelphia: Westminster, 1936]). Bultmann, like Brunner, was also trying to rehabilitate the orders of creation theology, although like Barth he actively opposed the antisemitism of the German Christians. For a careful account of Bultmann's use of this framework, and his relationship to the Confessing Church, the German Christians, and to Barth and Gogarten, see David W. Congdon, *The Mission of Demythologizing: Rudolf Bultmann's Dialectical Theology* (Minneapolis: Fortress, 2015), 143–59. See Hart for a detailed account of the relationship, interaction, and correspondence between the Barth and Brunner during the volatile year of 1934 (*Karl Barth vs. Emil Brunner*, 150–64).

16. In the following essays, Barth criticizes his colleagues' use of natural theology or makes critical references to the orders of creation: *The First Commandment as an Axiom of Theology* (May 10, 1933); *Theological Existence Today!* (June 24, 1933); "Barmen Declaration" (May 1934); *Nein!* (1934); "Gospel and Law" (Oct, 1935); "Das Halten Der Gebote," in *Vortrage und kleinere Arbeiten 1925–1930*, ed. Harmann Schmidt (Zürich: Theologischer Verlag Zürich, 1994), 99–139. See Hart's book-length study of the relationship between Brunner and Barth (*Karl Barth vs. Emil Brunner*), which argues that this 1934 debate was the culmination of disagreements dating back to 1924, and connected to a number of issues at the heart of Barth's move away from his colleagues. These issues included: the nature of dialectic and revelation; the relationship between theology and philosophy; the location of anthropology within theology; the task of theology. For an account of Barth's developing opposition to the orders of creation in these works see Neal, "Be Who You Are," 27–42.

2. Playing the Neighbor in an "Order of Praise"

to locate the law of God within a sphere of life that is separable from the revelation of God in Christ is to separate the sphere of divine law from the sphere of gospel and thereby to provide the grounds for an ethics of self-justification in which individuals must in some sense cooperate in their own salvation.[17]

In §18, the reasons Barth gives for his rejection of the orders of creation as an ethical framework reiterates and builds upon concerns and objections cited in these debates. Here, however, they are tailored to support his description of an "order of praise" that hinges on a dialectic of grace and law operative in his account of Christian ethics, as Barth continues to redirect readers from improper objects of theological reflection such as social institutions.

The neighbor within an "order of praise"

Throughout his first volume of *Church Dogmatics* Barth reminds his readers of their complete dependence on and necessary orientation toward the voice of the divine Other heard within Christian discourse, without which theologians will produce (natural) theologies that reflect only themselves and their worlds.[18] In §18, Barth turns to the theologian's dependence on and responsibility for the human other, now broaching the question of the identity of the neighbor for whom all would-be hearers of the divine address are responsible and the question of the nature of that obligation. The orders of creation was an obvious ethical framework for many of his contemporaries and one among several frameworks that Barth here quickly dismisses (I/2, 404–6) as a recourse to natural theology. Surprisingly—after all the polemics I have rehearsed above—he neither names nor dialogues with contemporaries who use the rejected framework, but identifies only their authorizing source:

> we shall have to treat with some reserve the advice frequently given by Luther, that we must seek our neighbour within the orders of life and society [*der Lebens- und Gemeinschaftsordnungen*] in which we actually find ourselves: the husband in his wife, the children in their parents and brothers and sisters, the master in the servant, the inferior in the superior and vice versa, the national in the fellow-national and so on. (I/2, 416 [459])

While he brushes these orders aside as a marginal distraction, unworthy of further polemical attention, this dismissiveness is part of his rhetorical performance. Barth notes elsewhere:

---

17. See especially *The First Commandment*, in *The Way of Theology in Karl Barth: Essays and Comments*, ed. H. Martin Rumscheidt (Allison Park, PA: Wipf and Stock, 1986), 69–76, and "No!" in *Natural Theology*, esp. 86–7, 90.

18. All parenthetical references inline are to *Church Dogmatics* I/2, while page references to *Die kirchliche Dogmatik* appear within brackets inside parenthetical references.

If one occupies oneself with real theology one can pass by so-called natural theology only as one would pass by an abyss into which it is inadvisable to step if one does not want to fall. All one can do is to turn one's back upon it as upon the great temptation and source of error, by having nothing to do with it and by making it clear to oneself and to others from time to time why one acts that way … If you really reject natural theology you do not stare at the serpent, with the result that it stares back at you, hypnotises you, and is ultimately certain to bite you, but you hit it and kill it as soon as you see it![19]

As with religious experience and the faculties of the self, so also with such social institutions: Barth will not give false sources for theological reflection sustained attention, but says only enough to redirect his readers, himself looking where he wants them to look.

Barth's objections to this framework are a familiar part of his critique of natural theology. The "orders of creation" assume that knowledge of and obedience to the will of God is humanly achievable, that knowledge of God's commandments with respect to our fellow human beings can be discerned from the creaturely sphere through human faculties unaided by God's self-revelation in Christ (I/1, 405). The framework thus opens up a misdirected course to self-justification propelled by "the idea that the neighbour is one to whom we have a definite duty, who has a claim upon us." The "neighbor" thus comes into view as the embodiment of the law (of a duty or obligation), and, as such, as "a Law separated and emptied of the Gospel," in which the love of God is sought through one's own efforts and labor (416). To be oriented toward the neighbor located within these orders of society is, therefore, to be oriented improperly. Relying on the resources of the self, one remains caught within the limits of self-knowledge. Furthermore, one remains within the confines of social relationships that provide no escape from human lovelessness and the isolated pursuit of self-reflection, self-discovery, and self-justification—instead they often serve to instantiate it (404–5).

Barth redirects his readers from societal institutions to the biblical texts, where they will be confronted with and be taught how to identify and respond to their neighbor. In the process he transposes the discussion of ethical obligation from a Lutheran framework that separates law and duty from gospel and grace, into a Reformed framework that emphasizes the role of divine agency in the efficacious communication of grace through mundane creaturely media.[20]

---

19. Barth, "No!" in *Natural Theology*: 74–6.

20. For a discussion of Barth's theological immersion in Reformed theology, beginning in the early 1920s as he prepared for his first faculty position at Göttingen, see Bruce L. McCormack, *Karl Barth's Critically Realistic Dialectical Theology* (New York: Oxford University Press, 1995), 332; John A Vissers, "Karl Barth's appreciative use of Herman Bavinck's Reformed Dogmatics," *Calvin Theological Journal* 45, no. 1 (April 2010): 79–86; Cornelis van der Kooi, "Herman Bavinck and Karl Barth on Christian Faith and Culture," *Calvin Theological Journal* (April 2010): 72–9; Kooi, "The Concept of Culture in Abraham

The two commandments, the love of God and the love of neighbor (as presented in Mt. 22:35-40; Mk. 12:28-34; Lk. 10:25-37), provide the biblical framework for addressing the question of how a life in conformity with God's revelation in Christ ought to be lived (367). Through a confrontation with Christ, who delivers these commands, readers will be directed out of their misguided searches for duty-fulfillment.

We cannot, Barth argues, know or enact this love of God and neighbor without first being redirected out of our self-love and self-justification by an act of divine love, an act that precedes and enables our responding love, an act that is mediated through our fellow neighbor. He thus construes the two commandments as a divine speech-act leading to a two-sided human response: the love of God is the inner and hidden reality of which the love of neighbor is the outer sign and external manifestation (368–71). Playing on the "order" language of the framework that he has rejected, Barth replaces talk of divinely imposed orders of creation, discernible to all, with talk of a divinely imposed "order of praise" (*Ordnung des Lobes*) (424 [468]), "order of grace" (*Ordnung der Gnade*) (409 [451]), and "order of humiliation" (*Ordnung der Demütigung*) (394 [433]). This order, we shall see, is constituted by the gratuitous divine revelatory act, that simultaneously humbles the subject and reorients him or her in a hopeful search for the divine subject revealed and concealed in creaturely forms.

Barth begins with the inner reality, by way of an analysis of the first commandment of Mark 12:29-31 to love God with all one's heart, soul, mind, and strength (381–401). In this analysis he continues to castigate the self-absorbed human subject, who must now be reminded of its utter incapacity to discern and fulfill the divine command to love God and neighbor. Barth posits that we can love God only in response to a preceding and enabling divine act of love in which we see our neediness reflected, with humbling results (380). Furthermore, he asks whether all our endeavors to love are not haunted by the question of whether we have truly escaped the isolation of self-love—by whether what we love is an objective "other" (386–7). Echoing his depiction of the human side of the revelatory event (§6), he writes:

> If love, *as distinct from the illusion of self-love, is love for another*, and if this other is God the Lord, then our loving must be defined as the nature and attitude of man, conscious that he is of a different kind from that object. Love to God takes place in the self-knowledge of repentance in which we *learn about ourselves by the mirror of the Word of God* which acquits and blesses us, which is itself the love of God to us. The man who loves God *will let himself be*

Kuyper, Herman Bavinck, and Karl Barth," in *Crossroad Discourses between Christianity and Culture*, ed. Jerald D. Gort, et al. (New York: Rodopi, 2010), 37–51; Paul T. Nimmo, "Bavinck, Barth, and the Uniqueness of the Eucharist," *Scottish Bulletin of Evangelical Theology* 29, no.1 (Spring 2011): 108–26; John Webster, *Barth's Earlier Theology: Four Studies* (New York: T&T Clark, 2005), 15–39.

> *told and will himself confess* that he is not in any sense righteous as one who loves ... he is a sinner who even in his love has nothing to bring and offer to God. (390, italics added)

This humbling self-discovery redirects the self from its improper fixation on a now devalued object toward the proper object of love, for "grace points them away from self, frightens them out of themselves, deprives them of any root or soil or country in themselves, summons them to hold to the promise, to trust in Him, to boast in Him, to take guidance and counsel of Him and Him alone" (394). The divine act of love enables obedience to the command it imposes by lending to the self both direction and desire, setting the self on a search for the divine other:

> We cannot be satisfied with repentance as such (especially if it is sincere). We cannot be satisfied with self-knowledge (especially if it does not mean assurance but a burning need). Beyond our own quite conscious lovelessness, and therefore without even dreaming that with our love we can offer anything to God, we begin genuinely, and in need, and with a consuming desire to know, to ask about the One who has first loved us. (391)

Yet this seeking, although divinely evoked, remains a human activity and effort to love, allowing no reason for self-congratulation. Properly humbled subjects will not rest assured that theirs is a proper seeking and therefore a proper loving, nor will they pause to reflect on such a question. They must not be distracted by the search itself, becoming fixated once again upon the self, succumbing to the allure of self-justification. Even so, Barth anticipates that we will nevertheless and inevitably be so distracted. The love for God (*the* great commandment) thus requires a repeated redirecting of the self away from its self-fixation, and thus the human activity that seeks to fulfill the commandment is an activity that is propelled by this need and hope for divine aid:

> Yet this being and activity acquires a direction at the point where everything is done for us, the direction Godward in Jesus Christ ... What matters is emphatically not the fact that we are seeking. What matters is that if we accept and adopt this direction, we are always seekers. Of course, that means that we are seeking. But in all that seeking we are again in the sphere of our lovelessness and unworthiness of being loved. In spite of our seeking, we can still be rejecting. Our seeking may be upright, inward and profound, but as such it will stand in constant need of the forgiveness of sins. (392)

Barth thus prescribes for would-be lovers of God a ceaseless activity, compelled by desire and hope, in need of continual reorientation by the signs of the biblical witness. They are not to await the assurance that they are moving in the proper direction, but are rather to persist in seeking with the hope of being led to and found by God. It will be a quest in search of and hope for continual redirection, and requiring endless labor:

How can love to God be inactive? It is all activity, but only as man's answer to what God has said to him. As this answer it is a work, and it produces works. But it is a work, and produces works, in the fact that it is the witness of God's work, and therefore a renunciation of all self-glorying and all claims. (401)

This loving quest is, thus, precisely what theological activity aspires to be, as Barth portrays it throughout *Church Dogmatics* I.

The Good Samaritan as a model neighbor

With the second great commandment, Barth configures the love of neighbor as the outer sign of this inner quest. The neighbor functions as the material and tangible reference point, divinely imposed on the subject—the object toward which would-be lovers of God direct their seeking activity, the mirror in which they are both humbled and redirected. The narrative template for Barth's exposition of the second commandment is the Lucan pericope (Lk. 10:25-35) in which Jesus tells the parable of the Good Samaritan to help a lawyer identify the neighbor whom he is to love (417–19). Barth depicts the scene in a section of fine print.

In Barth's re-description, the Lucan narrative is a scene in which Jesus redirects the self-justifying search of a lawyer of Israel by disclosing to him the neighbor whom he must love. The lawyer is "a doctor of the Law in Israel": "outward and by appearance, by his very calling, he belongs to the community of Yahweh," and claims to be "a prominent member" of it, a participator in its divine promises, and one who knows and is able to recite the commandments of God (417). The lawyer asks Jesus how he might inherit eternal life. When Jesus asks him what answer the law provides, the lawyer recites the two great commandments, the love of God and the love of neighbor. But when the lawyer asks Jesus who his neighbor is, he shows himself to be neither ready for, nor capable of, fulfilling these commands. Not knowing who his neighbor is, he does not know who God is. He approaches Jesus as one who seeks, but his search is misdirected, for while it is Jesus to whom he brings these questions, he does not see and recognize Jesus as the one whom he ought to seek. Remaining preoccupied with himself, he comes to Jesus seeking to "justify himself" (v. 29), not knowing that "only by mercy can he live and inherit eternal life." Since he does not know his neighbor and therefore does not live by mercy, he lives instead "by his own intention and ability to present himself as a righteous man before God" (417).

Jesus responds to the lawyer's misdirected inquiry ("who is my neighbor?") by telling a parable that holds a mirror up to the lawyer, reflecting the lawyer's own neediness and gesturing to the true neighbor who is able to help. "A man who fell among thieves" lies half-dead and neglected by the passing priest and Levite, but is attended to "without hesitation and with unsparing energy" by the Samaritan. When Jesus asks which of the three proved himself a neighbor to this man, the lawyer replies "he that showed mercy on him" (418).

Barth's re-telling of the parable hinges on this precise identification, for, contrary to the exegesis of many of his contemporaries, this identity of the neighbor is

> the only point of the story, unequivocally stated by the text. For the lawyer, who wants to justify himself and therefore does not know who is his neighbour, is confronted not by the poor wounded man with his claim for help, but by the anything but poor Samaritan who makes no claim at all but is simply helpful. It is the Samaritan who embodies what he wanted to know. This is the neighbour he did not know. (418)

Barth plays the part of one whose own expectations and assumptions have been unsettled by this disclosure, by Jesus's surprise reversal and reorientation of the lawyer's search for self-justification. He writes:

> All very unexpected: for the lawyer had first to see that he himself is the man fallen among thieves and lying helpless by the wayside; then he has to note that the others who pass by, the priest and the Levite, the familiar representatives of the dealings of Israel with God, all one after the other do according to the saying of the text: "He saw him and passed by on the other side;" and third, and above all, he has to see that he must be found and treated with compassion by the Samaritan, the foreigner, *whom he believes he should hate, as one who hates and is hated by God*. He will then know who is his neighbour, and will not ask concerning him as though it were only a matter of the casual clarification of a concept. He will then know the second commandment, and consequently the first as well. *He will then not wish to justify himself, but will simply love the neighbour, who shows him mercy. He will then love God, and loving God will inherit eternal life.* (418, emphasis added)

One does not discover one's neighbor on a quest for self-justification or as part of a dispassionate theological exercise; rather one is discovered *by* one's neighbor when such self-affirming exercises are interrupted by the benefit that the other confers on the self, a benefit that exposes the self's neediness.

Having foregrounded this gospel of grace embodied in the neighbor, Barth locates within the parable the law that the neighbor imposes. He continues: "in fact the lawyer does not see his own helplessness. He does not see that the priest and the Levite bring him no help and the Samaritan does. He does not really know his neighbour" (418). In another surprising turn in the narrative, Jesus gives a challenge to this man, who is incapable of recognizing himself in the mirror held up to him and, thus, incapable of fulfilling the two commandments. Jesus commands him to "Go and do thou likewise"; be a benefactor to another, imitate the Samaritan, and thus be one who brings "comfort, help, the Gospel to someone else" (419). This is surprising, Barth explains, because Jesus does not impose the law on the lawyer: he does not command the lawyer to love God and neighbor, as Jesus's hearers (and Barth's readers) might expect. Without waiting for the lawyer to properly recognize his neighbor, Jesus summons him to act and imitate the merciful acts of another, and in this way to seek and find his neighbor:

> We see and have a neighbour when we show mercy on him and he therefore owes us love. We see and have a neighbour when we are wholly the givers and he can only receive. We see and have him when he cannot repay us and especially when he is an enemy, someone who hates us and injures us and persecutes us (Mt. 5:43f). (419)

Thus the obligation imposed upon the lawyer as a misguided and needy subject is a performance aimed at imitating the example of the Samaritan benefactor.

Barth pauses to ask why Jesus should demand this sort of merciful activity of one "who obviously does not see or have a compassionate neighbour, who lacks all the necessary presuppositions." Barth's answer, delivered in a final narrative twist, is to direct the reader to the one who delivers the summons:

> On His lips the "Go and do thou likewise" is only Law because it is first Gospel. The good Samaritan, the neighbour who is a helper and will make him a helper, is not far from the lawyer ... He stands before him incarnate, although hidden *under the form of one whom the lawyer believed he should hate, as the Jews hated the Samaritans*. (419, emphasis added)

Barth thus presents Jesus as the paradigmatic figure of the neighbor, of whom the Samaritan is a reflection. But we never learn, Barth notes, whether the lawyer does in fact attempt to imitate Christ and thus perform truly the law he recites so well (419). The inner orientation of this lawyer, who is summoned by Christ to enact outwardly the part of the neighbor, remains concealed from the view of the reader.

In the exposition of the second commandment that follows, Barth reproduces the dialectical relationship between gospel and law that he finds within the narrative. He imitates its order in the very structuring of his exposition, for he talks first of the benefit (or gospel) conferred by the neighbor, and only then of the command (or law) this benefit imposes. The Samaritan and the fallen Israelite function as figurative representations of the two sides of a dialectical event in which the subject is confronted by the neighbor. The Samaritan represents for Barth the benefit the neighbor confers while the fallen Israelite foregrounds the neediness that the neighbor also embodies, the very revelation of which is itself a benefit.

The neighbor is a revelatory event mediated not through any specific group of persons, but through "the fellow-man who emerges from amongst all others as my benefactor" (421). In my neighbor, I am confronted by a benefactor who confers a gift that exposes my own neediness and reminds me of the gift embodied in the incarnate Word. As such the neighbor's benefit can only be received and cannot be earned, and this conferral imposes on me the obligation to act as a neighbor in turn. In this capacity, embodying both gospel and law, my neighbor "proclaims and shows forth Jesus Christ within this world," facing us as "the bearer and representative of the divine compassion" and as "the instrument of that order which is so necessary and indispensable for us in this time and world, in which God wills to be praised by us for His goodness" (416). As such, my neighbor imposes on me the obligation to also be "a bearer and representative of that divine mercy in the world" (421). In this precise sense Barth refers to the neighbor as a sacramental event in which "I am actually placed before Christ" (429)—the material reference point for my Godward-directed loving activity.

Barth elaborates on the nature of the revelatory benefit conferred: my neighbor is a mirror that reflects my own need and, in so doing, is a sign that points to the humanity of Christ. I have a neighbor when I recognize in the will and activity of the other the misery and neediness that I share with him or her:

> His actual misery consists in the fact that he wills, wills to live, and yet–with or without mask, openly or secretly, perhaps indeed without knowing it himself–he cannot, cannot live, and is therefore caught in an always hopeless and hopelessly repeated and varied attempt to do so. If I recognise him in this, if with whatever feelings I see this as his oppression, shame and torment, I recognise in him my neighbour. (429)

This reflection has its efficacy not in the specific emotive responses it might evoke in me, whether pity, surprise, horror, resignation, or even admiration (428–9), but rather as it unsettles, humbles and redirects me toward the neighbor. In fact, I may well dislike what I see of myself in this mirror and might prefer to remain alone:

> This neighbour will cause me a really mortal headache. I mean, he will seriously give me cause involuntarily to repudiate his existence and in that way to put myself in serious danger. In face of this neighbour I certainly have to admit to myself that I would really prefer to exist in some other way than in this co-existence. I would prefer this because from this neighbour a shadow falls inexorably and devastatingly upon myself. (431)

Furthermore, this shadow undermines any sense of superiority I might have over my neighbor. There is a leveling effect to this shared fellowship in misery that is profoundly disconcerting, allowing no one person any advantage over another (430–1). To love one's neighbor is therefore to submit to this humbling order that the neighbor imposes on oneself (434–5).

This confrontation with my neighbor reflects not only my sin and need but Christ's redemptive work, which meets that need:

> The neighbour shows me that I myself am a sinner. How can it be otherwise, seeing he stands in Christ's stead, seeing he must always remind me of Him as the Crucified? How can he help but show me, as the reflection of myself, what Christ has taken upon Himself for my sake? The divine mission and authority which the neighbour has in relation to me, the mercy which he shows me, is not to be separated from this revelation. (431)

The neighbor is, in this gratuitous revelatory sense, the revelatory sign of the grace of God embodied in the humanity of Christ:

> And his benefaction to us as a suffering fellow-creature in need of help consists in the fact that even in his misery he shows us the true humanity of Jesus Christ, that humanity which was not triumphant but submissive, not healthy and strong, but characterised by the bearing of our sins, which was therefore flesh of our flesh—the flesh abandoned to punishment, suffering and death. Our fellow-man in his oppression, shame and torment confronts us with the poverty, the homelessness, the scars, the corpse, at the grave of Jesus Christ. (428)

The mirror of the neighbor thus establishes between self and other a shared fellowship with the human misery and need of Jesus. Reflecting my own neediness, my neighbor reminds me of the forgiveness I have received: "Whether willingly and wittingly or not, in showing it, my neighbour acquires for me a sacramental significance. In this capacity he becomes and is a visible sign of invisible grace, a proof that I, too, am not left alone in this world, but am borne and directed by God" (436). As a sacramental event, this reminder is something of which I am in continual need.[21]

It is in recollecting Christ's mercy that the divine command is communicated in this confrontation with the neighbor. Following the dialectic from gospel to law, Barth speaks next of the duty to the other, and here an epistemic veil intervenes in Barth's account, for we cannot know if our neighbor is aware of the grace of which she or he has reminded us, and out of this ignorance our responsibility to the neighbor arises.

> The fact that in our need we look to God in Jesus Christ and listen to His Word and then love God afresh and this time truly, is something which, if it happens, we can only accept as grace. And that is how we stand here and now towards our neighbour, with the difference that while we can, of course, accept grace for ourselves, we cannot accept it for him. We can know that God loves him, and that His Word is for him. But we cannot know that in his need he looks to God and listens to His Word and is comforted. (438)

---

21. Barth's minimal but strategic uses of sacramental language to describe the neighbor in this ethical context is very much in keeping with the central commitments of his doctrine of revelation, discussed in Chapter 1. For a discussion on Barth's lack of precision in the use of the language of sacrament to refer to the intersection of divine and human action in a revealing and reconciling event, see W. Travis McMaken, *The Sign of the Gospel: Toward an Evangelical Doctrine of Infant Baptism after Karl Barth* (Minneapolis: Fortress Press, 2013), 186–7. This book provides a helpful account of how Barth's view of sacraments changed as he undertook his christological reformulation of the doctrine of election in *CD* II/2.

Because we do not know this, and because our neighbor has conferred this benefit on us, we must expect to find in our neighbor one who shares with us the continual need of this reminder of God's grace; we must act as those who hope to become signs to our neighbor of Christ's redemptive love (438).

The performance that Barth now prescribes for himself and his readers embraces the entire self. I am not to pronounce commandments and laws to the other (for Jesus did not impose the law on the lawyer), but rather, in my speech, acts, and attitude, I am to imitate the neighbor(s) modeled for me in the biblical narratives (439). Barth presents an ethic for a specifically theological and ecclesial practice, and so the role to be performed is that of witness to Christ (a role best modeled for Barth by the biblical authors). As would-be neighbor and sign, I must speak to the other of the grace I have experienced. While this does, admittedly, require *some* talk about one's self, it must above all be talk of oneself as a recipient of divine aid; it is therefore an indirect reflection on the self, channeled through the language of Christian discourse, but spoken specifically in regard to the effects of the biblical and ecclesial witness to Christ on the self. Moreover, my speech must be accompanied by acts of assistance directed toward the need of my neighbor as that need comes to external expression in "specific sicknesses, derangements and confusions of his psycho-physical existence" (444). Such effort at providing temporary and partial mitigation and relief of the neighbor's need might itself function as a sign of hope to him or her that this need will find its limit in Christ (445–6). Finally, in my entirety I must enact the sort of attitude, disposition, and mood that corresponds to these words and acts, and I must model for the reader the proper orientation: "The neighbour hears my few words and enjoys my little assistance. But he also notices that I myself look and listen where my words and deeds seem to invite him to look and listen" (447–8). And so in speech, word, orientation, and disposition, Barth instructs his readers to do as he seeks to do— to model a life reordered by grace and its proper orientation toward the divine benefactor.

What Barth calls for here is a performance that cannot live up to the norm it aspires to imitate. Barth reminds the reader that the efficacy of this activity is not something over which his readers have control: "if there is to be a real praise of God and love of our neighbour in our activity, there has to take place an activity of God which we with our activity can only serve, and which from the standpoint of our activity can only have the character of a miracle" (450). It is thus a role to be enacted in faith and hope for this miracle:

> We have to trust in the fact that Jesus Christ will be present in this meeting with my neighbour. It will be His business, not mine, and however badly I play my part, He will conduct His business successfully and well. We have to rely on the fact that it is Jesus Christ who has given me a part in His business; that He has not done so in vain; that He will make use of my service, and in that way make it real service, even though I do not see how my service can be real service ... These are not guarantees. They can only be an assurance. But this assurance is required of us when we are commanded: Thou shalt

love thy neighbour as thyself. It is only in this assurance that obedience is possible. (453)

Thus Barth prescribes for the reader a ceaseless imitative performance. Neither my inability to become what I attempt to enact, nor the necessity of the miracle in giving my activity its efficacy, relieves me of the responsibility of playing the part of the neighbor. Like the lawyer in the parable, I may not even recognize my neighbor, for I may be on a misguided quest for self-justification; and yet nevertheless I am summoned to act, and so to imitate the model-neighbors presented to me in the biblical witness. A ceaseless activity of speech, act, and attitude is required: the inner reality of the subject's search for (love for) God must be expressed in the outer sign of activity directed toward the other.

The Jewish Samaritan and the völkisch *church*

Having followed Barth's construal of the neighbor to its performative conclusions, we are now in a position to see Barth's own theological description of the neighbor as itself the discursive performance of one who hopes to be a neighbor to the reader. In the Scriptures he hears the voice of neighbors who set him on a search for his neighbor: "Who and what a neighbour is, we can best realise from those who founded the Church, the biblical prophets and apostles. What they do is the purest form of that work of divine mercy which is assumed by the children of God. They bear witness to Jesus Christ ... But the same thing happens wherever the Church is the Church" (422). Continuing along these lines, Barth directs his readers to their neighbors:

> For if in the prophets and apostles we see men to whom Jesus Christ has become a neighbour, and they themselves have become helpful and compassionate neighbours by bearing witness to Him, if it has become a general possibility in the Church that men can have this function, then we must obviously be prepared and ready for the fact that man, our fellow-man generally, can become our neighbour, even where we do not think we see anything of the Church, i.e., in his humanity he can remind us of the humanity of the Son of God and show mercy upon us by summoning us in that way to the praise of God. (425)

Barth draws the reader into a mimetic chain of recognition and re-description, and incites the reader to join with him on this path. Performing the role of the dogmatician, he plays the part of one confronted by a neighbor in the authorial voices of biblical narratives, as these voices speak to him of the neighbor they have encountered in Christ. In turn he plays the neighbor to his readers, giving witness to what he has heard, inviting them, also, to recognize themselves in the lawyer and fallen Israelite, and to hear along with Barth the command to "Go and do thou likewise." For if the lawyer, who seeks to justify himself (recognizing neither his own inability and need nor Christ's ability to meet it), must recognize himself in the man fallen among thieves, so too must the readers. And regardless of whether they recognize themselves in this mirror, they must hasten to play the neighbor to another (422).

When read with his contemporary context in mind, Barth's performance can be seen as enacting the sort of subversions and reorientations that he finds within the parable. Barth's identification of the neighbor effaces the boundaries of the visible Church, along whatever lines they might be drawn, and it relocates those who might be deemed "outside" to stand now within its boundaries as the potential neighbors who give witness to Christ's grace. The implications of this account for contemporaneous efforts to enforce racial exclusions from church office are not far from the surface. The relationship of the fallen Israelite to the Samaritan enables Barth to argue that while the neighbor embodies a proclamation of the Word in his or her speech, deeds, and disposition, the neighbor need not actually be a member of the visible Church in order to do so. In fact, the neighbor may well be one who is perceived as indifferent or even hostile to the Church, one whom members of the Church consider to be hated by and to hate God, just as the lawyer thought of the Samaritan—and also of Jesus (422, 418–19). The true status of the other's relationship to God cannot and does not need to be known for him or her to acquire this function (429, 438). The other's capacity to become such a divinely enabled medium of grace resides neither in his or her self-awareness nor in our knowledge of him or her (and certainly not in any ethnic or religious differences), but in the revelatory act of the Word, and thus in the mystery of God's freedom.

Since the status of the other remains concealed from the self, the apparent "outsider" must not be treated or regarded as such:

> It is in the light of this [divine] summons, of the fact that simply as he is, as a man, he can be a neighbor to me here and now at any moment, as the Samaritan was to the man half-dead by the roadside, it is in this light, and not in the light of the fact that he is an outsider, that I must regard him from within the Church. (423)

To view apparent outsiders in this way is to view them "in the reflection of the human nature of Jesus Christ." And we are not simply to await this divinely enabled moment of recognition but must "expect to find" such a neighbor in every individual (425).

In subtle ways Barth's description of the neighbor, construed as a sacramental medium, turns the tables on contemporaneous discussions about the racial delineation of a *völkisch* church, wherein race was said to trump baptism. Barth can be read here as inviting his readers in Germany to recognize themselves in the self-justifying Jewish lawyer of the parable, who does not know his neighbor and so does not recognize Christ. The contemporary Jewish "foreigner" is aligned, through the Samaritan, with Christ, both of whom the lawyer thinks he should hate as the very objects of God's hatred.

2. Playing the Neighbor in an "Order of Praise"

This sort of reversal appears to be in play in Barth's description of the "hidden neighbor": at one point he refers to the Gentile outsiders within the nation of Israel, figures in the Old and New Testaments who are presented as "strangers who from the most unexpected distances come right into the apparently closed circle of the divine election and calling and carry out a kind of commission, fulfill an office for which there is no name, but the content of which is quite obviously a service which they have to render" (425). He names the well-known biblical figures of Balaam, Rahab, Ruth, the Queen of Sheba, Naaman, the wise men, the centurion of Capernaum, the Syro-Phoenician woman, the centurion at the cross, and finally, the paradigmatic figure of "Melchisedek, King of Salem, and a 'priest of the most high God,' who brings bread and wine to Abraham, blesses him and receives from him a tithe (Gen. 14:18f.)," who as such is the "hermeneutic key to this whole succession" (425).

The contemporaneous rhetoric relating to nation and blood is not far from the surface here, nor are the debates about the place of Jewish Christians in the sacramental and clerical life of the church. Barth shifts quickly to talk of the New Testament equivalent term for "neighbor"—"brother"—and he invokes the language of "blood relationship" to refer to the relationship made possible between Jesus and those whom he calls into relation with himself. To be brother to Christ, Barth states, is to recognize Christ in the other: "in every man we have to expect a brother (for that only means a neighbor in the full sense of the word)" (426–7).[22] In this way Barth detaches the biblical notions of neighbor and of brother from any association with contemporaneous appeals to societal institutions of shared blood and nationhood, and he situates the terminology of neighbor, brother, and blood within a christological revelatory framework in which there is no "outside" to the sphere of God's grace, of the shared sacrificial blood of Christ, and thus to the sphere of the Christian's ethical obligation.[23]

---

22. Similar language in an earlier excursus (417–19) appears to have in view Barth's contemporaries' preoccupation with the concept of *Volk*. Here Barth refuses any appropriation of orders of creation from Luther and wants to detach notions of "a national community of blood" from Old Testament accounts of the neighbor. It is true, he notes, that in the Old Testament the fellow-Israelite is the primary referent for those passages that speak of the neighbor who is to be loved. He continues: "But note that in the Old Testament the 'people' is not primarily a national community of blood. The 'neighbour' also includes the frequently mentioned and by no means unimportant 'stranger within thy gates.' And the nation itself and as such is primarily the people of God ... Even in the Old Testament it is only secondarily that it is this within the framework of a closed, but never absolutely closed, national community of blood ... In light of the New Testament the secondary definition of neighbour cannot become primary (not even by extending it to all sorts of other orders of life and society)" (416).

23. While my reading points to ways in which Barth subverts antisemitic rhetoric, his reading of the parable nevertheless participates in the traditional Lutheran distinction between Law and Gospel to organize the relationship between Christianity and Judaism, a

I have made explicit the subversive dynamics of Barth's construal of the neighbor, when read within in its immediate discursive context. However, these subversive features, by their very subtlety, lend support to the criticisms that Barth's opposition to the antisemitism of the German church and state in the 1930s was far too restrained. My intent, in foregrounding them, has not been to contest these critiques but rather to make explicit the critical potential of this depiction of the neighbor.[24] Barth's account of the neighbor in §18 pushes at the

move which was commonplace in Protestant debates about the mission to the Jews and also in their inter-religious dialogue with Jews. For a discussion of Jewish-Christian dialogue in the Weimar Republic (1918–1933), including different Protestant positions in relation to rising antisemitism, see Ulrich Rosenhagen, "'Together a Step towards the Messianic Goal': Jewish-Protestant Encounter in the Weimar Republic," in *The Weimar Moment: Liberalism, Political Theology, and Law*, ed. Leonard V. Kaplan and Rudy Koshar (Plymouth, UK: Lexington Books, 2012), 47–72. Protestant theologians who were engaged in inter-religious dialogue with German Jewish intellectuals and eager to maintain a mission to the Jews (which the German Christians would later reject) were motivated in part by a shared objection to the rise of antisemitism. These Protestant participants fought antisemitism along with other racial ideologies that had become influential in the Weimar period (59). But they were always quick to highlight the differences between Judaism and Christianity, which they mapped onto a distinction between Law and Grace, with Judaism being depicted as pre-modern and legalistic (56–7). Barth's use of the parable of the Good Samaritan can be understood as a continuation of this trajectory of resistance to antisemitism. It remains within the framework of a Law/Grace distinction, but I have suggested that it destabilizes the commonplace alignment of Judaism with legalism and Christianity with grace: anyone anywhere in any religion might become the representative of grace; those who treat the other as an occasion for fulfilling the Law of God are in fact engaged in a legalistic pursuit of self-justification. Still, this subversion participates in the linkage of Judaism, by way of the lawyer, to self-justifying legalism, even if it takes the further step of incorporating all self-justifying efforts into that ambit.

24. While Barth's construal of the neighbor as mirror and sign has this positive critical potential in §18, it also has the negative potential to lend itself to precisely the sort of abstractions for which Barth's doctrine of Israel has been criticized. Barth has been accused of producing a doctrine of Israel in which the Jew is constructed as a mirror that effaces the will and agency of actual individuals. Friedrich Marquardt first raised this question, addressed more recently by both Sonderegger (*That Jesus Christ Was Born a Jew*) and Rogers (*Sexuality and the Christian Body*), of whether Barth's depiction of Jews and his doctrine of Israel is precisely the sort of abstraction his theology seeks to avoid, one that conceals the concrete lives of actual Jews by construing them as a mirror that reflects the will of another. In Rogers's words: "Despite himself, Barth throws up a conceptual screen onto which he can at once *project* a partial abstraction ('Israel') and *hide* actual human beings ('the Jews') behind it." Rogers argues that the concepts "man" and "woman" as used by Barth are susceptible to a similar critique (140–50). In III/1 we shall see Eve's agency utterly effaced in order that she might be a static mirror that supports Adam's figural connection to Christ.

limits of contemporary socio-cultural and theological frameworks, renegotiating the boundaries that exclude the Jewish other. I will exploit this critical potential in my subsequent chapters in order to unsettle the androcentric and heteronormative framework of Barth's account of sexual difference.

Conclusion

In *Church Dogmatics* III, Barth will continue to configure the activity of the human other as a benefit that imposes an obligation upon the self. However, with the introduction of sexual difference, the paradigmatic neighbor becomes someone of the opposite sex, and Barth's reading of the encounter of Adam and Eve in Genesis 2 will provide Barth the biblical template for this shift. Several features in Barth's depiction of the neighbor in §18 will provide a critical frame of reference for analyzing Barth's later account of inter-human fellowship and the normative place he gives to the relationship between the sexes.

First, the neighbor functions simultaneously as "a sign instituted by Christ" pointing to his suffering humanity and as a mirror within which the subject recognizes his or her own humanity (435). We have seen Barth describe biblical texts and proclamation in a similar way. In this capacity, the neighbor represents to the self a shared fellowship between self, other, and Christ. The neighbor communicates something new and unsettling to the self, undermining any basis for superiority or precedence of self over other. The self receives the gift of God through the other and is compelled to respond in an imitative activity by coming to the aid of another. I shall track this recurring pattern of dependency, responsiveness, and ethical obligation in future chapters.

Second, Barth describes this encounter as a revelatory event in which God selects one specific person from the many to be a neighbor to the self on any given occasion. The dialectic of veiling and unveiling is discernable here. The divine act is never fully transparent to the self, for it always remains concealed in the creaturely medium that reveals it. As we saw in the previous chapter, where that medium is human activity, it is human self-determination that conceals in a creaturely veil the divine determination of the subject. The divine act of grace cannot, therefore, be anticipated in advance, nor can one ever be too certain one has encountered it. This obscurity is in part what motivates the seeking, loving movement toward God that is to be expressed in activities directed toward the neighbor. One cannot anticipate who will be selected to fulfill this function—one cannot anticipate who will become the neighbor that one seeks; therefore, the sphere for this search has no clear boundaries. At the same time, the other's self-awareness and consciousness of the divine act is also *not* transparent to the self, and, furthermore, the other's self-awareness does not prevent him or her from being used by God for the benefit of the subject. Especially significant for my interests, Barth states explicitly that the self cannot assent to God's grace on behalf of the other. It is because of this opacity that the other always represents to the subject an obligation and responsibility.

Third, the inaccessibility of the other's interiority has the strategic function for Barth of destabilizing the visible boundaries of the church, since it does not allow these visible boundaries to demarcate the sphere of God's revelatory activity and the responding human ethical activity. Barth notes that "the Samaritan in the parable shows us incontestably that even those who do not know that they are doing so, or what they are doing, can assume and exercise the function of the compassionate neighbor" (422). He is emphatic on this point: even one who is hostile to the church can at any moment become a neighbor and testimonial of the grace of Christ, and so must not be regarded as an outsider. Thus Barth insists that his reader must expect to find a neighbor in every other person (423, 425, 427, 429). The apparent "outsider" must be treated "as if" she or he were within the church. Within Barth's immediate context this account destabilizes ethnic and religious divisions, and it allows the other to put into question existing assumptions and patterns regarding social orders. We shall see, however, that while Barth may have been comfortable with destabilizing and relativizing ethnic and religious differences, he was later uncomfortable with doing the same to sexual difference.

Finally, the neighbor-event demands of the self a ceaseless activity in pursuit of one's neighbor. The benefit conferred through the other imposes on the self the obligation to play the benefactor to another. While this encounter constitutes the self as necessarily dependent on the conferral of grace through another, it also demands a constant activity: the subject ought not to await either the certainty of a divine disclosure through the other before acting, or any assurance beside that of a hope that keeps seeking the redirection of a God who intends to be found. We shall soon see this model of seeking subjectivity in Barth's reading of Adam, but not so much in Eve. Accordingly, this activity will become a masculine prerogative.

Chapter 3

REORIENTING THE AGENT IN THE DOCTRINE OF CREATION

Introduction

Barth's theological description and agential ordering of sexual difference is found in the third volume of *Church Dogmatics*, "The Doctrine of Creation," in which Barth discusses sexual difference in three different locations. Much of the opening part-volume is devoted to a very lengthy exposition of the first two chapters of Genesis (III/1, §41), and it is here that he first broaches the topic. Adam is a model of human freedom and precisely as such is placed in an ordered fellowship with a sexually differentiated human other. This exegetical and figurative reading of the creation of Adam and Eve lays the biblical groundwork for the two subsequent discussions of the same material. In the theological anthropology of the second part-volume, Barth presents the marital relationship as the fullest realization of human co-existence and fellowship, patterned after Christ's saving fellowship with the Church, itself temporally prefigured in the relationship of Adam and Eve (III/2, §45.3). In the fourth part-volume, the special ethics of the doctrine of creation, sexual difference (and with it the relation between the sexes) is construed as the gift of the Creator, and as such it imposes a set of obligations that the agent is to perform in obedience to the divine command (III/4, §54.1).

Barth lays the groundwork for his doctrine of creation in *Church Dogmatics* III/1, where he continues the work of humbling and reorienting a human subject inclined to put itself at the center of the cosmos. He directs readers away from mundane sources for natural or anthropocentric theologies, fixing their focus instead on Christ, veiled as the secret at the center of the doctrine of creation and unveiled in the doctrine of redemption. Barth opens the part-volume by evoking the first article of the Apostle's Creed, which he uses to frame his dogmatic reflection as a confession of belief that creation is the work of God. He finds Christ prefigured within the first article, for he construes the profession of faith in God's creative activity as an anticipation of God's redemptive activity in Christ, itself confessed in the Creed's second article. In so doing Barth aspires to be a human witness to the work of Christ, becoming the eyes that recognize this hidden gift in multiple creaturely media, and the mouth that professes gratitude.

I will highlight the stance Barth occupies as he inhabits this creedal perspective, evokes biblical models for this stance, and, in so doing, enacts the pattern of agency he finds appropriate for doing theology. Barth holds up signs of God's grace that, in benefiting the recipients, impose upon them the obligation to imitate that benefit. Creation itself is such a sign and benefit that must be accepted and confessed in faith. The benefit of the existence of the cosmos and our place within it must be recognized as God's good gift, in spite of all the ambiguity that confronts us in that cosmos, and it must be confessed as such, in obedience to the obligation that it imposes. Readers, themselves recipients of God's many gifts, are to be redirected out of self-love and self-service into humbled dependence on and responsibility for a network of creaturely entities and actors. The sexually differentiated other will be located at the center of this network, as the locus of the human being's conformity to the *imago dei*, Christ himself.

Barth's account of the *imago dei* in Genesis 1 plays an important part in his efforts to redirect his readers away from resources for a natural theology. He will not allow the *imago dei* and the divine likeness to anchor in the human being a created capacity for knowing and obeying the will of God. The *imago dei* is Christ himself, and the human creature acquires a divine likeness to Christ through no inherent capacity, but only in a divinely enabled response to the gift of God in the sexually differentiated other.

Mythology receives sustained attention in this part-volume because Barth views it as another improper resource for theological reflection, one which Barth aligns with the anthropocentric projects and natural theologies that the faithful dogmatician must shun. Barth's expositions of his doctrine of creation (§40 and §42), and his exegesis of Genesis 1 (§41), refuse mythologies of all sorts, and he labors to distinguish Genesis 1 from "mythology" as a genre.

Barth explicitly refuses to allow any positive place for maternal imagery in his reading of Genesis 1, an interpretive move that is entangled in his critique of mythology. At the center of Barth's doctrine of creation is a paternal Creator set in antithetical relation to mythological imagery linking maternity and the divine. It is widely recognized that Barth's rejection of both myth and maternal imagery is a response to the ideology of National Socialism and its elevation of the relation between maternity, earth, and blood. This interpretation has been used to excuse—and approve—Barth's rejection of maternal imagery in his reading of Genesis 1–2.[1] In this chapter I aim to complicate this interpretation by arguing that Barth's unexamined assumptions about the fecundity of the female body play

---

1. See especially Walter Brueggemann ("The Loss and Recovery of Creation in Old Testament Theology," *Theology Today* 53, no. 2 [1996]: 177–90), who sets Barth's reading of Gen. 1 in the rhetorical context of the 1930s and tracks Barth's influence upon Gerhard von Rad and a long line of Old Testament scholars who likewise find in Gen. 1 a masculine logic with a macho, intrusive God and a suppressed feminine-maternal imagery—a dominant trajectory in Old Testament scholarship that did not meet resistance until a 1970s paradigm shift began incorporating feminist concerns in its resistance to this interpretive trajectory.

an important part in the ways in which Barth both evokes and rejects maternal imagery.[2] The elevation of maternity and mythology in the rhetoric of the German Christian movement and National Socialism is indeed a significant factor behind Barth's aversion to maternal imagery, as we shall see. However, I will show that Barth's objection to this elevation is deeply impacted by the correlation he perceives between imagery of the fecund female body and a natural theology in which the creature has innate capacities for the work God does with it. We will see, then, that in his interpretation of both the *imago dei* and of maternal imagery in Genesis 1, Barth has in view the threat of natural theology and its elevating of the creature to the status of collaborator in the work of God.

The first section briefly surveys some views of mythology, sexual difference, and maternity in Barth's immediate intellectual context, in order to foreground the subtle ways in which his doctrine of creation and its reading of Genesis 1–2 function as an implicit critique of his contemporaries' views.

The second section locates the vantage point Barth occupies in ecclesial discourse as he orients himself in the first article of the Apostle's Creed. With his sights already set on the second article, Barth gives theological significance to the cosmos only as it functions to conceal and reveal the grace of God enacted in Christ. This christocentric orientation is central to understanding how Barth conceptualizes the *imago dei* and the divine likeness of the human creature.

---

2. See Catherine Keller's criticism of Barth for his effacement of maternal imagery (*Face of the Deep: A Theology of Becoming* [New York: Routledge, 2003], 90–5) and Willis Jenkins's defense of Barth on this point (*Ecologies of Grace: Environmental Ethics and Christian Theology* [Oxford: Oxford University Press, 2008], 161–4). Keller finds in Gen. 1 a theological imaginary that has no place for the imagery of maternal generativity, while Jenkins faults her for ignoring Gen. 2, where he finds precisely such imagery: "Keller somehow misses the aqueous, generative metaphors of this second saga, where humans arrive with the rain and attend a womblike garden overflowing with surprising new life and rivers of water" (162). He argues, contra Keller, that Barth's objection to maternal imagery should be read as Barth's "fearful triumphant rejection not of the divine feminine but of Nazi geopolitics" (162), and that the sort of typologically feminine moments that Barth effaces in Gen. 1 he goes on to celebrate in Gen. 2. While much of my reading of Barth will resonate appreciatively with that of Jenkins, this chapter and the next show Jenkins's criticism of Keller's thesis to be mistaken, insofar as it attempts to dismiss Barth's treatment of maternal imagery as merely a response to an over-evaluation of maternity in Nazi ideology, rather than as a betrayal of problematic assumptions about the generativity of the female body and its incompatibility with the phallic imagery he deploys here for his creator God. In this chapter I address some of the texts upon which Keller focuses, while in the next chapter we will see that the problems Keller identifies in Barth's reading of Gen. 1 are—contra Jenkins—still very much in play in Barth's reading of Gen. 2. Furthermore, we will see that Jenkins is mistaken to find an embrace and celebration of maternal imagery in the aqueous imagery of the garden, for Barth will continue to reject the imagery of wombs and will turn both mist and river into actors in which Adam sees himself reflected.

In the third section I turn to Barth's reading of the Genesis creation narratives in which he finds an authorial vantage point that reflects the position he occupies. He sets these creation narratives in a figural relation to Yahweh's saving history with Israel, which in turn prefigures and culminates in the saving work of Christ. Myth-production emerges as a foil to both the biblical creation narratives and the proper orientation of the dogmatician who is undertaking work on the doctrine of creation. Maternal imagery appears in Genesis 1 as the residue of a mythical-matriarchal worldview that bears a threat to divine potency which the dogmatician must neutralize.

The fourth section turns to Barth's identification of the relationship between the sexes with the divine likeness of the created human in Genesis 1. I will look at Barth's efforts to detach sexual difference from reproductive or parental functions and to present the divine likeness as the divinely enabled response to a miraculous gratuitous divine conferral. Here again Barth redirects his readers from improper resources for theological reflection, refusing to allow the divine likeness to be located in creaturely faculties or capacities.

Myth, maternity, and sexual difference in contemporaneous scholarship

Barth was writing during a period of great interest in ancient mythologies, evident in theological and biblical scholarship and also in popular culture. Newly discovered Assyrian and Babylonian myths were front and center in studies of Genesis, with scholars attempting to determine the nature of the dependency of Old Testament texts on Babylonian-Assyrian culture.[3]

Over the previous two centuries "myth" had developed as an analytical category in hermeneutics, bridging the gap between the literal meaning of biblical narratives and their applicative meaning or religious significance. This category enabled scholars to access empathetically the literal and grammatical sense of the text by engaging it as an expression of the sensuous, childlike consciousness of a primitive mind; at the same time it allowed narratives like Genesis and the miracle stories in the gospels (which had history-like features) to retain abiding religious

---

3. Gunnlaugur A. Jónsson, *The Image of God: Genesis 1:26-28 in a Century of Old Testament Research*, trans. Lorraine Svendsen (Stockholm: Almqvist & Wiksell International, 1988), 15–58. See Suzanne L. Marchand, *German Orientalism in the Age of Empire: Religion, Race, and Scholarship* (Cambridge: Cambridge University Press, 2009) for an extensive study of the practice of oriental studies in Germany between the eighteenth and early twentieth centuries, and of the attention given to the nature of the dependency of Old Testament texts upon Egyptian, Persian, and Assyrian cultures. For a description of Barth's critical use of Delitzsch and Gunkel, see K. E. Greene-McCreight, *Ad Litteram: How Augustine, Calvin, and Barth Read the "Plain Sense" of Genesis 1–3* (New York: Peter Lang, 1999), 203–5.

meaning for the scholars, while obviating the burdensome question of its ostensive reference to historical events.[4]

This interest in mythology, intersecting with the rise of German nationalism and its reconfiguration of Jewish and feminine alterity, promised resources for displacing the Hebrew Bible's story of origins and buttressing conservative views of femininity. Having left Germany in 1935, Barth wrote his doctrine of creation in Switzerland at a time when the Second World War had put feminist emancipatory efforts on hold. While in Germany, he had witnessed conservative forces dismantling the advances gained by the German Women's Movement since the early days of the Weimar Republic. The rapid rise of women in the workforce, ongoing since the late nineteenth century and increasing during the First World War, had challenged traditional views of the place of women in society, while the immense loss of young men in the war challenged the normality of marriage itself. An increasingly vocal conservative movement pushed for the restoration of women to their place of domesticity in a male-dominated world, where the task of raising children was an urgent one, due to wartime losses and a birthrate in decline since the mid-nineteenth century.

Within this context feminism was viewed by many as a threat, and it provoked an exaggerated defense of a traditional patriarchal ordering of the family, accompanied by hyper-masculine rhetoric and the alignment of femininity with maternity. Older nineteenth-century views of the natural character of the female sex and its social roles were reconfigured with motherhood as the primary identity, role, and vocation for women. The psychological orientation of women to this role was deemed symptomatic of their proper place in the orders of creation. The orders of creation thus established an influential framework for repressing both feminist and Jewish emancipatory efforts to attain equality.[5]

---

4. Hans Frei (*The Eclipse of Biblical Narrative: A Study in Eighteenth and Nineteenth Century Hermeneutics* [New Haven: Yale University Press, 1974]) has narrated the gradual dissolution of the cohesion between the literal meaning of biblical narratives and their reference to actual events, a dissolution accompanied by the collapse of figural interpretation, which once unified the canon by weaving the different stories into one common narrative that embraced and incorporated the world of the reader (see esp. 1–23, 183–201, 233–81). See David Ford (*Barth and God's Story* [Frankfurt: Peter Lang, 1985], esp. 49–52), who finds in Barth's reading of biblical narratives an exception to Frei's modern trajectory, insofar as it recovers a figural reading of narratives lost to the modern period. He notes that while Barth does not share with many of his contemporaries and predecessors a concern with verifying the events of biblical narratives by referring them to what historical critics can reconstruct, he does have an alternative external reference to the text: the resurrected Christ, who is both a character in the gospel narratives (and who is prefigured in Old Testament narratives) and a living person.

5. On the gains made by feminist groups in Germany during the First World War and the gradual recognition by nationalist men of the inevitable inclusion of women in the public sphere and their efforts to mobilize women's organizations for nationalist ends,

This period's overvaluation of maternity, antisemitism, and heightened interest in mythology and prehistory came together in a strand of popular scholarly publications on prehistoric matriarchies. At a time when antisemitic contempt for the Hebrew Bible fueled interest in alternate myths of origin, a number of scholars, including some supporters of the Third Reich, pursued a theory of societal evolution (based on a study of ancient myth, ritual, and religion) in which a matriarchal goddess-worshiping society preceded a patriarchal society where male gods dominated. Their publications solidified the contemporary equation of femininity, maternity, and earth and aligned it with the agenda of the Third Reich, in order to offer the groundwork for a fascist understanding of myth and symbol in Germany. This literature found an (idealized) vision of maternity in this former matriarchal culture. Woman in her function as mother symbolized core values in need of retrieval to correct an overemphasis on male virility and intellect. These scholars lamented the eclipse of the place of the mother in the reigning masculine virility of the current culture. The monotheistic and paternalistic faith of the Jews was accused by many of destroying the privileged societal place of the mother, and her close relationship to blood, earth, and instinct.[6]

This strand of scholarship had come to the attention of Charlotte von Kirschbaum, and so it was likely known to Barth also, considering her indispensable role in keeping Barth apace with scholarly trends.[7] Barth was also familiar with (and drew on) the commentaries of scholars like Hermann Gunkel and Franz Delitzsch, who found a residue of matriarchal mythologies in the Genesis creation narratives.

---

especially toward the end of that war, see Matthew Stibbe, "Anti-Feminism, Nationalism and the German Right, 1914–1920: A Reappraisal," *German History* (June 2002): 185–210. On the construal of sexual difference and the feminine stereotypes circulating in the 1920s and 1930s, see Suzanne Selinger, *Charlotte von Kirschbaum and Karl Barth: A Study in Biography and the History of Theology* (University Park, PA: Pennsylvania State University Press, 1998), 92–100; Sheila Briggs, "Images of Women and Jews in Nineteenth- and Twentieth-Century German Theology," in *Immaculate & Powerful: The Female in Sacred Image and Social Reality*, ed. Clarissa W. Atkinson, et al. (Boston: Beacon Press, 1985), 226–59; Marion A. Kaplan, "German-Jewish Feminism in the Twentieth Century," *Jewish Social Studies* (January 1976): 39–53; and Doris L. Bergen, *Twisted Cross: The German Christian Movement in the Third Reich* (Chapel Hill: University of North Carolina Press, 1996), 61–81, 119–41, 182–205.

6. Cynthia Eller ("Matriarchy and the Volk," *JAAR* 81, no. 1 [March 2013]: 188–221) describes this politically conservative strain of scholarship, its growing popularity in the early decades of the twentieth century, and the hopes of some scholars that the mythic and symbolic expressions of these ancient societies might play a role in establishing a new Aryan religion.

7. The 1861 work by Johann Jakob Bachofen, a key influence in this strand of scholarship, is mentioned by Charlotte von Kirschbaum in her correspondence with feminist Henriette Visser't Hooft Boddaert regarding the images of men and women offered by mythologies in the 1940s (Selinger, *Charlotte von Kirschbaum*, 75).

Within this context, Barth's doctrine of creation positions the project of myth-making as yet another dangerous distraction to dogmatics. He links myth with philosophy as partners in the same anthropocentric agenda. He reconfigures the influential notion of a conflict between myth and reason, together with its accompanying historical narrative in which mythical thinking gives way to rational thinking that makes possible a scientific worldview.[8] He considers myth and philosophy as allies in the same misguided and self-absorbed anthropological project, and he secures Genesis 1 as the biblical warrant for his rejection. Furthermore, he appeals to some of the scholarship in comparative mythology in order to claim that the author of Genesis 1 is both familiar with and critical of a contemporaneous mythical and matriarchal worldview.

Barth detaches Genesis 1 from its entanglement with the category of myth by positioning the creation narrative as a critical rejection of Babylonian-Assyrian mythology and its gods, and by setting it in a figural relation to the history of God's saving work, as narrated in the biblical stories of Israel and the life of Jesus. Dogmatics and biblical saga thus emerge as properly oriented responses to the divine address—and critical challenges to the self-absorbed projects of myth-making and philosophizing.

Barth's critique of the hermeneutical category of myth is entwined with his subtler critiques of antisemitism and of the configurations of maternity and sexual difference found in the scholarship on prehistoric matriarchal myths, as well as in rhetoric repudiating the feminist movement. Against such a backdrop, Barth's lengthy exegesis of an ancient Israelite story of origins can be read, in part, as his own act of resistance to a climate that sought myths of origin in non-semitic pasts. In his exegesis of Genesis 1–2, Barth tells a counter-story of origins, performing the role of one who witnesses to the Word that he hears in the human words of creedal and biblical sources, and particularly in the Genesis creation narratives.

Barth's negative view of maternal imagery in his reading of the creation stories is integrated with his efforts to situate the creation sagas in a critical relationship to myth. In a cultural context in which female identity and maternity were closely connected, Barth rejects any positive incorporation of maternal imagery into the Genesis creation sagas, and he is silent on the relation of maternity to female identity. We shall see that for Barth, the imagery of the fecund female body carries with it the threat of a capacity within the creature to collaborate and cooperate in God's creative and sustaining work. He therefore has difficulty allowing any place for maternal imagery in his theological imaginary, which at times seems dominated by a patriarchal reproductive logic.

---

8. On the pairing of myth and reason in Barth's intellectual context, see David W. Congdon, *The Mission of Demythologizing: Rudolf Bultmann's Dialectical Theology* (Minneapolis, Fortress, 2015), 461–4 and Robert Erlewine, *Judaism and the West: From Hermann Cohen to Joseph Soloveitchik* (Bloomington: Indiana University Press, 2016), 14–51.

Christ concealed in the first article

Opening *Church Dogmatics* III/1 with a recital and exposition of the Creed's first article ("I believe in God the Father, creator of heaven and earth") (3), Barth distinguishes his doctrine of creation from the productions of the isolated, self-absorbed exponent of natural theology, to whom he now attributes the equally anthropocentric project of myth-making.[9] Philosophizing and myth-making are not the sort of pursuits that follow an encounter with the divine subject attested in ecclesial discourse (9). He assigns his doctrine of creation and its foil to very different intellectual trajectories. Kant, Ritschl, and Troeltsch are among the figures Barth locates on a philosophically oriented trajectory in which he also situates the nineteenth-century inheritors of Schleiermacher, who imitate the epistemic orientation of this trajectory (47):

> Although the statement of the dogma is formally approved and accepted, it is understood as a conception of man, who in this statement informs himself both about himself and also about the rest of the world, and whose task it is, as these theologians see it, to give himself this information ... As he sees it, he may and must "postulate" an extra-mundane cause of the world, and he makes the corresponding "religious statement," whose main features he "recognises" in essentials in the biblical account, and the Church's conception, of creation. (9)

With this caricature serving as the foil to his own dogmatic approach, Barth continues his pedagogical chiding of people who construct accounts of creation from their own anthropological resources, through which they discern and discover for themselves the nature of God and creation, rather than assuming the stance of those who must first hear and be taught by the biblical and ecclesial witness.

As the primitive, imaginative, childlike production of the same self-referential epistemic hubris (84–7), myth is "the contemplation of man and his cosmos as self-moved and self-resting, the contemplation of his emergence as one of his own functions" (85). Barth contrasts mythological stories to the "history" [*Geschichte*] in which God discloses Godself to human beings in concrete events in time. Myths, as he construes them, are interested only in timeless and eternal truths, and any history-like features that some may have are mere covers for non-historical esoteric speculations that point to timeless truths beyond the features of the story (84–7).[10] Barth writes: "Never is man more himself and at home in his world, never

---

9. All parenthetical references inline are to *Church Dogmatics* III/1, while page references to *Die kirchliche Dogmatik* appear within brackets inside the parenthetical references.

10. At the time Barth was writing *Church Dogmatics* III/1, Bultmann's work, which drew upon existential philosophy to detach the kerygma of New Testament texts from their mythological worldview, was gaining significant attention. Bultmann is mentioned only

does he have in his own strength a better understanding of himself and his world, than as an inventor and author or an intelligent hearer and reader of myth" (85).

Barth locates himself and his forthcoming retelling of Genesis 1–2 in a different trajectory that includes the Didache, Irenaeus, Tertullian, Calvin, Melancthon, and Quenstedt—those who "do not put man and his elevation to humanity into the centre of the quest for the meaning of creation, but God's dealings with man in the history of the covenant" (47). This trajectory he traces back to the "great crowd of witnesses" to God's acts in history named in Hebrews 11. This "crowd of witnesses" now serves as the biblical model for his dogmatic vantage point and his christocentric reading of the Genesis creation narratives. The epistle's profession, "by faith we understand that the worlds were prepared by word of God" (Heb 11:3 [NRSV]), precedes a re-description of salvation history which functions for Barth as the biblical author's

> long recital of acts of faith on the part of men of the old covenant—a recital designed by the writer as an appeal to Christians not to cast away their confidence (10.35f.), but, in the presence of a great cloud of witnesses, to run with patience the race which is set before them, looking into Jesus, the author and finisher of the faith (12.1f). This recital (11.3) of faith in God the Creator is obviously introduced by the writer as an illustration of the faith which, having its source and perfection in Jesus Christ, was tested by the ancients and has now to be tested by Christians. Whoever rightly and patiently, and therefore with certainty, believes in the fulfilment of the promise which was given in faith, believes that the world is created by God's Word. (4)

Playing his part as a confessor of the First Article's ancient communal witness to God's activity in history, Barth subtly positions his christocentric doctrine of creation as an imitation of the exemplary faithful witness that he locates in the authorial voice of Hebrews 11-12.

The first's article's biblical cosmology, the heavens and the earth, denotes the totality of all reality that is distinct from God while at the same time providing an orientation and vantage point for the human creature. But the human being, concealed and prefigured at the center of the cosmos (standing under the heavens

---

once in III/1, within a list of scholars who deal with myth (III/1, 181). David Congdon, however, has carefully uncovered the relationship between Barth and Bultmann and their respective theologies, and he finds in III/1 an implicit (albeit misguided) critique of Bultmann's program of demythologization (*The Mission of Demythologizing*, 130–59, 180–2, 461–4, 599, 708–13). See Kenneth Oakes (*Karl Barth on Theology and Philosophy* [Oxford: Oxford University Press, 2012] 200–7) for a discussion of the relation between theology and philosophy in *CD* III, especially in §42, where Barth names as "philosophy" any worldview that does not circulate around the central figure of Christ, any worldview that is not articulated from a confessional stance that sees God's gracious activity in Christ reflected in creaturely reality.

and upon earth), is revealed in the second article to be none other than the incarnate Christ (his life from conception to death and resurrection) (17–19), and not those who profess the faith of the Creed. It is this particular human being who is to serve as the central point of dogmatic reference, for "the reality of creation is and can only be known with clarity and certainty in the person of Jesus Christ" (28).

Having decentered the self in his doctrine of creation, Barth now follows the activity of the protagonist of the Creed's saving narrative arc, the same protagonist of the biblical story of creation that he will soon retell. God wills not to be alone in the isolation and self-sufficiency of the divine inner self-relation of Father, Son, and Holy Spirit (5–7), and so God produces the creaturely other in an act that corresponds to the constitutive act wherein the Father willed from eternity not to be alone but to generate his own other in the Son (13–15, 96). The divine subject that Barth has pursued in these many pages is a subject in pursuit of others, one who wills not to be alone, interiorly or exteriorly, one who wills to hear the voice of another. Thus:

> as God in Himself is neither deaf nor dumb but speaks and hears His Word from all eternity, so outside His eternity He does not wish to be without hearing or echo, that is, without the ears and voices of the creature. The eternal fellowship between Father and Son, or between God and His Word, thus finds a correspondence in the very different but not dissimilar fellowship between God and His creature. (50)

The incarnate Word reiterates his inter-trinitarian hearing-and-speaking in the sphere of humankind, himself the human paradigm of an eternal movement. Barth positions himself and his readers as the creaturely ears that hear and the creaturely mouths that profess the benevolence of this divine address. He prepares them to seek in the Genesis accounts the activity of one whose rejection of isolation and pursuit of fellowship produces alterity both internal and external to the divine life, and thus to anticipate a human existence that reflects this search.

Observing that the biblical writers seldom directly reflect upon the human being as the glory, climax, and goal of creation as is done in Genesis 1–2, Barth secures additional biblical examples for the perspective and voice of the Creed's first article. In Psalm 104—the most striking scriptural text on creation—the human creature is "completely lost in a host of other creatures." Likewise, in the speech of God in Job 38–41,

> unforgettable things are said about the earth, the sea and the stars, the foolish ostrich and the spirited horse, and finally the hippopotamus and the crocodile; but man seems to be ignored, except that it is he, in the person of the murmuring Job, who must constantly allow himself to be led *ad absurdum* by the question whether he had conceived, elected, determined and posited all these things. (20)

Readers are thus directed outward, as the eyes that recognize in the cosmos the products of a divine benevolent activity that has human welfare in view—a divine activity that everywhere points to the activity of Christ. Barth writes, "As Luther so profoundly emphasises, man is only the eye and ear, the reason and sense, to perceive the greatness and glory of it; and only the mouth appointed to praise this work" (21). Barth himself, then, mimics the stance of the Psalmist and Job, having eyes that are ready to see signs of divine grace (gifts and as such prefigurations of the incarnate Christ) throughout the creaturely sphere that Scripture and Creed present to him, and mouth and pen to respond as a grateful witness.

This is the vantage point, anchored in the Creed, that Barth will occupy when he surveys the creation stories through the biblical writer's gaze. By setting the Creed's two articles in a christocentric, prefigurative relationship and securing this relationship as a vocalization of the great crowd of witnesses in Hebrews, he fixes his eyes upon the second article's account of Christ (who is the author and finisher of a proper profession of faith [Heb 12:1-2]) (18–19). Through the two articles he traces the narrative arc of God's history of saving activity which culminates in Christ, and in so doing prepares his readers to anticipate an inseparable relationship between his doctrine of creation and his doctrine of reconciliation, between creation history and covenant history, and to locate the hermeneutical key to the Genesis creation narratives in Christ, for "Jesus Christ is the key to the secret of creation" (28).

Barth's reading of Genesis 1–2 is framed within this multi-layered effort to articulate the inseparable relationship between the doctrine of creation and the doctrine of reconciliation. Having situated these doctrines within the Creed's narrative of triune activity, he turns to the Bible's "historical narrative" [*Geschichtsschreibung*], in which the triune God is the central actor. Here he distinguishes the Genesis creation narratives [*Schöpfungsberichten*] from other history-like narratives of the Old Testament, while at the same time emphasizing their history-like features in order to disentangle them from the genre of myth which he reduces to the encapsulation of timeless truths. What myth lacks is that which the biblical creation narratives seek: "God and His activity, the distinction and confrontation between the Creator and the creature, the liberty of another divine reality which encounters man and his world and sovereignly decrees without reference to them" (86). Myth's protagonist is thus supplanted by the divine protagonist's confrontation with the reader through the vehicle of the Genesis creation narratives.

Barth distinguishes the creation history of Genesis 1–2 from covenant history of the biblical narratives that follow. Both feature the divine protagonist, but creation history prefigures and anticipates the divine activity of covenant history (reflecting and buttressing the prefigurative relationship between the first and second articles) (59–82).

Barth assigns to creation history its own distinctive genre: the poetic and imaginative genre of "saga," set in contrast to myth (84–7). The creation sagas tell the story of unmediated divine activity to which there are no human witnesses, and so they rely on the imagination. However, the imaginations of those ancient narrators are constrained in their service as witness to God's covenant-making activity, for they write as those who have been "encountered by God, the Lord, The Creator of heaven and earth." In this encounter, they are situated within the confessional community of Israel that has produced these other narratives of God's saving history (91).[11] Thus Barth will read Genesis 1–2 as the imaginative but faithful response within a larger community of witness to God's self-disclosing covenantal acts in covenant history.

Barth thus locates in the Genesis sagas a narrative vantage point that models and validates the vantage point that he himself occupies, as a dogmatician reciting the Creed's first article. The narrator of Genesis "has neither the time nor the desire to be occupied with the origination of the world and man in general, but with that of the world and the man whose existence will receive its meaning in the execution of God's covenant" (267). Barth's distinction between saga and myth gestures to his earlier distinction between the *philosophical* trajectory that self-confidently discovers the cosmos from its own anthropological resources and the *ecclesial* trajectory that in faith professes what it has learned from the great crowd of witnesses to God's covenant activity.

Situated within the covenant community of Israel, the narrators of biblical saga play their faithful part within the great crowd of witnesses, as they produce stories of origins that prefigure and point to the covenant history of Yahweh with Israel.[12] Barth in turn plays his part as he finds within their communal witness to both creation history and covenant history prefigurations of the latter history's culmination in the life, death, and resurrection of Christ. Furthermore, Barth claims that only the reader who has been encountered by the God of this covenantal history (standing in the company of the great cloud of witnesses, together with Barth and his Genesis-narrator, as a beneficiary of this communal history of the covenant) will recognize in Genesis 1–2, *not* the myths of origin, the mere coverings of an esoteric timeless truth, *but* the faithful witness to the creating activity of the God and Father of Jesus Christ (91–2, 86–7).

Having construed saga as a divinely guided, communally contextualized, exercise in imagination, Barth's reading of Genesis 1–2 employs contemporary interpretive tools in order to imaginatively and empathetically appropriate the gaze of the narrator—to imagine the divine activity through the perspective of

---

11. For a helpful discussion on Barth's understanding of Genesis 1–2 as saga in its relation to historical referent, see Greene-McCreight, *Ad Litteram*, 179–90.

12. Kathryn Tanner notes that Barth follows the lead of biblical scholars like Gerhard von Rad when he finds in the creation accounts of Genesis a text written later than key biblical narratives of Israel's history and thus a text that reflects retrospectively on the significance of creation for the history of Israel that follows. Thus in Barth's reading, subsequent books of the Hebrew Bible are the best commentary on Genesis, and Barth sees himself to be extending this principle when he reads New Testament texts as the best commentary on books in the Old Testament ("Creation and Providence," in *Cambridge Companion to Karl Barth* [Cambridge: Cambridge University Press, 2000], 111–26, esp. 113–14).

the narrative.[13] Barth assumes the modern theory of authorship of Genesis 1–2, he speaks freely of P and J passages, and he refers at times to the author and at other times to the editor or redactor of the text. But ultimately he is interested in the perspective of the text itself. He constructs the "literal" grammatical sense of the text using a variety of available hermeneutical tools (such as word searches and textual reconstruction), pre-modern works, and modern Jewish and Christian commentaries that rely on historical-critical methods. However, his overarching goal is to find creation's prefigurative relationship to covenant history, and so he will situate the biblical narratives in an inter-textual canonical frame of reference that occupies a critical relation to ancient and modern worldviews.[14]

Barth distinguishes and unites the two creation sagas by depicting the first as a temple structure and the second as a liturgical scene within that structure. Both derive their theological significance by gesturing to God's salvation history in Christ. The first saga (the priestly Gen. 1:1–2:4a) promises and prepares for the covenant in its depiction of creation as the sphere within which the covenant will be actualized. Prophetically prefiguring the covenant history as its telos, the plot moves to its climax when God invites the first man and woman into the sanctuary of creation and into the divine rest—to which no labor on their part has entitled them (98–9; 233). The second saga (Gen. 2:4b-25) places Adam and Eve at the liturgical center of this cosmic-temple structure, where they are "a unique sign of the covenant and a true sacrament" (232), in so far as they anticipate (through Adam) key moments in the gospel plot of Jesus's life, death, and resurrection (232–3).

Barth's account of sexual difference and its ordering is developed most fully in his reading of the second saga, and as such is saturated in christological significance, apart from which Barth's account of sexual difference and the relationship between the sexes cannot be properly grasped. In the next chapter we will see that Adam is a model human agent precisely as he points beyond himself to Christ.

---

13. Frei (*Eclipse of Biblical Narrative*, 245) delineates the role that empathy played as a first hermeneutical step for romantic readers of myth as well as for mythophiles. Barth's way of inhabiting the perspective of the narrator can be seen in continuity with this interpretive trajectory. However, as Greene-McCreight notes, unlike many romantic readers, Barth is not interested in the inner life of the author, nor does he equate the plain sense of the text with what author is trying to convey (*Ad Litteram*, 207).

14. It is widely recognized that Barth revives an interpretive practice that finds the narrative arc of Christ's life, death, and resurrection prefigured in the Old Testament. For a detailed account of the modern decline in figural readings of the Old Testament, see Frei, *Eclipse of Biblical Narrative*. For Barth's retrieval of this interpretive practice see Ford, *Barth and God's Story*, and Greene-McCreight, *Ad Litteram*, 210–13. Greene-McCreight, informed by Frei's work, provides a lucid analysis of Barth's exegetical practices, especially his re-appropriation of a figural reading of the Old Testament. She looks at Barth's return to a strategy of incorporating figurative reference into the "plain sense" reading of the narrative, a strategy resting on the assumption that the plain sense of Scripture resides in its function to give witness to Jesus Christ.

In the remainder of this chapter, I highlight two key features of Barth's exegesis of Genesis 1 that are informative for the gender dynamics of Genesis 2. First Barth's rejection of interpretations that find maternal imagery in the narratives discloses his underlying assumptions about female bodily passivity that come to the fore in his later discussions of sexual difference in *Church Dogmatics* III/2 and III/4. Second his identification of the relation between the sexes as the divine likeness itself (reflecting but not identical to the *imago dei*) will exhibit the characteristics of neighbor-love that I pointed to in my previous chapter. In these features Barth will sustain his rejection of an orders of creation framework for locating social relationships. Divine likeness will depend on a continual divine, revelatory activity and will never be an innate possession or human capacity or faculty.

Myth-critique and matriarchal repression in Genesis 1

Most of Barth's effort to render a clear distinction between the creation sagas and mythology is exhibited in his reading of Genesis 1 and is most clearly evident in his interpretation of Genesis 1:2: "And the earth was waste and void; and darkness was upon the face of the deep; and the Spirit of God moved upon the face of the waters" (102). Barth recognizes with Gunkel features of a mythic cosmology in three components of this verse: its references to "waste and void" (*tohu wa-bohu*), to darkness over the face of the deep, and to the brooding "Spirit of Elohim." Barth argues that this mythic cosmology is incorporated into the saga not as a positive appropriation, but rather as a critical rejection of competing stories of origin (108). He objects to readings in which a primordial chaos exists prior to God's creative activity or is the first step in God's creative activity. He insists that the features of this verse are antithetical to the picture presented in verse 1 and in the rest of the saga of an Elohim who creates an orderly, limited, and secure cosmos by the power of divine fiat. For Barth there can be no place within this saga for a God who makes positive use of chaos and darkness or for a God who relates to the chaos that this verse depicts. God will only say "No" to chaos and to any cooperation with it by speaking an orderly creation into being. Barth thus construes verse 2 as a summation of all that God rejects when in verse 3 God first speaks, ushering into existence the beginning of all things that are not-God.

Gendered assumptions are already at play here, as features of verse 2 evoke, for Barth, maternal imagery embedded in the mythological worldview that verse 3 rejects. In verse 2 "the Spirit of *Elohim* is condemned to the complete impotence of a bird hovering or brooding over shoreless or sterile waters," an activity Barth finds akin to a "passive contemplative role and function [*passiv-kontemplative Rolle und Funktion*]" (107 [118–19]). Such imagery suggests the powerlessness of this God's activity to effect a limitless and unproductive chaos, imagery completely antithetical to the Old Testament Elohim whose "creation means the irruption and revelation of the divine compassion" [*Schöpfung heißt Einbruch und Offenbarung des göttlichen Erbarmens*] (110 [122]). The maternal imagery of a brooding dove hovering over a "World-egg" is clearly too impotent for the irruptive and explosive activity of Barth's paternal creative Elohim. So, Barth's narrator describes a God who elects to be the God who loves in freedom and therefore to create an orderly and secure world—a God who, in so doing, simultaneously elects the sort of world and sort of God he will not be (thereby rejecting a chaotic and threatening creation, and also rejecting a passive and impotent mode of being).[15]

At the same time, maternal imagery has too much generative capacity for Barth to risk its association with the material that God creates and manipulates in further creative activity. Barth rejects any positive associations of this watery chaos with "a world-egg or a mother-womb which bears the future" (104). This watery boundless chaos must be viewed as sterile and barren, as completely lacking in internal resources for the production of the orderly world that God creates. Thus Barth takes comfort in commentators who foreground the paternal character of the saga, using them to support his claim that in verses 2 and 3 the narrator rejects myth and its matriarchal imagery: "All explanations of the origin of the world in terms of divine conception and birth are superseded when the 'And God said' is put at the beginning" (114).

Barth's interpretive rejection of maternal imagery continues further on in his reading of the Genesis 1. In the emergence of animals from the earth on the sixth day (Gen. 1:24), Barth declares: "We are spared the thought of a bearing 'mother earth' as the principle of the world (Gunkel)" (179).[16] He makes similar assertions when discussing the Genesis 2 account of the construction of Adam from dust.

In the divine command directing fish and birds to be fruitful and multiply (Gen 1:22), Barth finds a prefiguration of covenant history that will have at its center "a God-like creature ordained for fatherhood and sonship and continuing its existence in the relationship of fatherhood and sonship" (169–71). Notably, he makes no reference to third parties or mother figures whose generative capacities are necessary to secure creaturely sonship, nor does he refer to daughters (198–9). Implicit in these words is a reference to Old Testament patrilineal genealogies.

---

15. As articulated in *CD* II/1, §28: "The Being of God as the One who Loves in Freedom" (257–321).

16. Catherine Keller (*Face of the Deep*) gives an insightful feminist analysis of Barth's idiosyncratic and phallocentric reading of Gen. 1:2 (90–5). Regarding Barth's "impotent," "hovering and fluttering," "passive contemplative," "Spirit of *Elohim*," Keller notes that "the gender of the bird itself slides menacingly between mother and male." Here "Barth bats a double-whammy for Protestant virility. An inadequate masculinity 'flutters' above an abortive femininity ... Any concept therefore of a generative chaos, a spontaneous natality, must be sterilized. As to any God who demonstrates queer male or any female propensities—Barth kills both birds with a single stone" (94). Keller links Barth's treatment of chaos and maternal imagery to his §54 ordering of sexual difference in terms of sequence (III/4, 169). She asks, "Does Barth's gender logic only make explicit and literal motives that otherwise remain metaphorically indirect, to be teased out of the small print of bigger matters?" Keller finds in the subordination of woman to man Barth's "social template of chaos-control" (95). Woman does not represent chaos except when she gets out of order (96).

Later on, we see that his silence on the part of mother-figures is not an oversight. In his discussion of Adam's begetting of Seth (Gen. 5:3), Barth takes up the topic of human fatherhood and sonship and explicitly evokes Old Testament patrilineal genealogies to legitimize his own silence regarding the maternal function in human procreation. Of Adam's begetting of Seth, Barth declares "[woman] is not mentioned in Gen. 5:3, in the table which follows, or—significantly—in any of the genealogical tables of the Bible" (199). This is a bewildering statement, considering that it requires Barth's effacement of the role of four women in Matthew's genealogical table that ends in the birth of Christ—"the key to the secret of creation." But Christ's own genealogical table must be discretely ignored in order for Barth to fend off the threat he perceives in the maternal body.

Barth's rejection of any positive place for maternal imagery in the creation narratives is, as we have seen, embedded in his critique and rejection of myth, and we hear in his refusals echoes of the contemporaneous interest in matriarchal myths of origin that he wants to disavow. However, there is far more to Barth's objection to maternal imagery than his aversion to the valorization of the maternal and the mythological in contemporary trends (such as National Socialist ideologies). There is also more to it than his anxiety regarding the dependency of Genesis 1–2 on ancient mythologies, although this factor also undoubtedly plays a significant role. Barth's ambivalent assumptions about maternity (both its generative passivity and its generative capacities) prompt him to repudiate any association of maternal imagery with God's activity or with the material that God uses when drawing some creaturely entities out of others. It prompts him also to evict mothers from all genealogies. For the capacity of a woman's body to conceive might suggest a capacity of creaturely material for the creative work God does with it, which in turn might lend support to an anthropology in which human beings have a capacity for (or a point of contact with) the revelatory and redemptive work of God. Thus Barth must dissociate the imagery of maternal fecundity from his picture of the creation of some creaturely entities out of others, and he must guard against such threatening imagery by resorting at times to a phallic fantasy of a paternal reproduction that requires no third-party collaborators.

Sexual difference and divine likeness in Genesis 1

Barth's reading of God's creation of man and woman in Genesis 1:26-31 is shaped by similar worries about the threat posed by the attribution to creatures of any capacity for understanding God's work. Barth locates the divine likeness [*Gottebenbildlichkeit*] of the human being in the relationship between man and woman (194).[17] This human being-in-relation is not itself identical to the image of

---

17. Barth departs from both Luther and Calvin when he follows the new approach of Dietrich Bonhoeffer and Wilhelm Vischer to the *imago dei*. In his Commentary on Genesis 1:26-27, Luther gives to the image of God in the unfallen Adam a holistic reach, for it entails

God (a status Barth reserves solely for Christ), but rather it is a likeness, a reflection, an analogy, a sign of that image. As such it corresponds to the image of God, but only as it is divinely enabled so to do (197). As with all Barth's creaturely signs, its revelatory function does not rest in an innate capacity, for such would support a natural theology, and so Barth has much to say about where this divine likeness does *not* reside.[18] Barth rejects both dominant and marginal interpretations, for the divine likeness resides in no attribute or characteristic that the human being

an excellence in physical and mental capacities that enabled him to rule the animals. While Luther allows that Eve was also made in the image of God, he declares that she did not possess the glory and prestige of Adam, and he evokes as analogy the moon's lesser excellence in relation to the sun (*Luther's Works*, Vol. 1, *Lectures on Genesis: Chapters 1–5*, trans. George V. Schick [Saint Louis: Concordia, 1958], 55–70). While Calvin connects the capacity for relationship with God to the *imago dei*, he does not connect it to the free fellowship between the sexes in the way that Barth does. See Susan E. Schreiner (*The Theater of His Glory: Nature and the Natural Order in the Thought of John Calvin* [Durham, NC: Labyrinth, 1991], 65–7) for a discussion of Calvin's view of the *imago dei*. Barth makes explicit his affinity with Old Testament scholar Vischer (a close friend of Barth and Bonhoeffer) on the *imago dei*, and finds that Bonhoeffer comes closest to his own view of the text (III/1, 194–6). He also notes that he is saying something more than Vischer and Bonhoeffer when he finds sexual difference to be the only genuine distinction between human beings (III/1, 196). Vischer locates the *imago dei* of Gen. 1 in the direct relationship between God and the human being, and he uses I/Thou terminology to describe it. Vischer speaks of the equality of male and female and does not attempt to subordinate the latter to the former, and he too evokes Song of Songs 2:26 in order to show the reciprocal character of their relation. See Wilhelm Vischer, *The Witness of the Old Testament to Christ*, Vol. 1, *The Pentateuch*, trans. A. B. Crabtree (London: Lutterworth Press, 1949), esp. 47–64. Dietrich Bonhoeffer (*Creation and Fall: A Theological Interpretation of Genesis 1–3* [New York: Macmillan, 1959]) likewise does not share Barth's interest in subordinating Eve to Adam. Bonhoeffer, like Barth, insists that the *imago dei* is not something the human being possesses but is given to the human being by God. Bonhoeffer names it freedom for the other, resembling Barth very closely here. Human freedom for God is expressed in freedom for the other human creature. Bonhoeffer does not find a hierarchy in sexual difference, nor does he explicitly attempt to privilege the male position in any way, even though he invokes Ephesians 5 to set the relation between men and women in analogy to Christ's relation to the Church (35–9).

18. In translating image and likeness, Barth notes that he prefers "*Urbild und Vorbild*," instead of the usual translations, "*Bild und Gleichnis*" or "*Bild und Ähnlichkeit*" (197 [221]). But in his exposition of this phrase he indicates his preference to speak of the human being's *Gottebenbildlichkeit* [divine likeness]: "Man is not created to be the image [*Bild*] of God but—as is said in vv. 26 and 27, but also in Gen. 5.1 … in correspondence with the image of God [*entsprechend dem Bilde Gottes*]. His divine likeness [*Gottebenbildlichkeit*] is never his possession, but consists wholly in the intention and deed of his Creator, whose will concerning him is this correspondence" (197 [222]; see 184, 198, 200).

possesses: it is not located in the soul, the intellect, the spiritual faculties of memory, intellect, and love, in moral integrity, in holiness, in a Hegelian spiritual actualization, in physical form or appearance, or in dominion (192–7).[19] Barth also rejects Gunkel's physiological interpretation of the *imago dei,* thus refusing any association of divine likeness with physical attributes, and he is careful to separate the divine command to be fruitful and multiply from his account of divine likeness. Of the divine likeness he says: "It is not a quality of man. Hence there is no point in asking in which of man's peculiar attributes and attitudes it consists. *It does not consist in anything that man is or does*" (184, my italics). Rather it resides in something God must repeatedly enable the human being to do.

Barth describes the divine likeness in the same terms he favors for depicting the human subject's proper orientation to and encounter with the divine subject. Divine-likeness resides in the human subject's hearing and responding to an address, becoming a "Thou" when confronted by an "I."[20] Since Barth consistently

19. Gunnlaugur A. Jónsson (*Image of God,* 1–68) follows a trajectory of interpretations of the *imago dei* of Genesis 1:26-7 that includes the innovative relational interpretation articulated by Vischer and Bonhoeffer that in turn influenced Barth. By Barth's time the *imago dei* was a contentious hermeneutical point for theologians and biblical scholars. A key consequence of the impact of Darwin's theory of evolution within Old Testament scholarship was the concern to explain Genesis 1:26-27 specifically in terms of what distinguishes the human being from other animals. The dominant interpretation was to associate the *imago dei* with spiritual qualities, specifically mental endowments (especially from 1882 to 1928), although the specific qualities varied between authors (43). Against this backdrop the association in the work of Bonhoeffer, Vischer, and Barth of the *imago dei* with human relationality was one innovation among a number of others. Barth does not appear preoccupied with using his discussion of divine likeness to distinguish and elevate human beings above animals (especially when compared to Vischer and Bonhoeffer); in fact he makes a point of noting that it is associated with sexual difference, a feature that humans share with animals, and hence requires divine activity to enable it to point beyond itself to Christ (III/1 185).

20. Selinger follows an evolution in Barth's view of the *imago dei*: In *Göttingen Dogmatics* and *Christliche Dogmatik* he discusses it in relation to other issues and has a largely conventional configuration in terms of the creative activity of human beings in their dominion over the world (*Göttingen Dogmatics,* 163 and *Christliche Dogmatik,* 372). In *CD* I/2, 193-4 Barth does not find super-/sub-ordination present until after the Fall. Beginning in III/1 his overall account remains consistent, but he now introduces the sexually differentiated, hierarchically ordered relation into his discussion (*Charlotte von Kirschbaum,* 116–20). Selinger is especially interested in the role von Kirschbaum played in this evolution. Barth does not mention von Kirschbaum in III/1 when he cites Vischer and Bonhoeffer as sources for his new reading. However, Selinger argues that von Kirschbaum was an important influence on Barth's framing of divine likeness in III/1. She notes that Barth *does* name von Kirschbaum in III/4 (1945) as an authority on the *imago dei* conceived as an I/Thou relation between man and woman, and refers to her book *Die wirkliche Frau*

depicts this relational activity, this proper mode of human subjectivity (a proper hearing and responding), as something that requires divine enabling, he can declare that divine likeness is not something possessed but something that God must continually re-gift.

As an addressed "Thou" and responding "I," ordered from and to the human other, the human subject's orientation to the other has its analogue in "the true confrontation and reciprocity" of God's inner-trinitarian life and the human's relationship to God. He writes:

> But what is the original [*Urbild*] in which, or the prototype [*Vorbild*] according to which, man was created? We have argued already that it is the relationship and differentiation between the I and the Thou in God Himself. Man [*Mensch*] is created by God in correspondence with this relationship and differentiation in God Himself: *created as a Thou that can be addressed by God but also as an I responsible to God*; in the relationship of man and woman [*im Verhältnis von Mann und Frau*] in which man [*Mensch*] is a Thou to his fellow [*des anderen Menschen*] and therefore himself an I in responsibility to this claim. (198/222; italics added)

The "I's" orientation to the human "Thou" reflects the "I's" orientation to the divine "Thou" engaged in an eternal inner-trinitarian dialogue. We hear in these words echoes of Barth's use of the two commandments in §18 for an ethical construal of love directed to neighbor, patterned after love directed to God. Both orientations are made possible only through a divine act of enablement. For only through a divine act can the human subject become a copy of the divine "prototype," and that prototype is Jesus Christ, himself the image of God, the incarnated divine "Thou."

In Barth's reading of Genesis 2, this construal of divine likeness as a divine conferral rather than a natural capacity or attribute becomes far clearer, as does its christocentric reference point, for—as we shall see—Adam is conformed to the image of God only when he is divinely enabled to recognize and properly respond to God's gift of Eve as his neighbor "Thou," and in this conformity he prefigures Christ. With Christ himself secured as the *imago dei*, Barth will carefully transpose the divine likeness of human beings from physiological, social, or philosophical frameworks into his christocentric ethical framework.

(1949) in particular (91–2). Selinger suspects that von Kirschbaum contributed to the new content Barth gives the *imago dei* in III/1, while her version is developed within the theological framework she acquired from Barth over a long period of time. She suggests that the two were mutually indebted to each other as they appropriated ideas from the movement of dialogical personalism of the 1920s and 1930s, especially as ideas found in Buber's foundational work and developed by Brunner, Gogarten, Bonhoeffer, and Vischer. Because Barth makes no use of this resource prior to III/1 (and it does not arise in his view of the *imago dei* articulated in *CD* I), Selinger wonders if von Kirschbaum brought this material to his attention, in her role as research assistant (89–92).

While in §18 Barth uses his account of intersubjective relationships (together with their revelatory function) to unsettle fixed ethnic differences, in §41 he uses it to secure sexual difference as *the one* structural difference dividing human beings, and in the process he continues to signal his concern to relativize ethnic difference: "the distinction of sexes found in man too is the only genuine distinction between man and man, in correspondence to the fact that the I/Thou relationship is the only genuine distinction in the one divine being" (197). In its function as the divine likeness, sexual difference shares the features Barth gives to the material media of a revelatory sign, whether those signs be biblical language, creedal language, or the neighbor of §18. Specific mundane creaturely media are divinely selected to become something more than they have in themselves the capacity to be—pointers beyond themselves to Christ. This sort of understanding of signification and its efficacy is at work in Barth's connection of the divine likeness to the sexual differentiation of human beings—but not of animals.

As significant as this difference is, Barth does not explain what marks or distinguishes the human sexes. This is something he will consistently refuse to do in his later discussions. He avoids resorting to scientific discourses, gender typologies, and social conventions to describe the difference. If he is assuming that physiological markers or reproductive functions have a part to play in this distinction, he does not mention them or attempt to give them theological significance, and he puts much effort into disentangling the divine likeness from sexual reproduction and the command to be fruitful and multiply (198–9). Instead his discussion of sexual difference here centers on the recognition and acceptance of the divine gift in the human other.

Conclusion

As we have seen, Barth's doctrine of creation continues the formative exercise begun in his prolegomenon of describing and enacting a pattern of agency he finds modeled in biblical authors and in the characters they construct. He positions himself as a proclaimer of faith in God's creative work: along with all who confess faith in the Creator, he hears, is taught by, and then re-describes the biblical witnesses to Christ, summarized in the Apostle's Creed. This dogmatic subject is always in motion, seeking to hear afresh those voices, continually declaring what he has heard, and always hoping to have heard properly.

Barth locates for his readers a number of biblical models of this confessional and dogmatic practice. Barth imitates these models in the hope that they are imposed on him from without, in the hope that he has heard and recognized in biblical voices something more than his own projections and constructions. In the next chapter we will see that Adam also serves as a biblical model for such a confessional practice.

I have foregrounded the revelatory character of sexual difference in its function as the divine likeness of the *imago dei* (Jesus Christ). While the distinction between the sexes is a mundane feature that human beings share with animals, it is divinely selected to do what it cannot in itself accomplish. This point will become clearer in Barth's discussion of Adam's naming of Eve, for as Adam accepts and responds to the divine gift of the sexually differentiated neighbor-Thou, he is conformed to the image of Christ.

At the same time, I have noted Barth's reticence at this point in describing the distinction between the sexes. As important as it is to Barth that the neighbor-Thou is paradigmatically someone of the opposite sex, Barth says as little as he possibly can about what he imagines distinguishes the sexes, and he will remain silent on this point in his later discussions of the topic. In order to resist what he finds problematic in the orders of creation framework and other natural theologies, he seeks to locate sexual difference strictly within an ecclesial confession of faith in the Christ to whom Scripture witnesses, and he makes no direct references to biological facts, observable bodily markers, scientific studies, romantic essentializations, or any particular scientific or philosophical framework. He assumes an unambivalent givenness to this difference, and will continue to do so in his reading of Genesis 2, where the sexual relationship is developed more fully as a scene of recognition and address, to which physiological markers and reproductive functions make no explicit contribution. He will continue the work he has begun in Genesis 1 of detaching sexual difference from the divine command that men and women be fruitful and multiply and from the Old Testament interest in patrilineage.

In this chapter I have argued that assumptions about a feminine passivity are deeply implicated in Barth's aversion to maternal imagery in the Genesis creation narratives. While his rejection of maternal imagery has much to do with his rejection of the valorization of maternity and myth in Nazi and German Christian ideology, I have argued that this alone does not fully explain what is at stake theologically for Barth. Whatever maternity might be or evoke for him (he devotes as few words as possible to it), I have suggested on the one hand that the maternal body is, for Barth, too capable of generating life to allow its association with the materiality that God uses in God's creative activity, lest it serve to buttress a natural theology. We will continue to see evidence of Barth's anxiety about female fecundity in his reading of Genesis 2.

On the other hand, I have contended that the maternal body is too passive in its generative activity for Barth to allow it any association with God's creative activity. At best it appears as an impotent masculine generativity. Paternal imagery better lends itself to this service for Barth, who prefers to describe patrilineages as if they progress without the need of maternal bodies (169–71; 198–9). Barth's theological imaginary has trouble, then, accommodating the fecund female body, and in the following chapters, we shall see that it also has trouble accommodating female agency.

Chapter 4

PLAYING ADAM AND SILENCING EVE

Introduction

Barth's figurative exegesis of the creation of Adam and Eve in Genesis 2, found in *Church Dogmatics* III/1 (§41.3), functions as the biblical template for Barth's theological anthropology in *Church Dogmatics* III/2, and he recalls it in his account of sexual difference (III/2, §45.3) and his ethics of creation (III/4, §54.1). Barth presents Adam as an exemplary model of the free and responsible human agent, locating him in a network of creaturely relations of dependency and responsibility. Adam prefigures Christ in this capacity, and Adam's agency is carefully patterned after Christ's agency.[1] Adam performs this exemplary function most clearly in his recognition and naming of Eve, and so Barth's account of sexual difference is framed in the revelatory, agential, intersubjective, and dialogical terms that I have foregrounded as features of the ethical framework he develops in §18 to override anthropologies constructed from natural theologies and orders of creation. Eve serves, on the other hand, as the paradigmatic female model of agency specifically in her silent decision to refrain from decision and to consent to be the object of Adam's election.

Barth's reading of the creation of Eve is the first in a series of examples that I will use in the remaining chapters to foreground Barth's ultimate inability to secure a coherent account of agency for women. As we shall see, in using Eve in this way, Barth's model of agency becomes a male prerogative, while female agency is reduced to a highly truncated iteration of the male. Barth's description of sexual difference and the relationship between the sexes is, therefore, plagued by his effort to maintain the complete humanity of women as fully functioning agents, while nevertheless securing some sort of agential prerogative for men that consequently diminishes and restrains female agency. In exposing this conflict of aims, I will point to the ways in which Barth's understanding of agency resists his own efforts to subordinate and restrain the ways in which women relate to men.

---

1. Bonhoeffer, in *Creation and Fall: A Theological Interpretation of Genesis 1–3* (New York: Macmillan, 1959), to which Barth refers several times, makes explicit what is implicit in Barth's reading, namely that Adam presents a position the reader can access and disturbs the reader as a critic (57).

Since much of what is problematic in Barth's description of the relation between men and women in *Church Dogmatics* III/2 and III/4 is already embedded in his reading of the scene of Eve's creation, it is not surprising that many critics consider his reading to be irretrievable. Most approach the scene of Eve's creation through the interpretive lens of the dialogical personalism that he uses in *Church Dogmatics* III/2, §45.2, to describe human relationality as a reciprocal seeing, hearing, speaking, and aid-lending. They give only marginal and passing attention to the narrative details of Barth's reading of this particular scene in Genesis 2, assessing it simply as one among a series of scriptural texts that Barth deploys to locate the relationship between men and women within a chain of analogous, hierarchically ordered relationships.[2]

Others, like Elouise Fraser, Eugene Rogers, and Graham Ward, give closer attention to Barth's reading of Eve's creation in order to argue that this scene fails to do the work he wants of it. Since the scene of encounter between Adam and Eve in Genesis 2 is not a dialogical exchange between two subjects, they argue that this creation scene cannot serve as the normative biblical example for relationships between men and women. Fraser and Rogers direct readers to egalitarian narratives that depict the I/Thou exchange missing in Genesis 2—narratives that do not lend themselves so readily to Barth's patriarchal and heteronormative framing of human fellowship. Ward locates in Barth's doctrine of the Trinity an economy

---

2. Elizabeth Frykberg, *Karl Barth's Theological Anthropology: An Analogical Critique regarding Gender Relations*, Studies in Reformed Theology and History Series (Princeton: Princeton Theological Seminary, 1993), 31–5; JoAnn Ford Watson, *A Study of Karl Barth's Doctrine of Man and Woman* (New York: Vantage Press, 1995), 7–18; Paul K. Jewett, *Man as Male and Female: A Study in Sexual Relationships from a Theological Point of View* (Grand Rapids: Eerdmans, 1975), 69–86; Paul S. Fiddes, "The Status of Woman in the Thought of Karl Barth," in *After Eve: Women, Theology and the Christian Tradition*, ed. Janet Martin Soskice (London: Marshal Pickering, 1990), 138–55; Clifford Green, "Liberation Theology? Karl Barth on Women and Men," *Union Seminary Quarterly Review* 29, no. 3&4 (Spring & Summer, 1974): 221–31; Serene Jones, "This God Which Is Not One: Irigaray and Barth on the Divine," in *Transfigurations: Theology and the French Feminists*, ed. C. W. Maggie Kim, et al. (Minneapolis: Fortress, 1993), 109–41; Cynthia Campbell, "*Imago Trinitatis*: An Appraisal of Karl Barth's Doctrine of the *Imago Dei* in Light of His Doctrine of the Trinity" (PhD diss., Southern Methodist University, 1981); Jason Springs, "Gender, Equality, and Freedom in Karl Barth's Theological Anthropology," *Modern Theology* 28, no. 3 (July 2012): 446–77; Robert Osborn, "Man and/or Woman According to Karl Barth," in *Theology and Corporate Conscience: Essays in Honor of Frederick Herzog*, ed. Douglas Meeks, et al. (Minneapolis: Kirk House, 1999), 236–56; Yolanda Dreyer, "Karl Barth's Male-Female Order as Asymmetrical Theoethics," *Hervormde Teologiese Studies* 63, no. 4 (November 2007): 1493–521; Alexander J. McKelway, "Perichoretic Possibilities in Barth's Doctrine of Male and Female," *Princeton Seminary Bulletin* 7, no. 3 (January 1986): 231–43; Lisa P. Stephenson, "Directed, Ordered and Related: The Male and Female Interpersonal Relation in Karl Barth's Church Dogmatics," *SJT* 61, no. 4 (2008): 435–49.

of desire where the encounter with alterity is expressed in a kenotic outpouring of self-giving love, an economy not plagued by notions of complementarity and hierarchy. Ward uses this trinitarian economy to expose the problematic character of the economy of desire enacted by Adam in Barth's reading of Genesis 2.[3]

---

3. Elouise Renich Fraser, in "Karl Barth's Doctrine of Humanity: A Reconstructive Exercise in Feminist Narrative Theology" (PhD diss., Vanderbilt University, 1986), draws on the gospel narratives of Jesus to correct Barth's gender hierarchy, while Eugene Rogers (*Sexuality and the Christian Body*) finds scriptures with same-sex egalitarian relationships to correct the heteropatriarchal constraints of Barth's I/Thou relation. Graham Ward ("The Erotics of Redemption: After Karl Barth," *Theology & Sexuality* 8 [March 1998]: 52–72) turns to the Barth's doctrine of the Trinity for an economy of desire that is egalitarian and inclusive of same-sex erotic partnerships. Ward's analysis is situated within the framework of Barth's doctrine of the Trinity and §45 and §54, and he only briefly touches on Barth's reading of Genesis 2, where he finds an economy of the same in which woman serves the narcissistic project of reflecting man's image. While I agree with much of what Ward finds problematic in the scene of recognition between Adam and Eve, I argue that up until this particular scene of Genesis 2, Adam models, for Barth, a mode of subjectivity that actually participates in the sort of economy of excess and self-giving that Ward finds within the Trinity. Only upon the arrival of a female other does this economy seize up. The overflowing service that Adam sees reflected in the activity of the river becomes self-serving as Adam finds in the static silent Eve a motionless mirror to reflect his own agential precedence and to secure his own god-like prerogative over another creature.

Christopher Roberts (*Creation and Covenant: The Significance of Sexual Difference in the Moral Theology of Marriage* [London: T&T Clark, 2007], 139–64; 186–219) defends Barth's account of sexual difference against the criticisms of Ward and Rogers, and Barth's reading of Genesis 1–2 plays an important role in Roberts's defense, although he too does not attend to Barth's full exegesis of Genesis 2, but only to the verses on the *imago dei* in Genesis 1 and the scene of Eve's creation in Genesis 2. His reading rests heavily on what he assumes must be Barth's own assumptions about the biological differentiation of the male and the female. He distinguishes "sexual difference" from social constructions of gender by linking it to "biological difference" (7), and, surprisingly, he finds Barth to be a resource for giving theological meaning to "biological difference," even though he admits that Barth does not explain or describe precisely what sexual difference entails other than some sort of precedence and subsequence; and he also admits that Barth does not want to express the difference in terms of biological functions, social roles, or complementary essences. Roberts does not appear to recognize that it is this reticence and Barth's explicit efforts to detach the theological significance of the relation between men and women from sexual reproduction that open Barth's account to critical reconstructions like that of Ward and Rogers (as well as my own). Furthermore, Roberts's critique of Ward and Rogers rests upon his collapse of Barth's sexual difference into his own "biological difference." He faults Ward's preferred trinitarian economy of desire (and its openness to same-sex partnerships) for a re-appropriation of Barth in which "the significance of the person's physical body disappears under so much symbolism, as if human materiality were indifferent to God's theological

I agree with these critics that Genesis 2 provides an inadequate example of the I/Thou relationship that Barth later describes, and, as we shall see, this is a point that Barth himself recognizes (III/1, 300) and attempts to redress with the Song of Songs. However, these critics focus specifically on the scene of Eve's creation, in

purposes." Yet Ward is appealing to the symbolic and figural strategies that Barth himself uses, and so Roberts's criticism could just as readily apply to Barth's figural reading of Adam and Eve, apart from which Barth's account of sexual difference acquires no theological meaning. It is only through these symbolic and figural strategies that Barth can resist a natural theology that detaches God's creative activity from God's revelatory activity in Christ. Thus, for Barth, Eve acquires her prefigural significance in two different human collectives (the community of Israel and the community of the Church), neither of which lend meaning to any distinctive female physiology; rather they lend meaning to the subordinate place she is to take in the scene of recognition and address. Yet contra Ward, Roberts declares that for Barth "the biological differences between the sexes mean something" and that "for Barth, biology was the material presupposition for the covenant." The latter statement suggests a misunderstanding on Roberts's part of what the creation-covenant relationship is for Barth. Barth never names "biology" as the material presupposition of the covenant (for this would entail a recourse to natural theology), but rather creation, understood as a history, a sequence of divine acts that include God's production of a human actor whose own sequence of activities (seeking, recognizing, electing, and naming Eve … but notably and explicitly *not* sexually reproducing himself via Eve) are central to Barth's theological framing of sexual difference and male precedence.

When defending Barth against Rogers, Roberts attends primarily to Rogers's argument that on Barth's terms, Christ is not fully human because he does not, like Adam, have a human wife to complete his humanity. Roberts's response is that, for Barth, marriage is not compulsory for human being-in-relation and that in Barth's view Christ could fully live out his humanity as a sexually differentiated but celibate male in the sense Barth has in view without ever marrying. While Barth does say something of this sort in III/4, this in itself does not adequately address the force of Rogers's argument. As will become clearer in III/2 and III/4, human-being-in-a-sexually-differentiated-relationship will have its normative center in a monogamous marital relationship between a man and woman. Because Barth's theological anthropology must keep Christ as its central frame of reference, Barth's account rests not on the gospel narratives of how Christ lived out his life as a celibate male in a small circle of men, but on Paul's marital metaphor of Christ and the Church. For Barth's account to work on his own christocentric terms, he must marry Christ off to some "type" of woman, and (the probably unmarried) Paul helps him find one. Of course, Paul's metaphor itself does not secure for Roberts a stable site of "biological difference," for Christ's bride, as a collective of many human beings, does not bear the female bodily markers or reproductive functions whose significance Roberts seeks to secure, and neither Paul's nor Barth's use of the metaphor make appeal to such markers and functions (in either Christ or his bride) as the point of their analogy. Roberts's polemical project of using Barth to secure a theological norm for marriage that gives theological meaning to "biological difference" is, then, a dubious one (185–219).

isolation from Barth's reading of the chapter as a whole, a decision likely prompted by Barth's own, later summaries which focus on this particular scene. My intent is to show that Barth's reading of Genesis 2 as a whole actually provides its own resources for unsettling and re-imagining the patriarchal and heteronormative features of his theological anthropology, resources that are overlooked when the scene of Eve's creation is read in isolation from Barth's reading of the entire narrative.

I will argue that the model of agency that Adam enacts provides its own correctives to Barth's construal of Eve, and I hope to show, furthermore, that in spite of Barth's unquestionably overt heteronormativity, his reading of Genesis 2 does much (inadvertently) to support the detachment of sexual difference and desire from the sort of bodily markers and reproductive ends that would demand the reader to line up on either side of an oppositional divide. In this respect, Adam might function much like Mary does for Barth in Luke 1, as an agential site all might occupy in relation to the human other, regardless of how the differences of that other might be constructed.

Barth situates Adam in a network of relationships to multiple sites of creaturely alterity, and these others (earth, mist, river, plants, and finally Eve) all function as divine gifts to Adam and signs of what he himself ought to be and do.[4] I will argue that Barth's construal of these others (Eve in particular) as gifts and signs of divine grace is open to a reconfiguration that neither privileges the male agent nor asserts a heteronormative paradigm for all human relationships. By recalling Barth's reading of the parable of the Good Samaritan and of Luke 1, setting them alongside that of Eve's creation, I will present a variety of scenes in which Barth imagines human fellowship patterned after Christ—a variety that destabilizes his own assertion that a hierarchically ordered heterosexual marriage resides at the normative center of human fellowship.

The first section of this chapter notes influential contemporaneous constructions of freedom, masculinity, and femininity in order to show that Barth's reading both humbles and constrains human freedom, while re-inscribing widely held assumptions about male activity and female passivity. At the same time, however, his reading resists the common conflation of masculinity with virility and femininity with maternity.

The second section follows Barth's model agent through the three scenes of Genesis 2, wherein Barth finds the biblical template for his understanding of human freedom and his command ethic. With Christ as the secret and hidden key to creation, as we saw in the previous chapter, Adam must prefigure Christ if Adam is to function as such a model of human agency in Barth's theological anthropology. Adam will need to perform this role within the ethical and revelatory

---

4. In his insightful and appreciative reading of Barth, Jenkins (*Ecologies of Grace*) gives careful attention to Barth's reading of Genesis 2, specifically as a resource for environmental theological ethics. His focus is not on gender, but I share with him an interest in the relationships of dependency and responsibility in which Barth locates Adam.

framework we have seen Barth use in my previous chapters. He will be humbled and decentered in a network of creaturely actors, many of whom function as signs of God's grace. The command of God will direct him to his human neighbor in whom he is to find fellowship with one both like and unlike himself.

The third section analyzes Barth's efforts to subordinate Eve to Adam by rendering her inanimate in this scene of encounter and as such a sign of the Church in its relationship to Christ, while the fourth section turns to his efforts to reanimate her through a figural reading of the Song of Songs. I note the difficulty his christocentric methodology raises for his efforts to secure a heteronormative love relation at the center of his theological anthropology.

In conclusion I recall Barth's earlier readings of the Parable of the Good Samaritan and of the encounter between Mary and Elizabeth, in order to foreground the distorting and eviscerating effects of Barth's subordination of female activity to male activity and to show that this construal of inter-human fellowship does not require the sort of sexually differentiated alterity that Barth wants to secure at its normative center in *Church Dogmatics* III.

Freedom, masculinity, and Genesis 2

In his re-description of the Genesis 2 account of the creation and naming of Eve, Barth presents a normative scene illustrating the boundaries within which human freedom and decision are to operate. His interpretation resonates with, yet departs suggestively from, a German romantic and idealistic trajectory of interpretation that includes Lessing, Kant, Herder, Fichte, Schelling, and Hegel. In this trajectory the Genesis creation narratives were viewed as mythical or figurative representations of philosophically valid insights into human nature and its historical development. As an exercise in moral freedom and deliberative thinking, the decision to eat from the tree of the knowledge of good and evil, in Genesis 3, was frequently viewed as an ambivalent, yet overall, gain for humankind. It represented the development from instinct and childlike innocence to the maturity of freedom and rational thinking, even as it entailed a necessary loss of primordial unity and happiness and precipitated the descent into division and strife.[5]

Although he makes no explicit reference to this interpretive trajectory in his exegesis of Genesis 2, Barth was likely familiar with it, for he discusses a number of its key figures at length in his lectures on nineteenth-century Protestant theology.

---

5. See M. H. Abrams, *Natural Supernaturalism: Tradition and Revolution in Romantic Literature* (New York: Norton, 1973), 199–255, esp. 200–17. Abrams writes: "After Kant and Schiller it became a standard procedure for the major German philosophers to show that the secular history and destiny of mankind is congruent with the Biblical story of the loss and future recovery of paradise" (217). Notable also within this tradition is the emphasis on a fall from unity into division and conflict (232), which Barth will also echo but locate specifically in the relationship between men and women after the Fall.

Against this backdrop (and with Barth's foil of the myth-philosophy pairing in mind), it is striking that Barth should locate the paradigmatic moment of human deliberation and free decision *not* in the eating from the tree, but instead in Adam's recognition and acceptance of Eve as the companion that God has chosen for him. Adam remains subjected to divine initiative and decision regarding what is good, and he is free only to recognize and accept gratefully what God has declared is good for him. Adam's verbal confession of this recognition is thus an exemplary model of human freedom. As we shall see, however, Eve's part is more constrained: she silently consents to be that which Adam has chosen. Barth does not look beyond this scene to Eve's initiative, speech, and act in Genesis 3, a blind-spot that he shares with this romantic and idealistic trajectory, which for the most part overlooked Eve's leading role in the latter deliberative scene.[6]

Barth's model agent also contrasts notably with an overtly virile and militaristic construal of masculinity, which was dominant in the National Socialist ideology of the 1930s and in the rhetoric, liturgical events, and meetings of a German Christian movement eager to raise its profile before the Nazi party. Nazi and neopagan critics accused Christianity of preaching weakness, humility, and defeatism—construed as a set of "feminine" traits that were antithetical to National Socialist values and that contributed to Germany's defeat in the Great War. In response, the German Christian movement portrayed itself as the "manly" church, populated and run by men exhibiting the soldierly qualities of ruthlessness, aggression, and the disciplined and enthusiastic following of orders.[7] They drew heavily on military and wartime associations in their use of flags, boots, marching formations, physical violence, songs, and slogans, and they aimed to give music and new hymns a manly

---

6. Patricia E. Guenther-Gleason (*On Schleiermacher and Gender Politics* [Harrisburg, PA: Trinity Press, 1997]) examines the disappearance of Eve from these retellings of Genesis 2–3, especially in Kant and Schiller (159–93). When Kant and Schiller present the fall as a gain for humankind, a movement from instinct to freedom, they do not mention Eve's complicity in it or her initiating role (169). Barth makes no mention of Eve's initiating activity in the scene with the serpent in Genesis 3. He focuses instead on Eve's inactivity and Adam's initiating activity in Genesis 2, and so he shares assumptions about female dependency on free male initiative that underlie this interpretive tradition's effacement of Eve in Genesis 3, while departing from this tradition in making Adam's relationship to Eve central to his human existence.

7. Doris L. Bergen, *Twisted Cross: The German Christian Movement in the Third Reich* (Chapel Hill: University of North Carolina Press, 1996), 63. Bergen notes that in much German Christian rhetoric and publications *männlich* and *mannhaft* were the adjectives used frequently to modify the nouns for church, Christianity, and faith: both can be translated "manly" or "masculine" and connote virility, bravery, and resoluteness. *Männlich* was often contrasted with *schwach* (weak) and *weichlich* (effeminate, soft, or weak) (62). For Bergen's full discussion of the gender dynamics of the German Christian Movement see 61–81, 119–41, 192–205. Barth will avoid such contrasting language in his depiction of both Adam and Eve.

style. The Confessing Church was also eager to demonstrate its manly image, and it directed little criticism at this aspect of its opponent's rhetoric.[8]

At the same time, women found a place in Nazi ideology and in German Christian rhetoric primarily in their role as mother-figures (physically and spiritually), as noted in the previous chapter. In the militaristic and antisemitic rhetoric of the German Christian movement this role came primarily in the form of a loving, self-sacrificing eagerness to preserve racial purity, both biologically and spiritually. Liturgical revisions celebrated this maternal role. The mother-figure served as a complementary foil for the combative ideal man. Women were viewed as the guardians of virtue and the religious conscience of the *Volk*.[9]

The warrior male and maternal female are not discernible in Barth's Adam and Eve. Instead he presents his reader with the farmer and his partner, bound to each other in (and humbled by) their service to the earth and its garden. Barth holds up a model of male agency that is humbled and exalted, dependent and lordly—a model that constrains the virile masculinity proliferating in the wartime imaginations. Likewise, Barth's refusal to conflate femininity with maternity was a much needed corrective to the reduction of femininity to maternity in the rhetoric I note above.

Nevertheless, we will continue to see in Barth's reading of Genesis 2 an interpretive pattern wherein Barth efface sites of maternal fecundity. In Chapter 3 I noted some points at which Barth's reading of Genesis 1 reproduces a patriarchal logic in the creative and vocal activity of a powerful God set in overpowering contrast to an impotent-because-maternal brooding contemplative spirit. This logic reappears in his reading of Genesis 2, where the generative female body surfaces, here and there, as a threat to divine creative potency that must be neutralized. We will see in the following pages that Barth has difficulty allowing a place in his theological imaginary not only for female reproductive fecundity but also for female agency.

Adam as a model agent

Barth's reading of Genesis 2 confronts the reader with a Creator-protagonist who establishes a covenant relationship with Israel in a history that culminates in the life, death, and resurrection of Jesus. As the prophetic prehistory of this covenant history, creation unfolds in three scenes or sequences of divine activity, with each sequence completing and fulfilling the preceding one in an overarching plot that produces signs which anticipate covenant history. Led by God through the plot toward his own completion in the advent of Eve, Adam functions as both a prefiguration of Christ and a mirror in which the reader might see (him)self—a reflection that intends to evoke in the reader both humility and hope.

---

8. Ibid., 61–8, 71–81.
9. Ibid., 120–6, 195.

In each scene Barth uses a number of exegetical tools to inhabit the narratival perspective he imagines the author to occupy before shifting to an explicit discussion of the figurative sense of the scene as it anticipates covenant history. From the prefigurative vantage point of each scene, Barth first imagines an author whose gaze pierces through the narrative of creation to the history of the covenant of God with Israel, encoded within the narrative. Barth then looks further into the covenant history's culmination and completion in Christ's life, death, and resurrection. Barth's grammatical and exegetical analysis of the narrative's "plain-sense" embeds this figurative logic of completion within the story-line itself, which serves as a biblical support for his resuscitation of an often abandoned interpretive practice.[10] He thus presents his explicit figural reading as if it flows obviously from the plain sense of the text, and in so doing, he plays the role he has prescribed for himself and his readers, obediently re-describing what the biblical crowd of witnesses compels him to profess: that creation is always-already revelatory of the covenant history toward which it moves and the Christ in whom it culminates.

The first scene (Gen. 2:4b-7) opens with an earth already created and in need of completion through further creative activity. Adam is this completion of the earth. Taken from the earth and gifted to it as its servant-tiller, Adam will aid the earth's production of the vegetation that God has planted. As a gardener-servant animated from a divinely selected clump of dead earth, Adam functions as a sign of God's good will for the earth and a prefiguration of the resurrection promised in the Christ who will be taken from Israel.

Adam is himself in need of completion, which God accomplishes through two further sequences of activity. In the second scene (Gen. 2:8-17), God plants a garden-home for Adam, in which he will receive the benefits of shelter and nourishment. Adam will in turn serve the garden by fulfilling his obligation as cultivator. Prefiguring the temple, the garden is populated with signs of God's good will and intent for Adam, gifts that set the constraints within which he may freely act.

In the third scene (Gen. 2:18-25), God completes Adam's creation (and with him the creation of the cosmos), by guiding Adam along a deliberative path to his first free decision: to accept God's gift of a human companion-helper, molded from a divinely selected rib, extracted from Adam's side, during a divinely imposed death-like slumber. The scene of Adam's recognition and naming of Eve features the seeking, hearing, acknowledging, and confessing activity characteristic of Barth's human subject from *Church Dogmatics* I/1, who requires divine intervention to recognize God's gift for what it is. In his vocal acceptance of God's gift, then, Adam

---

10. In regard to Barth's revival of a figural interpretive practice that finds the narrative arc of Christ's life, death, and glorification prefigured in the Old Testament, see Hans Frei, *The Eclipse of Biblical Narrative: A Study in Eighteenth and Nineteenth Century Hermeneutics* (New Haven: Yale University Press, 1974); David Ford, *Barth and God's Story* (Frankfurt: Peter Lang, 1985); K. E. Greene-McCreight, *Ad Litteram: How Augustine, Calvin, and Barth Read the 'Plain Sense' of Genesis 1–3* (New York: Peter Lang, 1999).

plays a part in his own completion, thereby prefiguring the resurrected Christ's election of a Church bled from his wounded side. For her part, Eve says and does nothing at all, her immobility illustrating the docility and restraint that Barth (now himself playing Adam) recognizes and declares to be biblically normative for female agency in its subordination to the divinely guided process of male decision-making.

With this overarching figurative movement of the plot in view, I turn next to the salient features of each scene which will display the christomorphic character of Barth's model agent and its sexed dimensions.

Scene One (Gen. 2:4-7): Adam taken from the earth

From the opening scene onward, Barth robs his exemplary human being of any recourse to an "independent position in the totality of creation" and any corresponding claim to a special dignity therein (235).[11] He highlights the relativity and dependency of Adam's humbled (yet exalted) position in both his origin and role within creation. Adam, along with all creaturely life, depends entirely upon the grace and vitality of a Creator who constructs all living beings from material that possesses no inherent capacity for the purposes to which God puts it. Adam's role is one of a servant. Unlike the first creation narrative, vegetation does not arrive merely as food to serve the needs of the animals and Adam; instead, it is presented as a living end in itself—as the divine gift without which a barren and lifeless earth cannot be completed and perfected, and for the service of which water and a gardener are in turn created. Yet Adam does not plant the vegetation, nor is he unique in his role as servant to the garden, and he is not even the first of the two servants to be named. Alongside the mist that God causes to arise from the earth, prior to Adam's emergence, Adam must perform "the concrete duty to cultivate and tend the things which God has planted" (235).

The source and manner of Adam's creation is likewise humbling and not unique to Adam. "He is not a new element planted by God like shrubs and vegetation" (235), but rather "he owes his existence wholly and utterly to the fact that from a particular handful of the dust of the earth God willed to make him" (236), and he shares with the animals both this humble source and animation by the divine breath. Adam does not possess the gift of breath and animation, but has it only as long as Yahweh continues to give it, for he shares with the animals the tendency toward dissolution back into the barren dust (235–9).

The entire arc of Adam's dependent and servile existence (from origin, to labor, to dissolution), in all its humility, is at the same time an exalted sign of hope, albeit not the only one, to the desert-like earth from which he is taken. The direct and personal way in which God animates Adam, breathing directly into his nostrils,

---

11. All parenthetical references inline are to *Church Dogmatics* III/1, while page references to *Die kirchliche Dogmatik* appear within brackets inside the parenthetical references.

signals Adam's peculiar exaltation among all God-breathed living beings. Adam's existence is a sign of God's decision to sustain living beings against the threat of their dissolution and to bring the earth to its completion (238). Death-like in its desert-barrenness, the dust of the ground (and all creation with it) has need of this gift:

> The hope of the *arid, barren and dead earth* is that it will bear the vegetation planted by God. According to the second account of creation, we must add that this is the hope of the whole creaturely world. It proceeds from death to life. But the realisation of this hope waits for man as the being which, earthy by nature, will triumph over the *aridity, barrenness and deadness* of the earth because God is his refuge and hope, because God has constituted Himself as such. His existence will be the sign which will contradict the whole earthiness of earth. His act will be an act of release for the earth too, and for the whole creaturely world. And what he will take with him when he returns to earth will be the promise of life for everything terrestrial. (237; emphasis added)

Adam is, himself, in need of a sign of this hope, and it is his fellow laborer, the mist, which bestows upon him this neighborly service (238). The mist, writes Barth, is "the companion and therefore the friend of man; the longed-for sign of the goodness of God and the coming perfection of the earth" (241). The mist promises to Adam that which Adam promises to the creation: "that the earth given to him should not remain arid; that it should constantly be a green earth and therefore first become moist, is the concern of man and the gift of God in this saga" (243).

The ethical dialectic of neighbor-love that Barth drew from the parable of the Good Samaritan is discernible here: as the beneficiary of the hope that mist manifests to him (gospel), Adam, in accord with the obligation embedded in the gift (law), imitates the gift, rendering this service to all of creation. But it is God who secures the hope, Barth hastens to remind the reader, for it is God who plants the vegetation and provides the gardener, and "it is not he [Adam] but God who will create the other condition for the fulfilment of this hope, who will provide a mist for the earth and therefore rain and the humidity without which the service and work of man would be in vain" (237). Divine determination makes possible creaturely self-determination.

Divine gratuity and creaturely incapacity form the subtext that propels the entire series of divine acts toward its fulfillment on the far side of covenant history. In Barth's stress upon the barren, desert-like incapacity of the earth to produce life of any sort (evident in the quote above), we hear an echo of his reading of Genesis 1:2 and another reminder of the challenge the maternal body presents for a theological imaginary that can secure divine agential potency only in confrontation with utter creaturely incapacity and need. We saw in the previous chapter that Barth portrays the chaotic boundless waters of Genesis 1:2 as barren, sterile, and unproductive, and he rejects readings that find in this verse the matriarchal mythological imagery of an egg or a mother-womb. Here again in Genesis 2, Barth prefers the imagery of an "arid, barren and dead earth [*die trockene, unfruchtbare, tote Erde*]" (237 [268–9]), to that of the womb:

> There is no place here, of course, for the idea of "mother earth" [*Mutter Erde*]. Gunkel's suggestion that it is given a "monotheistic turn" is quite inadmissible. It is quite impossible both in the sense and course of the saga and in the rest of the Old Testament. *It is not the earth but God who produces man*, and He does so according to His plan and decree, *in the free choice of a lump of earth and in the sovereign formation of this lump.* The Pauline association of creation with the resurrection of the dead (Rom. 4:17) is very much to the point in relation to Gen. 2:7 … For the sake of clarity it is best not to speak of a "deep sleep of creation" which man originally slept, "resting on virgin soil [*am jungen Erdboden ruhend*] … in full surrender to the blessed earth," as D. Bonhoeffer wrote in commenting on the famous painting of Michelangelo. What existed prior to the event described here was not man, either in the womb of mother earth [*im Mutterleib der Erde*] or sleeping on the earth. It was merely a lump of earth like others, but one out of which man was creatively fashioned by God. (244–5 [277]; emphasis added)

The inherent inability and incapacity of the creature to participate in the divine activity is better portrayed by the infertile desert than by the fertile female body, which retains its own generative resources. Thus, once again, Barth evokes imagery of maternal fecundity only to evict it from the creation narratives.

Barth's reading of the first scene of Genesis 2, with its logic of completion, clearly anticipates the figural reading, which Barth makes explicit before turning to the second scene. He plays the part of obedient witness to the signs of divine grace that Scripture imposes upon him, the part of one who finds in the mirror of the Word a sign pointing to Christ and (only as such) an indirect reflection of his own humanity.

In the narrator Barth finds one who, like himself, has no interest in a theological anthropology for its own sake, one who understands the first human being only as a player in the covenant history of Yahweh and Israel. Molded from a divinely selected handful of dust, Adam prefigures Israel's election from among all the nations as mediator on their behalf and sign of God's good will (238–9, 247–8). Looking further into covenant history than his narrator can see, Barth finds in Adam a type of Christ, elected from the community of Israel, whose arc of life, death, and resurrection represents the culmination and completion of the Creator's work. This arc the dogmatician finds encoded in the prehistory of Adam's movement through the narrative and Israel's movement with Yahweh through covenant history:

> We shall have to press forward to a final and deepest meaning of the content of the passage. He, Jesus Christ, is the man whose existence was necessary for the perfecting of the earth; *for the redemption of its aridity, barrenness and death*; for the meaningful fulfilment of its God-given hope; and especially for the

realisation of the hope of Israel. He is the man who, *taken from all creation, all humanity and all Israel*, and yet belonging to them and a victim of their curse, was in that direct, personal and special immediacy of God to Him a creature, man, *the seed of Abraham and the Son of David* ... He is the man who did not return empty handed, but with the spoils of hope, to the earth from which He was taken but for which He was also given. (239)

While Adam's origin from the dust and agrarian work are a sign to Israel and all of creation of God's good will to sustain life over against the threat of death, nevertheless the threat of dissolution into dust hangs over Adam, foreshadowing the threat of dissolution into the nations than hangs over Israel, and prefiguring Christ's death. Christ's resurrection alone secures the hope that both Adam and Israel anticipate. As Barth's reading progresses he finds additional pointers to this saving work of Christ. I will recall Barth's interest in the threat of death and dissolution later on when that threat reappears with the extraction of Eve from Adam's side.

Before moving to the next scene, we should note that in the above quotation, the origin of Christ's body from Mary's womb is not mentioned by Barth in this figural context. Adam's origin from the earth prefigures Israel's origin from the nations and Christ's origin "from all creation, all humanity and all Israel" (239). Barth has emphasized the divine selection of one specific clump of dust from which to construct Adam, and one specific group of people from which to take Christ, but he does not at any point note an analogy in the divine selection of one female body among the many from which to construct the humanity of Christ. If we recall from Chapter 3 Barth's elisions of the maternal imagery in Genesis 1 and his startling declaration that no genealogies in the Bible contain women, then his silence here about the part that Mary plays in the origin of Christ does not appear accidental. The generative fecundity of Mary's body resonates too closely with the imagery of a maternal earth that Barth rejects. By the end of the third scene of Genesis 2 we will have reason to suspect that the origin of Christ from a female body would also threaten to disrupt Barth's efforts to use Eve's origin from Adam to subordinate women to men.

Scene Two (Gen. 2:4-7): Adam gifted to the garden

With Adam's origin and agrarian work configured as a sign of the saving work of Christ, Barth's treatment of the next two scenes addresses the completion of Adam's creation as this sign and servant to creation. Scene two narrates the divine provision of a garden-home, which Barth portrays as the template of the temple, in which Adam's cultivating role prefigures the duties of priests and Levites (254). Here Adam is first confronted by the divine benefactor and law-giver, who sets the parameters in which human freedom will operate. And here Adam is to perform obediently his agrarian service as a liturgical sign of God's grace.

As Barth moves through this scene, he teases from the various furnishings of the temple garden an implicit anthropology (272–3) that centers on his understanding of freedom. Freedom is the decision to gladly receive the gift of God and to enact the obligation it imposes. The Creator bestows life and provides its necessities, and creaturely actors of all kinds respond in obedient conformity to the constraints communicated in these gratuitous provisions. As in the previous narrative scene, Barth ascribes an obedient activity to non-human creaturely entities, who in this way reflect to Adam God's intent for human freedom and activity, and thus function themselves as signs to Adam of the divine (good) will.

God remains the protagonist, planting the garden-home, causing a river to arise from and water the earth, and setting Adam within the garden to cultivate the earth. As the recipient of the divine provision of the gardener, the earth reciprocates by providing Adam a bountiful excess of plant life, fruit, water, and shelter. Mutual service (of the kind we have seen before) comes into view in a reversal of the order of service: the garden is "a place on earth where it is clear that the earth which man is ordained to serve is also ordained to serve him" (250–1). The garden thus becomes a locale where the required agrarian work does not disturb the Sabbath rest (249–51, 254).

The abundance of mist has formed an excess of water, which "Eden is not to keep to itself but to take its own share and then to pass on to surrounding districts," creating a flowing river that will move out to the far reaches of the earth, and by which Eden acquires its "symbolic or sacramental character." Thus it is that:

> Paradise itself is the place of glory. Not in the fulness and beauty of its own life, however, can it be made known as the place of glory but only in the selflessness in which it gives back what it was first given, only in the external and distant fulness and beauty of the river which flows out of it and divides, and of the blessing of this river. (255)

Barth, through Adam's eyes, sees in this river "the promise and revelation and gift" (256), of God's good will toward all of creation. Reflected in the river is the reach of Adam's own divinely ordained service, for it is "here that man first becomes a witness of this act of blessing and therefore realises what God has in mind for himself" (255).

The gospel/law framework of Barth's command ethic, implicit in his construal of these Edenic actors and signs, is made explicit when Barth turns finally to the two trees placed at what is identified as the garden's Holiest of Holies (256). The trees delimit the constraints of human freedom. Divine gratuity radiates from the tree of life, "a sign which speaks for itself," not mediating but representing the reality of the gift that Adam enjoys in the garden (256–7), while command and law are manifested in the prohibition against eating from the tree of the knowledge of good and evil. Yet gospel precedes law and the gift embeds constraints, for God announces the prohibition only after offering the gift of the fruit of every other tree. The prohibited tree thus confronts Adam with his limits: God alone decides between what is good and evil in the very activity of creating. From this decision God gifts existence and its necessary sustenance to the human creature. The limited choice that this gift and prohibition open up for the first man is therefore the question of whether he will gratefully accept the life ordained for him or instead usurp the divine prerogative by first judging whether this divine gift is worthy of grateful acceptance (257–60):

> Everything obviously hinges upon man's recognition and acceptance of the judicial office of God. And this raises the critical question whether he will do so. Will man acknowledge and praise [*erkennen und lobpreisen*] God as the One who has found concerning good and evil, salvation and perdition, life and death, so that all that he has to do is to rejoice and be thankful—consciously thankful— on the earth which has been created? Or will he hold aloof from this offer of supreme fellowship between God and himself and lay down the impossible but tempting condition that he must first know evil as well as good, that he must first know what God has not willed and rejected as well as what He has willed and created, and then when he has achieved a certain competence, a knowledge of what God knows, he will accept His judicial sentence and place himself on the basis of it? (260–1 [296–7])

The prohibition expresses God's will to protect the human being from attempting to occupy an impossible vantage point (261). The responsible free act is performed in the recognition and thankful acceptance of the goods selected and gifted by God. In scene two, Barth thus sets the parameters for human agency, the responsible free human act: Adam is "free to confirm, not himself, but God's decision accomplished in and with his creation." His freedom "is simply the freedom to be humble; his capacity to recognise and to praise the divine judicial office" (265). In scene three Barth locates the first free human act in Adam's recognition and naming of Eve.

Scene Three (Gen. 2:18-25): Eve taken from and gifted to Adam

In the saga's final scene, all other actors, coworkers, and signs fade from view as God leads a solitary and incomplete Adam on a search for the companion that God will eventually provide in order to complete Adam's creation. Adam's search provides a narrative template for the sort of ethical deliberation featured in Barth's command ethic, to which I turn in my final chapter. We can readily discern in Barth's re-description of the scene the central features of the revelatory event: human incapacity and ignorance, divine intervention, epistemic disclosure, and a gift that imposes an obligation in calling for a self-determining response.

The divine protagonist plays the leading part, bringing to Adam a series of animals and then the newly created Eve, who is constructed from Adam's side while he sleeps. Adam's own agency comes into view only as he responds to the creatures that God presents to him, first rejecting those in which he does not recognize his partner, and then gladly acknowledging and naming the partner that he recognizes God to have taken from his own body.

Along the way Adam remains ignorant of what he seeks, knowing only that he lacks something which he has not yet found (294). He is also ignorant of the manner of Eve's origin. That Adam sleeps while she is created and that the narrator uses the crude anthropomorphic imagery of divine rib-extraction together reinforce for Barth the epistemic limits of both Adam and the biblical narrator who, like Barth and his readers, are incapable of understanding the divine provision of Eve. They are no more a witness to her creation than they are to the creation of the heavens and earth. Finally, Adam is utterly incapable of producing for himself what he lacks, for once again God creates using material that has no inherent capacity for the use to which God puts it, Adam's body and rib, now serving as an analogy (like the barren earth, the virgin body, the post-menopausal body) for human incapacity in the revelatory event (294–7).

The naming of Eve is the event in which Adam declares his recognition and acceptance of God's gift of a companion. The revelatory structure of the event is evident in the language Barth uses. God remains the pre-emptive actor: having brought the animals to Adam, put Adam to sleep, and constructed Eve from his rib, he now presents Eve to Adam, rather than leaving Adam to discover her on his own. Adam lacks "the knowledge of woman given to man by God's revelation" (327), and is not capable of recognizing her for the helper he needs without divine intervention. Thus:

> It was not he who brought it about that "this" is his helpmeet, "bone of his bones, and flesh of his flesh," and is thus to be called and to be "woman." *And as he has not done it himself, he does not know it himself, but speaks prophetically when he makes this confession. But it is in his own freedom that he speaks prophetically, repeating what he has not discovered of himself, but what God has revealed to him* in and with his accomplished work as the necessary positive affirmation of his humanity. (327; emphasis added)

In these words we hear Barth's ongoing efforts to redirect misguided theological orientations, with Adam's body and first words now doing what Mary's body and "Let it be" did in Luke 1. Barth is clear that Adam's confession is an exemplary act of human freedom: "his responsible Yes to what God has willed and done" (298), "the declaration of his free choice and decision" (298), "the work of his most proper freedom" (327); and with this confession Adam (and only Adam) actively participates in his own completion. Barth writes, "he must be present with his knowledge and confession at the completion of his own creation. He must recognise and welcome the woman who will be the true helpmeet now given to him" (298). The contrast that Barth goes on to draw between what Adam must do and what Eve does not do in order for their creation to be completed is deeply troubling when we keep firmly in mind Barth's account of human freedom.

For her part in Adam's completion, Eve need say and do nothing at all: "Woman created by God and brought to man reveals herself by her existence. She convinces by her presence. She cannot be mistaken, but can be recognized without any effort on her part" (327). Seeking, recognizing, choosing, confessing—the hallmarks of

Adam's free decision—are utterly dispensable for Eve in the scene of Adam's first encounter with the partner most like himself. Indeed, no act of any sort is required for Eve to function as another (and ultimate) sign of God's provision, alongside earth, Eden, mist, and river, all of which function as signs of God's provision and mirrors reflecting God's purpose for Adam, precisely in the execution of their various divinely intended activities.

Voice and choice, free decision itself, are also missing in the "comprehensive" definition of woman that Barth constructs from Adam's vantage point: "The simplest and most comprehensive definition of woman is that she is the being to which man, himself becoming male, can and must say in the exercise of his freedom that 'this' is now the helpmeet which otherwise he had sought in vain but which had now been fashioned and brought by God" (300–1 [343]).[12] Adam's ethical decision-making process and his own free decision take center stage in this definition too. The absence of Eve's voice and vocalization, indeed her free decision, cannot be dismissed as an oversight on Barth's part. They are central to how he construes Eve in her sexual specificity:

> She does not choose; she is chosen. She is not asked to decide between the beasts and man ... Thus she is not called upon first to prove her humanity or to confirm it by any special recognition or confession. Being herself the completion of man's humanity, she has no need of a further completion of her own. Her Yes in this matter is anticipated by that of the man, which as we have seen is not directed to her but to God, but which as regards content is uttered with her in view. *His recognition [Erkenntnis] and acknowledgment [Bekenntnis] imply hers as well. As man chooses her, she has chosen him.* For as God has made her out of and for man, as man has to confirm this by his choice and explanation, she is this, and in her case the question of choice or explanation does not arise. ... *She chooses that for which God has chosen her. She thus chooses herself by refraining from choice; by finding herself surrounded and sustained by the joyful choice of the man, as his elect.* (303 [347–8]; emphasis added)

With this quote Barth secures for women, by way of narrative silence, a highly truncated version of human agency as he has hitherto construed it.

Eve's own free decision is, then, to refrain from the act of free decision. What she is robbed of here is ethical deliberation itself: the seeking that entails being divinely led; the divinely enabled recognition of the divine gift and its obligation; the free act of counter election, of choosing that which God has chosen for her; and the vocalization of that choice as an obedient and faithful confession. The ethical work entailed in the free decision is now presented as a distinctly masculine prerogative, performed on woman's behalf and in her stead.

---

12. Barth suggests that "partner [*Partner*] is perhaps the best modern rendering for the term 'helpmeet' [*Hilfe*]" (290 [331]).

Here Barth renders Eve the necessary appendage that occasions (and is subsumed within) Adam's first free act. Eve's decision is merely to consent to be that which Adam has freely recognized, chosen, and named her to be: to allow him to do the distinctively masculine busy-work of ethical deliberation on her behalf. Silence means "yes" in this fantasy of a love object whose own decision-making processes cannot possibly impede male desire. We will have to wait until Barth's special ethics for the relations between the sexes to view the ethical consequences of this normative portrait of female agency.

At this juncture in the narrative (and in *Church Dogmatics* itself) there is good cause to ask why Barth should present Eve, the mirror in which female readers should see themselves, in this way. After all, he not only describes this moment as "the divine initiative and attack upon solitary man" (302), but he also refers to it as the "pre-history" of the forthcoming history of the I/Thou relation between men and women. This encounter is the sign that points to and prefigures "creation history," in which the relationship between men and women plays its part. He also names it the event in which "the being of man becomes being in the encounter, in which man receives and will always have a neighbour [*Nächsten*]" (300 [343]). How can Eve's activity and speech be so utterly dispensable in so crucial a scene of recognition? Among the network of co-actors populating Barth's reading—mist, river, plant life, even the barren earth—how is it that Adam recognizes one most like himself in a being that says and does nothing at all? In so static a mirror, does he see anything other than his own decision-making and desire reflected?

Barth's reading of this creation narrative sets up an alternative possibility for construing this scene that he does not pursue. Considering the epistemic limits that shroud Eve's construction from a rib, we might ask, why does Barth fail to find those limits in this scene of encounter as well? Narrative silence might be read as an indicator of the inaccessibility of the interiority and free decision-making process of the other, representing that moment of vulnerability and suspense wherein Adam, having declared to God his grateful acceptance of his neighbor, waits in anticipation and hope that she will recognize and vocalize the same in regard to him. Such a reading would far better anticipate the inauguration of the I/Thou relation. In the next chapter we will see that this sort of vulnerability and epistemic limitation drives the "I's" need for the grace of the "Thou's" self-revelatory speech, and therefore propels the dialogical exchanges between "I" and "Thou." We will see this relational dynamic at play in both §45.2 and §54.1. Why then should Barth render Eve's response to God and Adam utterly transparent to the male gaze? Why does Barth's Adam hear in Eve's silence a reciprocating desire and decision?

We shall soon find the answer to these questions in Barth's uses of narrative silence to subordinate female to male agency. Barth's emphasis here on Eve's silence and inactivity anticipates his efforts to secure a Christ-like prerogative to Adam's decision-making at the expense of Eve's. But in truth the effects of this subordination—an agential evisceration—will prove impossible for him to incorporate into his later descriptions of the mutuality and reciprocity between male and female in the I/Thou relation in *Church Dogmatics* III/2 and III/4. Indeed, he will never even attempt to integrate female subordination into his depictions of this exchange.

Constraining Eve

In the scene of encounter between the first two human beings, Eve says and does nothing. Here narrative silence speaks loudly to Barth about the nature of woman, for in it he hears echoes of a biblical portrait of female identity. In this "still, quiet, soft and silent message [*stille, ruhige, sanfte, schweigende Botschaft*] of the work finished and presented by God," Barth recognizes "the σιγή [silence] (1 Cor. 14:34) and ἡσυχία [quiet] (1 Tim. 2:12), in which the New Testament does not see a lack but the distinctive features of woman" (327 [374]). Long forgotten are the voices of Mary and Elizabeth in Barth's reading of Luke 1, which some years earlier prompted him to question the association of women with silence. Yet we will see shortly that Barth is *not* completely comfortable with this inanimate female counterpart, for Eve does, after all, have work to do as man's "Thou" in a dialogical exchange. Barth will draw upon the Song of Songs for a supplemental account through which to animate Eve so as to configure woman in turn as a seeking, choosing, speaking actor—but not until he has used narrative silence to secure a subordinate role for women.

While Eve's silence plays an important part in Barth's efforts to prioritize male agency, gesturing to a broader biblical picture of idealized feminine restraint, he clearly does not find it to be sufficient for this purpose, for he must appeal to an order of origination to further secure Eve's subordination:

> The fact that the relationship is not one of reciprocity and equality, that man was not taken out of woman but woman out of man, that primarily he does not belong to her but she to him, and that he thus belongs to her only secondarily, must not be misunderstood. The supremacy of man is not a question of value, dignity or honour, but of order. (301)

Her subordinate status is evident, Barth explains, in that she is taken from Adam's body and gifted to him as the servant he needs in order to be completely human (303), in that her very name ("isha") means that she is "of man" and thus belongs to him and is created for his sake, as his glory (301–2). Along with Eve's silence, these factors indicate that the relationship between Adam and Eve is not reciprocal and that she is second to him in an agential order that Barth does not attempt further to describe.

In this order of origination Barth finds another clue to the normative biblical portrait of women. Evoking I Corinthians 11:7 he declares Adam the glory of God and Eve the glory of Adam. Barth writes:

She is his glory as he himself is the glory of God (1 Cor. 11:7). Without her he would be without glory. Without her he could not be the glory of God. It is the peculiar glory of her creation, i.e., that she was "taken out of man," that she completes the creation of man from man himself and that this is crowned by his own recognition and confession—it is this distinction, insurpassable in its own way, which, not for her humiliation but her exaltation, specifically and inexorably assigns her to this position. Only in this position does she possess her true humanity, but in this position she really does possess it. (303)

A dubious exaltation it is, if it can so readily be mistaken for humiliation, as Barth suspects—as dubious as this quotation's elision of Adam's origin from and relation to the earth. This elision replaces the earth with God, thereby aligning Adam's activity with divine activity.[13] Within the narrative's overarching sequences of completion, this implies that Adam is the glory of God—that Adam is in some sense the completion of a God who is never in any sense lacking or dependent upon the human creature for glory.[14] Up until this point, Barth's talk of glory and completion within the movement of creation history has served to manifest and fulfill the divine will and intent (not human will and intent). Thus, following Barth's interpretive pattern up to this point, Eve as the final act of divine creation, the final stage in God's work toward its completion, *ought* to be configured as the fulfillment of the overflow of divine glory in creative activity, with Adam as the preceding stage. That is, if Adam, taken from the earth and gifted to it as its completion, is a sign of Christ, then surely Eve, taken from Adam and gifted to him as his completion, is analogously *also* a sign of Christ, along the lines of the neighbor prefiguring the Christ-neighbor in the parable of the Good Samaritan. But by appealing to Paul's words in precisely this context, Barth temporarily suspends his own interpretive pattern in order to appropriate the divine prerogative and divine glory for the male Adam. Underlying this interpretive slide is, of course, Barth's intent to consign the christological prefigurative function to Adam alone and to subordinate Eve to Adam as a prefiguration of the Church. Strikingly, even

---

13. Earlier Barth repeats the same slide between earth and God when he states: "Woman is as little asked about her attitude to man as was solitary man about his attitude to God when after his formation from the dust of the earth God animated him by His breath" (303). In keeping with the parallel patterns Barth finds in Genesis 2, the comparison should be the relationship between Adam and earth, not Adam and God, for Adam is not asked about his attitude toward the earth/garden to which he is gifted as servant, any more than Eve is about her attitude toward Adam. This aspect of Adam's relationship to earth apparently does not merit mention nor does it trouble Adam's position in relation to the earth as the triumphant sign of Christ.

14. In Barth's analogical framework, the Father would find his glory and completion in the Son, and correspondingly God *ad intra* in God *ad extra*, but not God in Adam—only God in the Christ (the *imago dei*) whom Adam prefigures but to whom he is never identical.

ironically, she must lose the confessing function of a free and vocalized decision in order to serve this purpose—that is, she must refrain from giving witness.

Let us recall the multilayered parallels between Eve's origin from Adam and Adam's origin from the earth, conveniently forgotten by Barth at this critical juncture in the text. Previously, when describing God's activity in constructing Eve from Adam's rib, Barth had drawn attention directly to some of these parallels: "God used man for the creation of woman just as He used the dust of the earth for the creation of man. In both cases He fashioned the new out of the old" (297). Barth makes the structural parallels even more explicit a few pages later:

> It is to be noted that there is an analogy here to his own creation. As he was taken out of the earth, so now at the creation of the woman, in which his own creation is completed, he is himself what the earth was in his own case—the material which quite apart from its merits or suitability is used by God for His work and impressed into His service. What is meant by the statement that woman "was taken out of Man" is that God willed to complete man of and through himself irrespective of any capacity of his own. (302)

We can flesh out Barth's analogy here with other features from his reading of Genesis 2. In the construction of both Adam and Eve, the material from which God creates has no merit making it suitable for what God creates. Both scenes are haunted by the threat of death and the promise of God's intent to preserve life. Taken from the earth, Adam is placed by God in the garden as its completion, its helper, and its glory, just as Eve is brought to Adam as his completion, helper, and glory. Furthermore, Adam's name (*Adamah*), like Eve's, points to the source from which he is taken and indicates that he belongs to that source and is created for its sake and in service to its needs (244).[15]

However, at the moment in which Barth secures Eve's subordination to Adam, he elides these parallels. This elision serves to support the work he does shortly thereafter, when he shifts to his focused discussion of the figural dimensions of the text. Yet these figural connections are already quite obvious here, in his "plain sense" reading. For we hear echoes of Christ's death and resurrection in the threat of death *to Adam* that Barth finds arising in the scenes of both Adam's and Eve's origins.

As we saw in scene one, the threat of death and dissolution into dust lingers over Adam's origin from the barren dust, inscribing christological significance into Adam's very living and breathing body and pointing to the ultimate resurrection triumph over the threat of death. Adam is threatened by death again in the origin of Eve, for in the divine rib-extraction Barth diagnoses a potentially mortal

---

15. A comparison of these two passages, one on Adam's origin and name (244) and the other on Eve's origin and name (301–2), shows that only when it comes to the origin of woman does Barth import the language of order, superiority, and lack of reciprocity into otherwise analogous relations of origin, dependence, and service.

wound—a death from which Adam is spared, by the grace of God, as he once again triumphs over the barren earth that would consume him into its dust. Here again Adam is the beneficiary of christological affiliation that never accrues to Eve. Of his wound, Barth writes:

> He experienced a loss. He is no longer wholly himself, but has had to yield a part or member of his body. Is it not really death which has befallen him? But he does not have to die. He does not have to suffer because of his loss. He bears no wound, not even a cicatrised wound. He has not ceased to be wholly himself because woman was taken out of and from him. Indeed, is it not only now in contrast to woman, in whom he recognises something of himself, that he is wholly man, as man in relationship to woman? (296)[16]

Beholding Eve, then, Adam discovers that it is *his own* living and breathing body and its lack of a wound that functions as the triumphant hope-giving sign of God's preservation of life. Strikingly, Eve in her own particularity, does not represent to Adam this sign of hope—it would seem he has no need of her for this specific function. That is, she does not function as the river did earlier: in the river's *activity* of watering Eden and all of the earth, Adam saw a reflection of what he himself might be and do as a gift and servant to creation. In contrast, Eve functions as a mirror to Adam precisely in her *inactivity*—she is reduced to a blank slate that serves to remind Adam that it is he himself (but apparently not her) who is a (christomorphic) sign of hope. And so Adam alone emerges in triumph as the sign of God's life-giving will, the prefiguration of Christ. Thus, Adam, and all men with him, finally recoup the losses they sustained in the humiliation of their origin and service to the earth, in the humiliation of their need of the fellow laborers of mist and river. Eve (and all women with her) will have to live with and suffer under the loss of free decision itself, all the while being assured by Barth—and others who follow him here—that no humiliation accrues to them in the place men occupy over them.

Barth must here strategically neglect the sort of parallels which he elsewhere appreciates, for there can be no reversal of order between Adam and Eve if Adam alone is to prefigure Christ. Thus while Adam is taken from the earth, ordained to serve it, and in turn receives the service of the earth (250–1), Barth insists that no such reversal of order should be found in the narrative's depiction of Eve's relation to Adam. At the point in the narrative where Barth fears that a reversal of order (a reciprocity of service and initiative) might be perceived, he insists on the opposite. Upon arriving at Gen. 2:24 ("Therefore a man leaves his father and his mother and clings to his wife, and they become one flesh" [NRSV]), he cautions that while one might find here a dialectical reversal implying a woman in motion, and even

---

16. Barth makes much of a necessary *mortal* wounding of Adam for Eve to emerge, mentioning it several times, and without doubt he has in mind Christ's wounded body (297, 299, 302, 326).

a man following after her, the opposite is in fact the case. Barth feigns surprise at not finding here that which would undermine the male precedence he has hitherto secured for himself in the narrative:

> If what preceded has been carefully read and correctly understood, we are rather startled by this continuation. This description of the being of man and woman is hardly expected immediately after the description of their becoming ... Man is now the follower and adherent of woman, and the two are an absolute unity. We may well ask what has happened to the emphasised supremacy of man. We may well ask in what sense the passage can connect with a "therefore" the becoming in God's creation and this actual being of the relationship between man and woman? But the contradiction is only in appearance. (304)

Hence Barth secures in this text another iteration of male initiative, consistent with what Barth has already found, for

> The goal of the whole supremacy shown at this point is his subordination to this arrangement. It is only in this arrangement that it can and will be revealed and validly operative that he alone is the one who chooses. Only in the humiliation which he must experience in this event; only in the fact that—as the one who seeks, desires, sacrifices and is referred to her—he confronts the woman as the weaker partner, can he be her lord and stronger than she. Only in the consummation of this event does he gain and have the right, in virtue of his free thought and with his free word, to speak for the woman and in the express confirmation of his own humanity to acknowledge hers too. (306)

In yet another elision of woman's agency and capacity for decision-making, Barth here declares that Adam's own humiliation resides precisely—and paradoxically—in his submission to the very arrangement that secures the supremacy of his choice and voice over that of women. His supremacy is this humiliation, while woman's humiliation (her loss of voice and choice) is her glorification, a logic that could only resonate with the one holding the upper hand in this relationship.

Yet it is not surprising that Barth should declare his confidence that Eve could not have arrived on the scene with greater honor (299), for with this declaration he appropriates the prerogative he has secured for himself. Seizing his God-ordained initiative, he preempts any feminist criticism that might arise at the picture he has painted with the reassurance that, "from this standpoint it may be seen that in practice woman need not fear this pre-eminence," that "here is thus taken from woman the last pretext for anxiety, self-seeking or rejection" (306). And so Barth plays his part, speaking, choosing, deciding on women's behalf and in her stead what best suits her interests. The order prescribed in this Edenic scene does not allow man a tyrannical control over woman, Barth reassures, for like Christ he must have her interests in view (even if this should deprive her of desire, decision, and speech by which to discern and express those interests), and so she need not (ought not) defensively assert her own needs (306).

Barth's declarations of reassurance proceed as if untroubled by the possibility of a deliberative activity on the part of female readers, for he has not allotted them any part in the ethical process: they are simply (and with some measure of relief, he fancies) to embrace gladly the account of agency and subordination that he has chosen for them. This is Barth's answer to feminism, as we shall see in the final two chapters. Barth will continue to assume for himself and his sex the prerogative of declaring and deciding for anxious women (and envious feminists) the configurations of agency best-suited to their interests. Yet as we shall see in the following chapters, his description of the mutual self-revealing, aid-lending exchange in which this relationship is to play out actually does not allow for one partner to discern and decide what best suits the interests of the other.

Re-animating Eve

In an extended and complex discussion of the figurative dimensions of the third scene, Barth traces a prefigurative arc that runs from Adam and Eve, to Yahweh and Israel, to the groom and bride of the Songs, and arrives finally at Christ and the Church. In following this arc, he makes a number of interpretive moves to support the privileged place he gives to the marital relationship, detached from the production of progeny. He disentangles the sexual relationship from a reproductive framework, secures its christocentric reference in the Ephesians 5 bridal metaphor for Christ's relationship to the church, and locates in the Song of Songs the seeking, speaking, confessing (ecclesial) bride who is absent in Genesis 2. These interpretive moves are of particular significance for my critical intervention into his account for a couple of reasons. First, Barth weaves together Scriptural support for the privileged place that sexual difference and the marital relationship occupies, but in the very process of so doing he destabilizes sexual difference by detaching it from any naturalizing or reproductive discourses. One result will be an account of sexual difference that is highly unstable and far more open-ended than Barth wants to allow. Another result will be that marriage itself acquires a very tenuous connection to Christ. Second, Barth finds the *voice* of the bridal church prefigured, not in Eve, but in the seeking, choosing, speaking female agent of the Song of Songs. However, in so doing he undermines the claims he has already made about the significance of Eve's silence and her consent to refrain from free decision. He thus presents an incoherent account of female agency that we will continue to see in *Church Dogmatics* III/2 and III/4.

Peering out from the second creation narrative toward covenant history, Barth finds the dominant Old Testament picture of the sexual relationship not in the Edenic scene but in a relationship gone tragically wrong (and we might ask, how could it do otherwise under the terms Barth has set for its ordering?). For in the Old Testament's many snapshots of the sexual relationship Barth finds a divinely prescribed order utterly distorted by "conflicts between the blind dominion of man and the jealous movement for feminine emancipation" (310). He here uses the language of envy that features whenever he speaks of contemporary feminist activity, for when she is not consenting to the aims of male decision-making, woman is expressing her envy of a prerogative that she has mistaken for a slight to her dignity, or so Barth imagines.

Furthermore, within the Old Testament the theological significance of this unhappy disorder is inseparable from and prefigures the tragic situation of a God envisioned by the prophets as the seeking, desiring, electing, long-suffering husband, who remains faithful to the singular marital covenant he has established with an adulterous, harlot wife—whose desire is ever directed elsewhere and never reciprocates in kind. The histories of both the Yahweh-Israel covenantal relationship and the man-woman relationship gesture reciprocally to the other in both their misery and anticipation of a final redemption and restoration of each to its proper ordering of election and counter-election (318–19). Barth uses this analogical connection between the two marital pairs to support his claim that it is the relationship of election and counter-election that is key to the theological significance of sexual difference, and *not* the production of progeny.

As we have seen, Barth has already gone to some effort to detach sexual difference from sexual reproduction, and so now he must account for the interest the Old Testament takes in sexual reproduction itself. He therefore goes on to argue that the reproductive framework in which sexual difference is couched, complete with its prohibitions and restraints, embeds a prophetic anticipation of eventual redemption from the current fallen state of the relationship. In fact, so miserable is the current state of affairs that the biblical writers prefer to look away from eros and the vexed relationship between tyrant husbands and adulterous, jealous wives, and to console themselves instead with a sexual difference conceived in terms of paternity and maternity. For this latter difference bears the promise of a patrilineage that will produce the Messiah-Son—and hence the Old Testament interest in patrilineal lines. The longed-for advent of the Messiah-Son promises not only the restoration of the relationship of Israel to Yahweh, but also the restoration of the relationship between the sexes (315).

This restoration is, of course, accomplished in the advent of Christ, the incarnate triune Son, and in the ecclesial bridal community birthed on the cross from his wounded side. The arrival of this marital couple displaces any further theological function for patrilineage (and thus for sexual reproduction) and restores the sexual relationship to its proper interpersonal framework: one in which men are not tyrants when enacting their prerogative of seeking and deciding before and on behalf of women, and women are not rebels, enviously grasping after this prerogative for themselves. With these figural connections, then, Barth disentangles sexual reproduction from the theological significance of the sexual difference, while keeping a properly ordered marriage (minus then need for progeny) closely tethered to the difference.

Barth finds his warrant for these figural moves in Ephesians 5:22-33, where Paul uses the marital metaphor of Christ and his bridal Church as the normative picture for the relationship between husbands and wives. Paul relates husbands and obedient wives to Christ's relationship to the Church, and connects both pairs to Adam and Eve. Barth uses Paul's marital metaphor to control the christocentric reference of his figural commentary on Genesis 2, the Song of Songs, and all the marital metaphors used by the prophets, and in so doing he secures Christ as the secret key to the divine likeness of sexual difference (321–6). In these metaphors husbands prefigure Christ and wives the Church.

With these figural acrobatics, then, Barth bypasses the reproductive framework for sexual difference embedded in the divine command to the first couple to be fruitful and multiply (Gen. 1:28), while at the same time securing (the childless and unmarried) Christ as the central reference point for his future configuration of a relational theological anthropology that has the married couple at its normative center.

Genesis 2 points to this advent of Christ and the Church, the accompanying future displacement of sexual reproduction, and the restoration of the freely electing husband and the desire-constrained, demurely reciprocating bride. Genesis 2 and the Song of Songs alone escape the Old Testament's shadow of the devastated sexual relationship or so Barth claims. In these Scriptures Barth locates a marginal but prophetic picture of the sexual relationship, specifically in their preoccupation with desire, love, and interpersonal encounter for its own sake rather than for the purpose of producing a son. For Barth fancies a Genesis 2 narrator who, like himself, knows all too well the misery and strife of the relationship between the sexes and is well aware of the marital metaphor favored by the prophets—a narrator who in the figure of Adam and Eve imagines and anticipates that future restoration of both relationships (Yahweh and Israel, man and woman).

Seeing further into this horizon than the Edenic narrator, Barth discerns this restoration in Christ and his bridal Church. However, he requires the Song of Songs to complete the prefigurative arc: the Church cannot simply remain silent as does Eve, for the Church and its theologians have much to say. Thus if Eve is to prefigure the confessing Church, she must eventually find her voice, as also the celibate Christ must find a bride if he is to be the theological reference point for the sexual relationship. Barth secures this voice in his brief discussion of the Song of Songs, where he discovers erotic pursuit and desire undertaken for the dialogical and interpersonal encounter itself, rather than the production of a son.

Anticipating the account of the I/Thou relation at the heart of his theological anthropology, Barth's depiction of the Songs' bride and groom seems almost egalitarian in the reciprocity wherein agential precedence accrues to neither partner. Barth sees a bride who does what Adam does, and more: seeking, yearning, desiring, bypassing obstacles, hastening toward her partner: "The Song of Songs is one long description of the rapture, the unquenchable yearning and the restless willingness and readiness, with which both partners in this covenant hasten towards an encounter" (313). Barth now recognizes the sort of dialectical reversals he refused to allow in Genesis 2:

Indeed, we have here a note which cannot be heard in Gen. 2. For woman is now portrayed in the same rapture—one might almost say with the same eager: "This is now"—in relation to man. She now answers just as loudly and expressly as she is addressed by him. She now praises him no less than she is praised by him. It is she who now seeks him with pain and finds him with joy. The famous inversion is now found on her lips: "My beloved is mine, and I am his" (*Song of Sol.* 2:16); "I am my beloved's, and my beloved is mine" (*Song of Sol.* 6:3). (313)

With the Song of Songs Barth finally animates Eve. But what of the narrative silence with which he constrained any such activity in order to secure for Adam a Christ-like electing prerogative? In an interpretive move that can only surprise us, after all the normative work Eve's silence has played in subordinating woman to man, Barth now suggests that the shadow of the devastated sexual relationship actually haunts that very silence of Genesis 2, suppressing the prophetic light of a future restored order of election and counter-election. Of the dominant negative Old Testament perspective, Barth declares:

In sad contrast to the Song of Songs 2:11f., the winter is not yet passed, the rain is not over and gone, the flowers have not yet appeared on the earth, the time of singing has not yet come. The call: "Arise, my love [*Freundin*], my fair one, and come away," could have only a suspicious, deceptive, lascivious, or at least supremely indifferent, worldly connotation [*nur einen verdächtigen, verführerischen, lasziven oder doch höchst indifferent weltlichen Klang*]. The first woman's welcome to the first man, and the nakedness and shamelessness of both, are better ignored. The Song of Songs had better not be written, or not read if already written. But the Old Testament does occasionally look in the other direction. (315 [360–1])

For a passing moment, then, the voices of the Songs' bride and groom must stand in for speechless, desireless Eve and for an Adam who would prefer to speak directly to God rather than to her. In this alternate view of Eve's arrival, narrative silence is symptomatic of authorial angst over unbridled sexual expressions, and conceals Eve's vocal welcome, rather than revealing her consent to refrain from desire, election, and speech. Had Barth incorporated Genesis 3 into his discussion, he might have found further support for this gloomier reading, namely, in an Eve whose activity is directed elsewhere—conversing with a serpent, desiring fruit, seeking divine likeness, and leading Adam along after her on this quest. He might also have found in that silence a reminder of the inaccessibility of the will and desire of the other to the self's perception, knowledge, and control.

We must question, then, why Barth is so inconsistent in his reading of Eve, why at one moment this scene from Genesis 2 is normative for the properly ordered marital relationship, while at the next moment this scene is already tainted by the Fall. Does not the ordering Bath finds here instead reflect the distorted picture of the sexes Barth thinks himself to have found in the rest of the Old Testament, rather than the normative picture that he finds in the Songs? Is he reading the ordering of a fallen relationship of the tyranny of the man back into the Edenic scene, importing an order that eviscerates rather than guarantees woman's agency? Can an order that demands a silence from Eve, be anything but fallen? These are not questions Barth considers. This Edenic scene of encounter and Eve's silence will play a normative role in his future discussions of the ordering of the sexes.

Eve's silence thus aids Barth's figural reading of Old Testament covenant history while simultaneously securing support for male initiative. Yet at the same time, in his efforts to animate Eve and thus to affirm that women too are fully functioning agents (thereby securing the speech of an ever-witnessing Church), he undermines the very reading he used to subordinate Eve to Adam. The discontinuity between these two readings of Eve's "response" in Genesis 2 will reappear in Barth's future depiction of a relationship that is, on the one hand, mutual and reciprocal in its dialogical interaction, and, on the other hand, ordered to constrain female ethical deliberation, speech, and election.

Conclusion

With the second creation narrative, Barth finds another example of the humbled but hopeful model of subjectivity for the (now male) reader to occupy. Adam is humbled in his dependence on God's provision of creaturely others and his relativity alongside them, but Adam is exalted as a sign of Christ's resurrection—God's will to sustain life over against the threat of death. Divine gifting of creaturely others is key to Barth's efforts to resist a model of subjectivity that is inclined to mastery and self-love in lonely isolation, yet when the male subject acquires a silent immobile female partner, he recuperates some of his losses, becoming more god-like than Barth is otherwise willing to allow, as he speaks and acts for and on her behalf. Barth construes Eve as the silent motionless object and mirror of Adam's seeking, recognizing, electing, and confessing activity toward God.

I have gestured to an alternative way in which Barth might have read Eve's silence, in better keeping with patterns and analogies he finds within Genesis 2: namely as indicative of Adam's epistemic limitations and of the human subject's dependency upon the self-disclosing activity of the other. One might here recall the biblical models for human agency that Barth located in his earlier readings of Luke 1 and of the parable of the Good Samaritan, discussed in Chapters 1 and 2. In these alternate scenes of normative human agency, same-sex interactions between biblical characters provide an agential backdrop with which to contest some of the idiosyncrasies that arise in Barth's use of the Edenic scene to support the place and ordering he wants to give to the sexual relationship in his theological anthropology.

With his lectures on Luke 1 Barth shows himself not only to be capable of imagining fully functioning female agents, but also ready to present them as exemplary models for dogmaticians and preachers to imitate. Like Adam, Mary and Elizabeth freely choose and declare what God has chosen for them, and in this way they serve as models of faith, ecclesial proclamation, and theological speech. The two provide an example of fellowship, of reciprocal recognition and vocal confession of the promise of God, with each woman literally embodying the fulfillment of the promise, and each addressing the other as such.

In the naming scenes of both the Lucan and Genesis narratives, Barth draws a contrast between silence and speech along gendered lines, but for contrary purposes. Zechariah fails to serve as a model of faith and is struck dumb, his silence the consequence of his lack of faith, while Mary and Elizabeth pronounce their faithful hearing in the presence of a variety of others (God, each other, a broader family network). Furthermore, Elizabeth's vocalization in response to the divine command subverts the gender conventions that Eve's silence is said by Barth to instantiate: Elizabeth preempts her husband's voice and choice in order to obey the divine command, for it is she who names her son, and she does so in the company of family who register the subversion of the proper ordering of the sexes with discomfort. When Zechariah subsequently expresses his obedience to the divine gift and command by writing the name already announced by the preceding proclamation of his wife, he regains his voice and in turn becomes a vocal witness to God's grace—following after his wife in the sort of reversal of ordering that Barth will not admit in Genesis 2. In this reading of the Lucan narrative, Barth *can* imagine a female agent assuming the prerogative over her husband in her obedient decision and witness to the divine gift and command. He imagines her taking on the very role that he later bestows upon Adam and uses to secure the divinely intended ordering of the sexes that Elizabeth had earlier subverted.

The roles of Mary and Elizabeth, when compared to that of Zechariah, give Barth cause to question the way 1 Corinthians 14:34 is used to silence women in the churches. By *Church Dogmatics* III/1, however, he finds in Paul's prescription a special demand of female agency, and Paul's words here will play an important part in his future discussions.

In his earlier reading of Luke 1, then, Barth approaches the agential subordination of women as a social convention to be ignored in obedience to the divine command, whereas from *Church Dogmatics* III/1 onward he instantiates this female subordination within the divine command for the sexes.

In recalling Barth's reading of the parable of the Good Samaritan, we find another example of a same-sex ethical encounter that gestures to an alternate way in which Barth might have construed Eve's part in the creation narrative. Barth presents Eve as a sign of God's gracious aid that imposes an obligation on Adam (a sign of both gospel and law), and in this respect she has much in common with the Good Samaritan, who is a sign of Christ—representing both the divine gift and the divine obligation. Yet in the encounter between Adam and Eve, only Adam is a sign of Christ, even though Eve shares with the Good Samaritan the same features by which she might serve as such a sign.

As Barth reads the parable, the suffering fallen Israelite reflects the self's neediness and dependency while at the same time pointing to the suffering and needy humanity of Christ. The Samaritan benefactor points to the divinity of Christ and the benefit Christ confers upon the self, while at the same time directing the self to imitate Christ and hasten to the aid of others. Eve likewise serves as the paradigmatic neighbor to a needy Adam who passes through a death-like state in order to receive the aid of her presence. She shares some of these features of the Good Samaritan, in that she is said to be already human from the start, in no need of completion in her function as the completion of Adam's own humanity. We might, therefore, expect Eve to occupy a role akin to that of the Good Samaritan benefactor. A wounded, needy, lonely Adam resembles the fallen Israelite in that Adam must first encounter those who do not help him before he is aided by the anything-but-needy Eve, his own Good Samaritan. Having benefited from this gift, we might expect Adam to imitate Eve's service in turn. However, in Barth's reading, Adam alone serves as a sign of Christ, pointing to both Christ's humiliation and exaltation.

Barth's readings of these two earlier texts expose an interpretive path in Genesis 2 that Barth did not take: one in which the needy lonely Adam functions much like the fallen Israelite, Mary, and Elizabeth—as a mirror in which anyone might recognize themselves (regardless of ethnicity or sexual difference). In Eve they might recognize that human neighbor (regardless of sex or ethnic difference) who embodies the divine gift of fellowship and imposes the obligation to imitate that neighborly fellowship. Barth, of course, does not present Adam in this way. Instead, as a sexually delineated subject position, Barth's Adam is to be appropriated only by the male. However, Barth's reading of these other biblical narratives suggests a different reading in which Adam might mirror a subject-position that is open to all.

Interpretive idiosyncrasies arise in Barth's use of Scripture when the paradigmatically male subject encounters his female other, and these idiosyncrasies are put to the service of subordinating women to men. With these idiosyncrasies we arrive at the heart of Barth's gender trouble, for his depiction of Eve will provide the narrative template for the normative description of the leading, initiating, inspiring, commanding man and the self-restraining, following, obedient woman that we will see in *Church Dogmatics* III/2 and III/4. The tensions I have exposed here will recur whenever Barth attempts to assert the full humanity and dignity of women while simultaneously subordinating them to men.

Chapter 5

REORIENTING THE AGENT OF A THEOLOGICAL ANTHROPOLOGY

Introduction

In his theological anthropology of *Church Dogmatics* III/2 and its accompanying special ethics of *Church Dogmatics* III/4, Barth's figurative reading of Adam comes to fruition in a human agent who is set in motion by the creative and redemptive work of Christ and directed toward its human others in relationships of shared need and obligation. Recalling his figural reading of Genesis 2 through the lens of the Ephesians 5 marital metaphor, Barth installs the marital relationship, and with it sexual difference, at the center of inter-human alterity, relationality, and ethical obligation.

The tension I foregrounded in Chapter 4 reappears in discussions of the sexually differentiated relationship in both *Church Dogmatics* III/2 and III/4. On the one hand, there is the image of a seeking, desiring, choosing, and speaking bride of the Song of Songs, who does what Barth's model agent Adam does in freely electing the divinely gifted neighbor. On the other hand, there is the silent, immobile Eve, whose restraint secures for Adam the ethical prerogative to seek and choose for her and on her behalf.

This tension reappears at the heart of Barth's theological anthropology in *Church Dogmatics* III/2, §45.2 ("The Basic Form of Humanity") and §45.3 ("Humanity as Likeness and Hope"). In §45.2 Barth appropriates from Buber and Feuerbach an I/Thou phenomenological framework in order to construe human nature as the co-existence of an "I" with a "Thou," a framework that Barth finds to be anticipated, if not performed, in the Genesis scene of Adam's naming of Eve.[1] This relationship of self to other entails a mutual give-and-take based on a shared need and responsibility for the other, and Barth does not introduce sexual difference or the subordination of women to men into his lengthy description of this exchange. However, in the very next sub-section, §45.3, he identifies the interaction between

---

1. Mark McInroy ("Karl Barth and Personalist Philosophy: A Critical Appropriation," *SJT* 64, no. 1 [2011]: 45–63) draws attention to the critical dimensions of Barth's appropriation of personalist philosophy, noting the ways in which Barth restructures its central categories in a christological and trinitarian framework.

the sexes, and marriage in particular, as the occasion for the fullest realization of this co-existence and fellowship, and it is here that he reintroduces the ordering that he used in *Church Dogmatics* III/1 to structure Adam's relationship to Eve. With this move there arise again two conflicting accounts of agency for women. Barth refuses to explain how the relationship detailed in §45.2 is to be enacted under the constraints of order he belatedly imposes.[2]

As I explained in the book's Introduction, most interpreters of Barth on sexual difference are preoccupied with this particular section of his theological anthropology. The tension between mutuality and ordering in the sexual relationship has prompted most interpreters (whether critical or defensive) to focus on "order" itself as it functions in Barth's theology. Interpreters track a trajectory of dyadic relationships (most of them asymmetrical)—a pattern about which Barth himself has very little to say, aside from brief and passing comments. Some identify one or more mutual relationships (usually the immanent trinitarian relationship between Father and Son) by which to correct the hierarchal ordering of the sexual relationship. Others conclude that Barth's entire theological edifice is compromised by an intransigent hierarchy, ultimately grounded in the Creator-creature distinction that is instantiated in the person of Christ.[3]

---

2. Most embrace §45.2 as the central insight that Barth's theological anthropology lends to human fellowship, and they question the inevitability of the ordering imposed on it. However, some critics argue that §45.2 already embeds the problems that become explicit in §45.3: Elouise Renich Fraser, "Karl Barth's Doctrine of Humanity: A Reconstructive Exercise in Feminist Narrative Theology," PhD diss., Vanderbilt University, 1986; Fraser, "Jesus' Humanity and Ours in the Theology of Karl Barth," in *Perspectives on Christology: Essays in Honor of Paul K. Jewett*, ed. Marguerite Shuster, et al. (Grand Rapids: Zondervan, 1991), 179–96; Eugene Rogers, *Sexuality and the Christian Body: Their Way into the Triune Life* (Oxford: Blackwell, 1999); Rogers, "Supplementing Barth on Jews and Gender: Identifying God by Anagogy and the Spirit," *Modern Theology* 14, no. 1 (January 1998): 43–81. I address these arguments below, in the context of my reading of §45.2.

3. I discuss this scholarship in my Introduction. It includes JoAnn Ford Watson, *A Study of Karl Barth's Doctrine of Man and Woman* (New York: Vantage Press, 1995); Lisa P. Stephenson, "Directed, Ordered and Related: The Male and Female Interpersonal Relation in Karl Barth's *Church Dogmatics*," *SJT* 61, no. 4 (2008): 435–49; Elizabeth Frykberg, *Karl Barth's Theological Anthropology: An Analogical Critique regarding Gender Relations* (Princeton: Princeton Theological Seminary, 1993); Cynthia M. Campbell, "*Imago Trinitatis*: An Appraisal of Karl Barth's Doctrine of the *Imago Dei* in Light of His Doctrine of the Trinity," PhD diss., Southern Methodist University, 1981. Other critics and defenders who follow a similar interpretive trajectory include: Alexander J. McKelway, "The Concept of Subordination in Barth's Special Ethics," *SJT* (1979): 345–57; Alexander J. McKelway, "Perichoretic Possibilities in Barth's Doctrine of Male and Female," *Princeton Seminary Bulletin* 7, no. 3 (January 1986): 231–43; Paul S. Fiddes, "The Status of Woman in the Thought of Karl Barth," in *After Eve: Women, Theology and the Christian Tradition*, ed. Janet Martin Soskice (London: Marshal Pickering, 1990), 138–55; Gary W. Deddo, *Karl*

My attention to Barth's christocentric account of human agency over these past chapters has aimed, in part, to show that this analytical approach leads to a misdiagnosis: the problem is conceived as a systemic ordering that may, or may not, be correctable. If instead we follow the activity of the agent that constitutes the respective relationships (along with their ordering), the critical question is not whether Barth's analogy of relations is hopelessly compromised from the start. Rather, the question is whether Barth will allow women fully to appropriate the christocentric model of agency that he has prescribed, described, and attempted to enact since the opening volume of the *Church Dogmatics*—in truth, the only model of agency he has to offer.

In *Church Dogmatics* III/2 we find that Christ remains the secret and key to Barth's doctrine of creation and theological anthropology, as we saw in the previous two chapters, only now Barth makes explicit from the start that his methodological intention is to build his theological anthropology from christology. Barth's earlier, innovative reformulation of a classical Reformed doctrine of double predestination (II/2, §§32–35) drives the christocentric focus in *Church Dogmatics* III, and it helps to account for the limited attention he gives to the immanent Trinity as a model for human relationships. With election recast as the eternal decision and revelatory movement wherein God moves out beyond God's triune fellowship to create and sustain fellowship with the creature, Barth incorporates his doctrine of election into his doctrine of God, presenting it as revelatory of God's very nature as the one who loves in freedom. The doctrine of election therefore becomes the driving force for his christocentric construal of the revelatory center to dogmatic reflection, as a wealth of recent scholarship has shown. The incarnate second person of the Trinity is described as both the subject and object of God's eternal decree. As the electing and elected God, and the electing and elected human being, Christ is, from eternity, the one human being through whom all other human beings are elected (II/2, §33, 100–27). With his reformulation of the doctrine of election, it is now widely recognized that Barth's references to the immanent trinitarian relations play a limited role after *Church Dogmatics* II/2.[4] For my purposes, since

---

Barth's Theology of Relations: Trinitarian, Christological, and Human: Towards an Ethic of the Family (New York: Peter Lang, 1999). These share with the former the same focus on order and the tendency to allow the Father-Son relation to over-determine their readings of male-female ordering and to overshadow the pattern of Christ's activity.

4. For a description of the ongoing debate about the doctrinal and methodological implications of Barth's reformulation of the doctrine of election, and some representative essays and voices in the debate, see *Trinity and Election in Contemporary Theology*, ed. Michael T. Dempsey (Grand Rapids: Eerdmans, 2011). Scholars disagree over the extent to which dogmatic reflection on the immanent Trinity still contributes to the volumes following *CD* II/2, while some question whether his doctrine of election leaves any place for it at all. Bruce McCormack has argued that Barth's doctrine of election effects a revolution in his doctrine of God in that it rejects any place for an indeterminate state of being in the life of the Logos prior to the divine determination to enter time and become human.

Barth's doctrine of election sets limits on the role the immanent Trinity plays in Barth's theological anthropology, it constrains the sort of internal correctives to which critics have recourse.

In this chapter, I follow Barth's christological agent through the theological anthropology of *Church Dogmatics* III/2, §§43–45, tracking his patterns of relationship-constituting activity—as Son of the Father, as the eternally elected

---

After *CD* II/2 Barth loses interest in the significance of the immanent life of the Trinity, the *Logos asarkos*, and ultimately any talk of God in Godself isolated from references to God's self-revealing activity in relationship to creation. For McCormack and others, this opens up a reading wherein the electing decision and activity of God is constitutive of the divine essence, and not merely expressive of it in a way that might suggest divine essence precedes act. See Bruce McCormack, "Grace and Being: The Role of God's Gracious Election in Karl Barth's Theological Ontology," in *Orthodox and Modern* (Grand Rapids: Baker, 2008); McCormack, "The Ontological Presuppositions of Barth's Doctrine of the Atonement," in *The Glory of the Atonement: Biblical, Historical and Practical Perspectives: Essays in Honor of Roger R. Nicole*, ed. Charles E. Hall and Frank A. James III (Downers Grove, IL: IVP, 2004), 346–66; McCormack, "Seek God Where He May Be Found: A Response to Edwin Chr. van Driel," *SJT* 60, no. 1 (2007): 62–79; see also Paul T. Nimmo, *Being in Action: The Theological Shape of Barth's Ethical Vision* (London: T&T Clark, 2007), 4–12; Nimmo, "Barth and the Election-Trinity Debate: A Pneumatological View," in *Trinity and Election*, ed. Michael T. Dempsey, 162–81. While recognizing the profound implications of Barth's doctrine of election for the methodological function of the immanent Trinity in theological reflection after *CD* II/2, other scholars argue that Barth's continued references to the immanent Trinity and *Logos asarkos* after II/2 are not inconsistencies on Barth's part, but rather serve the significant, albeit limited, role of securing the freedom and independence of God over creation (Paul Jones, *Humanity of Christ: Christology in Karl Barth's Church Dogmatics* [London: T&T Clark, 2008], 60–116, 187–244, 190–2; Jones, "Obedience, Trinity, and Election: Thinking with and beyond the *Church Dogmatics*," in *Trinity and Election*, 138–61; Kevin Hector, "God's Triunity and Self-Determination: A Conversation with Karl Barth, Bruce McCormack and Paul Molnar," *IJST* 7 no. 3 [2005]: 246–61). Still others argue that Barth retains an indispensable place in his theology for talk of the immanent Trinity and the *Logos asarkos*, as necessary antecedents, presupposed in his doctrine of election: George Hunsinger, "Election and the Trinity: Twenty-Five Theses on the Theology of Karl Barth," in *Trinity and Election*; George Hunsinger, *Reading Barth with Charity: A Hermeneutical Proposal* (Grand Rapids: Baker, 2015); Paul Molnar, "The Trinity, Election, and God's Ontological Freedom: A Response to Kevin W. Hector," *IJST* 8 no. 3 (2006): 294–306; Molnar, "Can the Electing God Be God without Us? Some Implications of Bruce McCormack's Understanding of Barth's Doctrine of Election for the Doctrine of the Trinity," in *Trinity and Election*. For the purposes of my argument, this debate sheds light on the deep methodological and doctrinal commitments behind Barth's decision to build his anthropology on christology and not on the immanent Trinity, and it accounts for why he makes so few and notably underdeveloped references to the inner-trinitarian fellowship when speaking of an analogy of relations.

savior of humankind, as the man Jesus among his fellows. I attend to the ways in which Barth carefully (and often quite subtly) patterns human agency after Christ's activity. In so doing he positions himself, and his readers with him, as objects of Christ's self-revelatory, aid-lending activity, who must in turn become subjects by conforming themselves to this activity in their own turning toward the needy human "other."

In this context, Christ the Good Samaritan reappears in §45.1, calling the beneficiaries of his grace to "Go and do likewise." In Barth's appeal to this parabolic figure, we hear echoes from §18 of his earlier construal of the neighbor. Gospel precedes law with the divine unmerited gift of Christ's work embedding an ethical obligation. I show how deeply this ethical obligation is engrained in Barth's human agent, the "I" of §45.2, and I show how it is appropriated by the male agent to secure a Christ-like precedence over women in §45.3, thereby unmooring the would-be female agent from her christological anchor.[5] The tension between the reciprocity of §45.2 and the order of §45.3 thus arises from Barth's efforts to constrain in women the most important feature of the would-be-imitator of Christ, the ethical spontaneity that effects an initiating move toward and on behalf of others.[6]

As I follow Barth's christological and anthropological agents through *Church Dogmatics* III/2, I continue to argue that the privileged place Barth gives to sexual difference and the relationship between the sexes in §45.3 has a tenuous connection

---

5. Jason A. Springs ("Following at a Distance (Again): Gender, Equality, and Freedom in Karl Barth's Theological Anthropology," *Modern Theology* 28, no. 3 [July 2012]: 447–77) offers an insightful reading of the ethical dimensions of §45.2, with a particular eye toward correcting Barth's problematic ordering of the relationship between man and woman. Like my own reading, he is attentive to Barth's construal of human agency (specifically human freedom) and not to patterns of ordering. Thus, while he looks back to the immanent trinitarian relations in *CD* I he does so with an eye to deepening Barth's theological construal of human freedom in §45.2. The humanity of Jesus as the primary text for Barth's theological anthropology remains central to his analysis of human ethical activity (458–9).

6. Although I attend closely to the role that Christ's saving activity plays for Barth's construal of the human agent, I do not have space for a careful assessment of Barth's understanding of Christ's human agency in itself, after which human beings are to pattern their lives. Jones's *The Humanity of Christ* provides this assessment. Jones notes the limited attention *CD* III/2 gives specifically to Christ's human existence and the surprising brevity of the sections devoted to christology in this part-volume (117–19). He paints a broader picture of the ontological and agential complexity of Christ by drawing on Barth's doctrine of election in II/2 (see 60–116) and his discussion of Christ's human existence in *CD* IV (especial §59; see Jones 203–44). The electing God binds the human existence and agency of Christ eternally to the triune Son, such that the divine being-in-act constitutive of the person of Jesus Christ is the divine Son. The presence and prevenient direction of God qua Son defines Christ's entire being: the divine Son is the person of Jesus Christ, the principal agent in the life of the individual human that he assumes into union with himself (85–6).

to its christological mooring in §45.1, not only because Christ is not married to a member of the opposite sex, but also because sexual difference does not structure Barth's depiction of Christ's relationship to other human beings in §45.1.[7] We will see some surprising elisions and omissions with regard to the various gospel depictions of Christ when Barth attempts to secure a christological norm for his account of human relationships.

A christocentric method

The opening paragraph of *Church Dogmatics* III/2 (§43, "Man as a Problem of Dogmatics") sets Christ at the epistemological and methodological center of theological anthropology, as Barth goes about delimiting the object of his study and its in-built epistemological constraints. His readers must be ready to learn anew, for a *theological* anthropology will differ from other anthropologies insofar as the dogmatician refuses *to teach himself*, whether through self-reflection or through recourse to speculative theory, dominant worldviews, or the biological, psychological, and sociological sciences. Such resources can tell him no more about the nature of creaturely life than they can about the nature of the Creator. At best they provide a supplemental aid to what the dogmatician must first learn from the church's witness to Christ (19–26).[8]

Barth locates his confessional vantage point, once again, under the heavens and upon the earth of the Creed's first article (3–7), and he sets his methodological sights on Christ, the key to the knowledge of creation. The "heavens and earth," the sum total of all that is not God yet created by God, finds its significance for Barth as "one great parable" of God's activity for and on behalf of human beings (11).

Yet while Christ's human activity is framed and determined by the divine electing activity, God wills to secure an autonomous creaturely other in this one human being, to whom God grants space to live an existence in confrontation with the divine will and address (91). In time and space Christ humanly realizes his elect identity by learning obedience to the will of God—through his human will, judgment, and decision he acts in conformity with the divine will (98–9). Thus Jesus Christ is the God who elects the human Jesus through whom to establish fellowship with the creaturely other, and Jesus Christ is also the elected human who exemplifies the proper human response to God's election in his life and activity, which is performed on behalf of his human others (103–4).

7. Here I share with several recent works an interest in unsettling the heteronormativity of Barth's theological anthropology and ethics on his own terms. See Rogers, *Sexuality and the Christian Body*; Jaime Ronaldo Balboa, "'Church Dogmatics,' Natural Theology, and the Slippery Slope of 'Geschlecht': A Constructivist-Gay Liberationist Reading of Barth," *JAAR* 66, no. 4 (Winter 1998): 771–89, and Graham Ward "The Erotics of Redemption: After Karl Barth," *Theology & Sexuality* 8 (March 1998): 52–72.

8. All parenthetical references inline are to *Church Dogmatics* III/2, while page references to *Die kirchliche Dogmatik* appear within brackets inside the parenthetical references.

The human being is placed by God on earth, the sphere in which human activity plays its part and an arena accessible to human knowledge, and the heavens form the horizon that limits human self-determination and knowledge, for the heavens denote the sphere from which God speaks, directing the appropriate human response (11–16). With Christ as the hidden secret of this cosmology, the doctrine of creation requires an anthropological focus, and so Barth excuses himself from the task of a general cosmology. Shrouded in mystery, God's relation to the cosmos as such remains an inaccessible topic of the dogmatic reflection that is conducted beneath the heavens.

Barth depicts Christ, held up before him in the ecclesial witness, as a mirror that acts upon the dogmatician as it reflects. In Christ our dogmatician must recognize not only what he can never be (the Word of God made flesh), but also what he is and ought to be, yet cannot be, on account of his sin (27). He will recognize himself in this mirror (a seeing that can only be the result of the mirror's enabling revelatory activity) when he recognizes in Jesus Christ first the expression and performance of the attitude and will of God toward the human being, and then also that very human being that God willed and designed to be the object of and participant in God's covenant relationship. For the incarnate Word embodies and performs both the activity and will of God toward the human creature and the responding activity of the human creature toward God. Christ is therefore the central point of reference not only for an understanding of God but also of the human creature, and thus the criterion for constructing a theological anthropology and a corresponding ethic wherein the agent will seek to conform himself [and to a lesser extent herself] to the sort of activity he sees modeled in Christ (40–1).

This mirror has its own epistemic constraints, for it does not provide transparent access to self-knowledge, but gives at best only an indirect glimpse of what we ought to be. Jesus Christ, while utterly like us in his humanity, is nevertheless utterly unlike us in his divinity, having a different relation to God (as God's very self) (31–53). A theological anthropology must, then, begin with christology, and thus with the activity of the human being who is the divine address to all other creatures. From this picture the dogmatician must derive basic principles about human beings, precisely as hearers of the divine address that is embodied in and enacted by this one particular and unique human being. Both the similarities and differences between Christ and those who see themselves in him will be equally important to the way in which Christ is to function as a model and ethical reference point for Barth's description of the human agent (30–44, 53).

No other bodies of knowledge about human existence—psychological, biological, philosophical—shed revelatory light on the self, because at best they paint a portrait of human nature corrupted and distorted by sin and are themselves products of that distortion. We cannot recognize in them our own sinfulness unless we have already been enlightened and brought to repentance by a vision of ourselves in the mirror of the Word (26–40). Barth's insistence on this point will later contribute to his lack of descriptive words for the precise nature of sexual difference and the order it entails, for he will continue to refuse any recourse to a natural theology derived from other bodies of knowledge, all the while tacitly relying on the very assumptions that support these spheres of knowledge.

In keeping with this christological method for theological anthropology, the next two paragraphs (§44, "Man as the Creature of God," and §45 "Man in His Determination as the Covenant-Partner of God") each begin with a christological section from which Barth then develops some anthropological implications. The two commandments (love of God and love of neighbor) structure the ethically funded account of human agency that he develops in these two paragraphs, as they did explicitly in §18 and implicitly in §41. Together §44 and §45 give us a human agent who is constituted as the beneficiary of Christ's saving activity and is directed toward the neighbor. Having received from the Good Samaritan a gift it can never repay, the human being is commanded to imitate Christ to the needy other.

In §44.1 Barth begins with the divine identity and determination of Christ, God's revelatory address, by following his ecstatic movement toward (and for the sake of) the needy human creature, through the dogmatic registers of incarnation, election, and Trinity. In §44.3, he gives an account of the human agent, constituted as the object of this movement, who becomes a subject by responding in a countermovement of gratitude. With §45.1 Barth turns to the human identity of Christ, describing Christ's responsiveness to, and activity on behalf of, his needy human fellows. In §45.2 the human agent appears as the beneficiary of this gift that it can never return in kind, who must pattern its own (self-revealing, aid-lending) activity after the benevolent activity of Christ. Finally, in §45.3, Barth reintroduces the ordered relationship between the sexes as *the* relational site in which this imitation of Christ is most fully realized, thereby elevating sexual difference and the marital relationship to the center of inter-human alterity and relationality. These sections of *Church Dogmatics* will be considered further in what follows.

The love of God

The christological agent (§44.1)

While Barth does not develop his anthropology from his doctrine of the Trinity, but from the incarnate Christ, it is by way of his doctrine of election that Barth secures his anthropological mooring within the eternal movement and fellowship of the triune life. Christ embodies and lives out an ecstatic and gratuitous divine movement toward the creaturely other. Christ reiterates this pattern at every ontological level: in his incarnate identity as Word made flesh, in his identity as elected and electing God, and in his triune identity as Son (and spoken Word) of the Father. From any angle that Barth considers him, Christ is divinely determined to be on his way toward the needs of the creaturely other, and human agents are to conform themselves to this movement.

Barth uses the concept of history (*Geschichte*) to capture what is at stake for human beings as objects of this electing movement, and to depict the constitutive role the other plays for the self. His account echoes the imagery used in §18 to describe the divine benefactor's intrusion into the self-circularity of the subject:

"The history of a being occurs when it is caught up in this movement, change and relation, *when its circular movement is broken from without by a movement towards it and the corresponding movement from it, when it is transcended from without so that it must and can transcend itself outwards*" (158, emphasis added). Jesus Christ, the Word made flesh is "primal history" (*Urgeschichte*) (157 [188]), for Christ's person is the embodiment of this dynamic movement of Creator to creature and creature to Creator, a point Barth will repeat when he writes later of Christ's human agency. All other human beings are copies of this archetype, becoming a "history" as they are confronted by and drawn into this history (161).

In a passage that is key for capturing Christ's place as the central and model actor in Barth's theological anthropology, Barth draws analogies between Christ's incarnate movement as electing and elected God and his movement as Son of the Father, in order to secure Christ's divine and revelatory credentials (as this primal history) within the eternal, electing, triune decision of Father, Son, and Spirit. Reflecting on what it means for Christ to be the Word of God, he writes:

> The man Jesus, and again we start with Him, is the sum of the divine address, the Word of God, to the created cosmos. It is in this way that He is the primary object of God's eternal counsel, of the divine predestination and election. It is in this way that He is the embodiment of the divine will to save. It is in this way that He forms the Counterpart of man, and that it is really true in Him that man is with God, and derives from God and is elected by God. All this is concretely expressed in the fact that the man Jesus is the Word of God; that He is to the created world and therefore *ad extra* what the Son of God as the eternal Logos is within the triune being of God. If the eternal Logos is the Word in which God speaks with Himself, thinks Himself and is conscious of Himself, then in its identity with the man Jesus it is the Word in which God thinks the cosmos, speaks with the cosmos and imparts to the cosmos the consciousness of its God ... And the object of His election of grace is a creature which not only acts concretely but speaks concretely, acting as it speaks and speaking as it acts, the fountain of light as well as life within the created world. The Creator makes Himself heard and understood and recognised by becoming this creature, the man Jesus, and by acting as the Saviour of the creature in this man. (147)

The ecstatic pattern of the activity of the man Jesus is consistent with the incarnational movement of the Son outward toward the creature, as it is also with the pattern of activity enacted by the Son and Word of the Father from eternity. Thus Christ's orientation toward his fellows reveals an ontological openness intrinsic to the eternal being and decision of God, disclosing "a will which reveals as well as acts, and illuminates as well as quickens," and which "refuses to dominate by external means, but is ready to speak for itself, to teach, to convince, to seek and win recognition, and to conquer in this highly individual manner" (148).

Through these analogies, Barth not only secures the revelatory credentials of Christ, but also locates his model human agent within the inter-trinitarian relations, as the object of the trinitarian electing decision. From eternity this human being is already in the mind and will of God, as the object of God's election. From eternity God has elected to establish the union of this one human being with the Son, a union that does not consume but sustains the alterity of the creature (66–7). This one human being is oriented in his will, activity, and speech toward the well-being of his fellows. The dogmatician, therefore, has no need to peer behind Christ to the inner, strictly divine relationship of Father and Son for an understanding of human agency and fellowship.

The human agent (§44.3)

The human objects of this address hear in it a divine summons awakening them to the activity of responding subjects. Human existence is constituted precisely as an answer to this address, for there is no human subject for the dogmatician to consider apart from and prior to this awakening, responding, countermovement—no doer behind this deed (150, 152, 161–2). Both receptive and spontaneous, human beings are the recipients of a gift that imposes an obligation by calling them to respond accordingly: to conform themselves to the activity performed on their behalf by striving to act as those whom this revelatory address reveals them to be—beloved objects of God's love who must endeavor to love as they have been loved (170). As they do so they are called and drawn into Christ's history, transcending their own creaturely limitations, capacities, and possibilities in an ecstatic answer to the divine address (141, 174, 191, 158).

In Barth's description of human existence, first as gratitude (*Dankbarkeit*) and then as responsibility (*Verantwortlichkeit*) (166–202), we hear echoes of Barth's depiction of Adam's first free decision. Human existence is "a word of thanks" in response to "a Word of grace" (175). To be grateful is not only to receive and enjoy a benefit but to understand the benefit as a gift that one could not have acquired for oneself (167–8). A grateful existence is thus driven by the awareness of a debt to the benefactor that can never be fully discharged:

> If the obligation of thanksgiving could be fully discharged in an attitude towards the benefactor, there would be no real gratitude, just as a benefit which could be cancelled by an attitude on the part of the recipient would certainly not have been a benefit. In such a case both the benefit and the gratitude would simply have been the two sides of a transaction based on mutual self-interest. Where a genuine benefit calls for thanks, and where genuine thanks respond to a benefit, there arises a relationship which, created by one party, can only be accepted by the other, and not cancelled but continually renewed. (167)

Gratitude thus points to the asymmetrical and irreversible character of divine movement and human countermovement. This particular notion of a transaction based on mutual self-interest will be an important point to recall below, when we turn to the inter-human relationship of §45.2. There again Barth will want to avoid a relationship of transactional self-interest, and will prefer instead a relationship in which the partners imitate the gratuity of Christ's benefit. If human existence is one of gratitude for a benefit that can never be repaid in kind, it is also one of responsibility as it conforms and directs itself as an answer to the divine address which calls it into motion. The human existence Barth here prescribes is a life lived in response to divine grace, always reaching beyond the limits of its own sphere of possibilities, toward a fresh hearing of the divine address, always conducting, shaping, and expressing itself as an answer to a preceding divine directive (175).

Barth stresses the spontaneous cognitive dimensions of a life lived responsibly—the very dimensions that we have seen driving his dogmatic project throughout, and that will reappear in §45.2 in the "I's" self-revealing dialogical pursuit of its "Thou." Only as they move toward knowing and hearing the Word do human beings come to acquire a knowledge of themselves, reflected in Jesus Christ, who tells them that they are the objects of grace called to respond gratefully, that they are ecstatic beings who are always on the way to a center beyond themselves (176–8). With words that echo his early depictions of the lover of God in §18 and the would-be hearer of the divine address in §6, Barth captures something of the dynamism of this agent—one who must always seek the one whose gratuity makes possible the very seeking:

> Coming from where I can have nothing behind me but the Word of God, I find myself on the way to God, my Saviour and Keeper, apart from whom I can have nothing before me. There alone do I have the future of my being. There alone do I find myself before myself. But there where I am moving as I seek and know and call upon God, I do really find the future of my being as it must be saved and kept by God. Without God, and without seeking, knowing and calling upon Him, I could find there only my abandonment to nothing, my lostness. And then, moving to my future, I could only be nothing. (178)

We will see that the beneficiaries of divine grace live out their response not only in their movement toward a fresh hearing of the divine address, but also as they conform themselves to the gratuity of this address, by being a benefactor to other human beings. We will need to recall the actualism and dynamism of Barth's construal of a human agent always on its way, ever crafting itself as a response to and imitation of Christ's address. We will need to ask whether there can be any place in this picture of human agency for the sort of constraints which Barth imposes upon women.

The love of neighbor

The christological agent (§45.1)

With §45.1 Barth shifts his focus from the human agent as lover of God to the human agent as lover of neighbors. The human agent is constituted as such within the company of Christ's fellows and called to imitate his neighbor-love. Consistent with his christological method, Barth orients the discussion around the human existence of Jesus Christ. In Christ the Word of God accomplishes its self-disclosing, revelatory, and saving work in the veil of a creaturely neighbor (*Nachbar*), companion (*Genosse*), and brother (*Bruder*),[9] in whom human beings recognize one who is both like and unlike themselves. To hear the divine address spoken in Christ is to encounter our human neighbor and benefactor, Christ himself, who points us in the direction that his own activity is oriented—that is, toward our fellow human beings.

Barth recalls the two commandments to secure this correspondence between Christ's Godward and humanward determinations and thus also between the two orientations of human life lived in Christ's likeness. In their interconnectedness, the two commandments (to love God and to love one's neighbor) converge in the self-transcending "history" that is Christ's own person, as Barth writes:

> It [the two-fold command] has reference to God, but also to the neighbour. It has the one dimension, but also the other. *It finds in the Creator the One who points it to this creature, fellow-man. And it finds in this creature, fellow-man, the one who points it to the Creator. Receiving and taking seriously both these references in their different ways, it is both love for God and love for the neighbour. Thus the structure of the humanity of Jesus Himself is revealed in this twofold command.* It repeats the unity of His divinity and humanity as this is achieved without admixture or change, and yet also without separation or limitation. (217; emphasis added)

In pronouncing the two commandments (Mk. 12:29-31; Mt. 22:39) Christ speaks "the law of His own twofold yet not opposed but harmonious orientation" (216–75), which comes to us as an unmerited gift, redirecting us to an imitative love of God and of neighbor.

Christ again takes on the guise of the Good Samaritan, whose parable illustrates the inseparable relation between love of God and neighbor-love, and whose benevolent activity, witnessed in the Gospel narratives, we must follow if we are to learn who are our neighbors and how we ought to treat them. Barth writes:

> According to the New Testament, this sympathy, help, deliverance and mercy, this active solidarity with the state and fate of man, is the concrete correlative of His divinity, of His anointing with the Spirit and power, of His equality with God ... On the presupposition of His divinity, His humanity consists wholly and exhaustively in the fact that He is for man, in the fulfilment of His saving work. Similarly, His prophetic message and miracles, His life and death, stand under the sign of this relationship. He is wholly the Good Samaritan of Lk. 10:29f. who had compassion on the man who fell among thieves and thus showed Himself a neighbour to him. And if the parable concludes with the words: "Go, and do thou likewise," this is equivalent to: "Follow thou me," and in this way a crushing answer is given to the question of the scribe: "And who is my neighbour?" He

---

9. For his use and favoring of this constellation of terms see 133 [159], 135 [160–1], 160 [191].

will find his neighbour if he follows the man Jesus ... The fact that the Son of God became identical with the man Jesus took place *propter nos*, for the sake of His fellow-men, and *propter salutem nostram*, that He might be their Good Samaritan. (210)

With these words Barth secures as the object for human imitation the eternally electing, incarnating movement of the Son of God to humankind. Barth's depiction of the human interrelationships, soon to follow in §45.2, proposes an extremely modest imitation of this self-transcending, self-revelatory benevolent activity as the driving force of human relationality. The "I" follows the Good Samaritan as it seeks and comes to the aid of the "Thou" to whom Christ points.

Barth makes his transition to inter-human fellowship by way, once again, of the concept of the "analogy of relations." He does this by situating Christ at various points within a series of analogies that move through Trinity, election, and incarnation, finally securing Christ's revelatory credentials as the *imago dei* precisely in his relationship to his human fellows. In his humanward orientation, Christ is a "repetition and reflection of God Himself," in whose triune life there is likewise "co-existence, co-inherence and reciprocity" (218–19).

The appearance of this language and its trinitarian foundation at this moment in *Church Dogmatics* III/2, right as Barth transitions to his discussion of the human I/Thou relation, has encouraged many to identify the inter-trinitarian relation between Father and Son as *the* primary analogue, that is then reflected down the ontological ladder: in his relationship to his fellows, Christ reflects this primary analogue, and, in turn, so do human beings—in the "I" and "Thou," man and woman. But this reading misses what Barth is attempting to do here. Barth is not attempting to secure the inter-trinitarian fellowship of Father and Son as the basis for all inter-human relationality—far from it. Indeed Barth has remarkably little to say about what this Trinitarian co-existence and reciprocity means for human fellowship.[10] His sights remain set on what specifically the triune movement of the Word becoming flesh means for the human creature. He thus

---

10. The tendency among many critics (and defenders) of Barth's account to focus on the immanent Trinity, rather than Christ's saving activity, is in part prompted by the several places where Barth speaks of an analogy between the Father and Son and the I/Thou orientation of inter-human fellowship. In his reading of Genesis 1 in III/1, §41, Barth draws an analogy between the fellowship of one sex with the other, the *imago dei* (Christ) in his fellowship with the creature, and the inter-trinitarian fellowship (III/1, 185). Barth concludes his discussion of the relations between the sexes in III/2, §45.3 by referencing this earlier discussion and repeating this same connection. In both discussions, however, human relational orientation is a likeness of the relationship-constituting activity of Christ the *imago dei*: "As man generally is modelled on the man Jesus and His being for others, and as the man Jesus is modelled on God, it has to be said of man generally that he is created in the image of God" (III/2, 324). Barth goes on to write that God, as Father of the Son and Son of the Father, is both "I" and "Thou," confronting himself yet always one and the same in the Holy Spirit. He speaks of this "analogy of relations" also in III/2, 218–19, where again his

evokes the analogy of relations at this juncture (as he did earlier in speaking of Christ's divine orientation) in order once again to secure Christ as the singular locus of revelation as to the nature of divine and human existence, and thus as *the*

focus is upon an analogy between the pattern of activity exhibited by Christ as the incarnate savior and that exhibited by him as the electing and elected Son of the Father. By showing how Barth carefully patterns human agency after Christ's agency, I intend to show the very limited sense in which such references to immanent trinitarian relations actually contribute materially to the development of Barth's anthropology.

One passage in particular gives the impression that Barth's doctrine of the Trinity has a central part in shaping Barth's ordering of the relationship between men and women, even though the text comes many part-volumes later. IV/1, §59, 202 is the one text where Barth explicitly connects his *ordering* of the sexes to the ordering of the relationship between Father and Son *ad intra*. He presents Christ's obedience to God as an intra-triune event associated with the Son, and he claims in passing that if the subordination of Son to Father is no indicator of an inequality between the two then neither is it so with respect to the subordination of wives to husbands. With this statement Barth has feminists in his sights, and specifically their criticism that there is a contradiction between equality and order in efforts like Barth's own to hold together the full human dignity of women alongside their subordinate status in relation to men. Paul Jones (*Humanity of Christ*, 203–16, esp. 212–13) has argued that with this move Barth distorts what he is attempting in §59—namely a creative re-configuration of *Gehorsam* as a central category for thinking about God's obedient self-determination qua Son and the concurrent obedience rendered by the man Jesus. As Jones explains, §59 presents the Son's obedience as an event of divine self-determination, wherein the Son incarnate actualizes the electing will of the Father, as a responsiveness in finite space and time to the directive address of the Father. This self-determination of God (as the Son assuming human flesh) provides for Barth an economic insight into God's immanent life. Here Barth shows obedience to be a disposition predicable of the Son as such; otherwise the Son would be different from the God revealed in Christ. The humiliation and lowliness of the Son are dominant themes in Barth's conception of God, insofar as obedience names the Son's willingness to realize God's love in a very radical way, to the extent of an eternal ontological transformation wherein the Son assumes a human nature (Jones, 187–244, esp. 203–8). Jones draws attention to the distorting and doctrinally corruptive influence of Barth's sexism, exhibited at the end of this discussion in this particular passing comment on wives and husbands. It imports into the rich account that precedes it a distorting, crude hierarchy and rank, one that implies a chain of command. Jones notes also the flawed analogy at play here, wherein Barth transmutes a paternal relation to a marital relation, and renders fatherhood-sonship analogous to sexual difference hierarchically construed as heterosexual marriage, all for the sake of upholding social and cultural mores. He finds this distracts from Barth's careful efforts to depict the Son's obedience as the fulfillment and execution of divine decision (212–13).

In this chapter and the next, I will show that Barth's ordering of the relationship between the sexes persistently relies on precisely such superficial and underdeveloped claims as the sort Barth makes in IV/1, §59, 202—claims that prove unsustainable when interrogated in light of the detailed discussions of agency to which they refer. The force of such statements resides precisely in their superficiality.

interpretive key to theological anthropology.[11] By tracking a pattern of revelatory divine activity, reiterated at the levels of incarnation, election, and Trinity, Barth secures the dependability of the benevolent character of God in every relationship that God constitutes. Barth's claim is that in the life that Jesus lived among us, we encounter a divine movement toward ourselves that is consistent with and thus revelatory of God's way of being at every relational level. We may therefore rest assured that there are no surprises to be feared, no damning, indifferent, or rejecting God lurking behind the vision of this Good Samaritan neighbor who disposes himself so completely for our salvation (217–19). It is precisely in this sense that Jesus Christ is himself the *imago dei* (219), revealing God's goodwill to us and, like the parabolic Samaritan, calling us to conform ourselves to this gratuitous pattern by seeking and helping our fellows. In this way we become the divine likeness of Genesis 1.[12]

---

11. Paul Nimmo (Nimmo, *Being in Action*, 87–109) shows that the actualistic character of Barth's "analogy of relations" (as an analogy of events and activity) centers upon the repetition and reflection of a christological activity playing out in intra-divine and intra-creaturely spheres. Jesus is the central agent, wholly determined by a human "Thou." Human agents are conformed to the image of God as they act analogously to Christ's saving activity on their behalf. Thus the *imago dei* is this saving activity of Christ, and the ethical agent is called to bring itself into conformity with this image through its own decision and action.

For helpful resources on the centrality of Christ's activity in driving Barth's "analogy of relations" and his theological anthropology see: Eberhard Jüngel, "Die Möglichkeit theologischer Anthropologie auf dem Grunde der Analogie. Eine Untersuchung zum Analogieverständnis Karl Barths," in *Barth-Studien*, ed. Eberhard Jüngel (Zürich-Köln: Benzinger Verlag, 1982), 210–32; John Macken, *The Autonomy Theme in the "Church Dogmatics": Karl Barth and His Critics* (Cambridge: Cambridge University Press, 1990), 142–53; Keith L. Johnson, *Karl Barth and the Analogia Entis* (London: T&T Clark, 2010), 191–223. For a book-length investigation that recognizes the analogical crafting of human activity after divine activity, specifically with respect to Barth's ethics, see Gerald P. McKenny, *The Analogy of Grace: Karl Barth's Moral Theology* (Oxford: Oxford University Press, 2010).

12. Barth's description of the "analogy of relations" here in §45.1 has prompted many interpreters of Barth's ordering of the sexes to pursue analogies in ordering rather than analogies in patterns of activity. However, in this particular passage it is especially clear that Barth is following one divine actor through a nexus of relationships that his activity constitutes, for the purpose of securing the coherence and consistency of this agent's self-revealing activity. It is this same actor and pattern of activity that he follows through the christological sections of §44.1 and §45, and after whom he patterns his anthropological actor.

It seems that Barth at one point may confirm that the analogy of relations should be taken as relating to order, toward the end of §46 in his treatment of the doctrine of human soul and body. Here, Barth identifies several analogies (heavens-earth, Creator-creature,

With these analogies in mind, we can now recognize in Barth's subsequent account of human relationality (§45.2) a human "I" whose movement toward a "Thou" is (or ought to be) analogous to Christ's gratuitous, self-revealing, aid-lending movement toward humankind. This movement of the "I" on its way toward its neighbor is Barth's human model of neighbor love. Before we turn to §45.2, however, we should consider two features of Barth's discussion of Christ's relationship to his fellows, the one having to do with the prerogative Barth will secure for his sex and the other having to do with the privileged place that Barth gives to sexual difference.

First I would like to emphasize that it is the aid-lending orientation of Christ's activity that finds its analogue in the ethical impulse that drives "I" toward "Thou" in §45.2, and that reappears as a male prerogative in §45.3. The (widely recognized) tension between reciprocity and order comes into play when we move from the asymmetrical character of Christ's aid-lending orientation to his fellows in §45.1, to the mutual and reciprocal relationship of inter-human fellowship in §45.2, then back to the asymmetrical relationship between men and women in §45.3. As with all of Barth's analogies, the differences are as significant as the similarities. Christ's movement toward his fellows lacks the mutuality and reciprocity of the inter-human I/Thou relation in §45.2, for Christ does for his fellows what they cannot in turn do for him; they need from him what he does not need from them (212). Quite the opposite is said of the "I" and its "Thou" in §45.2, for "I" and "Thou" together share the same need for and obligation to the other. But Barth nonetheless attempts to capture in the mutuality of the inter-human relationship something of the gratuity of Christ's activity. Of Christ he writes:

Christ-church, male-female) all of which he finds illuminate his depiction of the human being as a ruling soul of a serving body, for all entail a seamless unity of ruling and serving activity. Barth does not develop any of these analogies; he simply draws attention to the correspondence in the ordering of activity. Here, however, Barth actually discourages precisely a reading of the analogy of relations based on order, and renders any such reading the result of a hasty and superficial move. Barth tells his readers here that he does not deduce his understanding of man as soul and body from these analogies; they at best cast only "a supplemental light," for "they say both too much and too little to permit us to draw direct conclusions about man from them" (III/2, 427). I would claim more—that they tell us nothing useful at all, precisely because they say both too much and too little and so obfuscate all Barth has said in the previous paragraph about the relationship between the sexes. In §45.2 he does not actually speak of a ruling man and a serving woman, rather he attempts to avoid such a notion by construing male privilege as a primacy of service directed to the needs of the other and patterned after Christ's saving activity; he does the same in §54. Here in §46 Barth tells us only that this "supplemental light" illumines "the order, rationality and logicality which consists in the ruling and serving which so mysteriously pervade the whole work of the Creator with His creation" (III/2, 427). As I noted in n. 10, the force of such language resides precisely in its superficiality, which has the effect of imposing a distorting framework onto Barth's carefully developed depictions of human agency.

> He moves towards the Thou from which He comes. Disposed by it, He disposes Himself wholly and utterly towards it ... He has only one goal: to maintain the cause of these men in death and the conquest of death; to offer up His life for them that they may live and be happy. He therefore serves them, without prospect of reward or repayment, without expecting to receive anything from them which He cannot have far better and more richly without them. (215)

In the next section I argue that this gratuitous responsiveness of Christ's movement toward the other is what the "I" will imitate in its own modest way, spontaneously moving to the aid of the other at the risk of not receiving the same benefit in turn. It is precisely this gratuitous, spontaneous movement that will coincide with the male prerogative, and with it the ethical impulse. With this move, we shall have to ask, what is left to women in Barth's theological anthropology if not to imitate Christ in precisely this movement?

Again, in the following language, we hear echoes of Barth's reading of Genesis 2, as he evokes the order of appearance and the language of origins between first and second Adam:

> The glory of His humanity is simply to be so fully claimed and clamped by His fellows, by their state and fate, by their lowliness and misery; to have no other cause but that of the fatal Adam whom He now allows to be really the first, giving him the precedence, ranging Himself wholly with him for his salvation as the second Adam. If there is indeed a powerful I of Jesus, it is only from this Thou, from fallen Adam, from the race which springs from him, from Israel and the sequence of its generations, from a succession of rebels, from a history which is the history of its unfaithfulness. He is pleased to have His life only from His apostles, His community, those whom He called His own and who constantly forsook and forsake Him. He is pleased to be called by them to His own life, to be given the meaning of His life by them. He is pleased to be nothing but the One who is supremely compromised by all these, the Representative and Bearer of all the alien guilt and punishment transferred from them to Him. (215)

In these two quotations above, we can glimpse more clearly the prerogative that Barth will attempt to preserve for men later on when he again appeals to the Ephesians 5 bridal metaphor, in which the husband gives himself for his wife as Christ gives himself for the Church. The incarnate Christ retains his indisputable precedence over his fellows as the divine address to them, and as such he is the one who discerns their neediness and orients his entire existence to meet those needs, and it is in this way that he allows these, his creatures, to be first, giving them the precedence that is always already his own. As we saw in *Church Dogmatics* III/1, Adam enacts his precedence (his always-already-first status) over Eve by treating her (always-already his second) as if she were his first—electing and speaking on her behalf with her own best interests in view. In Adam's singular ethical orientation toward Eve he prefigures Christ's relationship to his fellows.

Barth's emphasis, in the quotation above, on Christ's status as second Adam and on his origination from Adam and Adam's race is also noteworthy. As we saw in *Church Dogmatics* III/1 Barth argues that Eve's origination from Adam and the ordering by which she is second to Adam, together signal her subordination to Adam. Yet in the quote above, it is clear that coming second in an order of sequence does not impinge on the second Adam's role as the "powerful I," acting on behalf of the needy first Adam, any more than it impinged upon Adam's position over the earth from which he originated in Genesis 2. Once again, as I demonstrated in Chapter 4, we see that for Barth sequential order does not inevitably subordinate the second term, as it does so relentlessly when the second term is a woman (Eve and all her sex). A sequential or asymmetrical ordering of various relations or dyads is not itself the foundation for Barth's patriarchal account, for he makes orderings and sequences do whatever interpretive work he wishes of them in order to secure Christ at the center of his theological anthropology.

The second point to consider is Barth's lack of attention to or interest in sexual difference when he discusses Jesus's relationship to his fellows in §45.1. He makes no mention of Christ's specific sex, nor does he speak of sexual difference when discussing the fellows toward whom Christ so utterly disposes himself. If we look forward to Barth's discussion of the relationship between soul and body in a later paragraph (§46, "Man as Soul and Body"), we find a telling passage which suggests that Barth's silence over this particular detail is not merely an odd but accidental oversight. When discussing interconnection between soul and body, Barth observes that there are minimal details in the Gospels regarding the physical life of Jesus, his birth, family, health, hunger, thirst, and so on:

> It is clearly no concern of ours whether Jesus was ever sick. An impenetrable veil of silence lies over the fact that He was a male (Jn. 4:27). The noteworthy thing is the absence of both positive and negative information on both points. No attention is paid to the health or to the celibacy of Jesus, nor are these things even mentioned. The fact of His corporeality is crucially important. The substance and nature of this fact, which are so desirable and even necessary to a biographer, remain fundamentally hidden, and can be supplied only by an imagination whose methods have nothing in common with what the New Testament has to say to us. (330)

If the givenness of Christ's sex and his celibate status in relation to women merit no attention in the scriptural witness, and if, furthermore the very fact that they merit no attention is theologically significant for Barth, then we have to question why he gives sexual difference and the relationship between the sexes so central a role in his theological anthropology. Considering that Christ is the criterion for theological anthropology, should not this biblical veil of silence function to decenter sexual difference from the privileged place he wants to give it?

I would also draw attention to the ways in which Barth depicts Christ's relationship to his fellow human beings when sexual difference is not in view. In §45.1, Christ's "Thou" is not a single disembodied female character, even if it later acquires a dubious female identity in Barth's use of Ephesians 5. Instead, the language Barth uses to characterize Christ's relationship to his creaturely "Thou" resists the dyadic rigidity and fixed alterity of his later depiction of the sexual relationship: Christ "interposes Himself for Adam, for the race, for Israel, for His disciples and community" (215–16). "If we see Him, we see with and around Him in ever widening circles His disciples, the people, His enemies and the countless millions who have not yet heard His name" (216). As such, "Jesus has to let His being, Himself, be prescribed and dictated and determined by an alien human being (that of His more near and distant fellows)" (214–15). Christ's others are not themselves divided by sexual difference in the imagery Barth uses here, a silence that is noteworthy when we recall Barth's insistence (at key points in III/1, III/2, and III/4) that sexual difference is the one structural difference cutting through every other difference among human beings. Instead, differences in relational proximity to Christ seem more significant to Barth than does sexual difference. As Barth visualizes it, the divine electing address incarnate in Jesus is dynamic in its reach, transgressing dividing lines of proximity, reaching out not only to his most intimate circle of disciples, but well beyond, to those who hate him, and further to those who have not yet heard of him. In the remaining pages I will continue to draw attention to the ways in which Barth depicts Jesus's relationship to his fellows, for here we find an important resource for correcting his heteronormative framing of human fellowship.

The human agent

In §45.2 Barth presents to the reader an account of the human "I" whose movement toward its other parallels Christ's movement toward his fellows, not only in imitating his gratuity, but in the self-revelatory character of that movement. The burdens and needs of the human other are the object and focus of human agency. The christological "I" that funds his anthropology is the Christ who suffers for the needs of his suffering fellows, and this divine-human gift demands of the beneficiary the recognition of what she or he owes to these same others. The parallels between the human "I" and the christological "I" will play a central part in my interpretation of Barth's account of sexual difference and the relationship between the sexes. We will need the excessive (and often repetitive) detail he offers in §45.2 to cast light on the murky, mystifying, and minimal words he gives to describing the difference and order between the sexes in §45.3 and §54, for there Barth exhibits a descriptive reticence that he does not display in §45.2.[13]

    13. While many critics find the reciprocity and mutuality of §45.2 to be the corrective to Barth's ordering of the sexes, not all critics agree with this assessment. Fraser and Rogers argue that the problems of §45.3 are already rooted in §45.2, specifically in the loss of key features of its christological grounding in the §45.1 depiction of Christ's fellowship with other humans. What Barth does in §45.2, they suspect, aids rather than undermines a framework and ethical trajectory resistant to a strong account of gender equality. Fraser finds that Christ's prioritizing of the "other" in §45.1 gives way in §45.2 to the priority of the

Barth begins his reflection by presenting to his readers a familiar but distorted pattern of human agency, inviting them to recognize themselves in it, before introducing them to Christ, who will redirect them to their neighbors. We meet again the isolated and lonely self, who acts always in service of its own needs,

"I," which in §45.3 becomes the priority of the male ("Karl Barth's Doctrine of Humanity"; Fraser, "Jesus' Humanity and Ours in the Theology of Karl Barth," 179–96). While Fraser's analysis and critical intervention into Barth's ordering of the sexes share features of my own reading (in its attention to the dominant function of Christ and in its use of §18 for a critical correction), she too focuses on order's instantiation in binary pairs. As a result, she sees in the I/Thou relation of §45.2 an order that prioritizes self over "other," and so she does not recognize the subtle ways in which the spontaneous activity of the "I" toward the "Thou" reflects the gracious movement of Christ toward and on behalf of the needs of his others. She therefore looks to §18 and §45.1 to find a critical corrective to the prioritizing of the "I" beginning in §45.2. She does not recognize that the agency and orientation she appreciates in these other paragraphs are actually present also in §45.2 (and indeed in many of the relational sites she finds to be problematic). The divine agent's movement toward the creaturely other is that which constitutes the many relationships Fraser finds to be problematically ordered, and it is this movement that propels the human "I" of §45.2 toward its "Thou." This movement of the agent toward and on behalf of the needs of the other (what she calls the priority of the other) plays out in the registers of Trinity, election, incarnation, and anthropology. The problem is not that the "I" in §45.2 occupies a privileged place over the "Thou," but rather that the agency exhibited in §45.2 and patterned after the movement of the divine agent comes to be fully appropriated only by the male in §45.3.

Rogers argues that the communal features of Christ's relationship to a wide range of people in §45.1 gives way to a dyadic I/Thou exchange in §45.2 that loses its christocentric focus, which then in §45.3 takes a heteronormative turn as it fixes marriage as *the* paradigmatic ethical relationship. Rogers argues that Barth's use of I/Thou phenomenology stands in tension with his commitments to Bible, Trinity, and church and also with his christocentric method precisely because of its dualism. I/Thou phenomenology, when used as a lens for reading biblical narratives, tends to reduce co-humanity to co-individuality. It thus effaces the ecclesial nature of the biblical healing stories, which center on a Christ working mostly in crowds; it hides the presence of third parties and ecclesial mediation (disciples, crowds, friends). In spite of the bridal imagery of Ephesians 5, it does not capture God's relationship to Church and Israel (which would demand the second-person plural instead). As an imitation of the *imago dei*, it falls short of the likeness to the triunity of the creator, for it elides the place for the work of Holy Spirit which is not easily reducible to a "Thou" (a place analogous to those very third parties he elides in Scripture). Thus, by framing fellow-humanity in terms of a binary I/Thou encounter, Barth wanders from his christocentric focus (and its embeddedness in biblical narratives); he replaces the community with a single other who, in §45.3 becomes a member of the opposite sex. Rogers argues that had Barth been true to his basic commitments, and had he not been so fixed on establishing a basis for compulsory heterosexuality, he might have seen in the I/Thou relationship the condition for the variety of relationships that Christ enacted (*Sexuality and the Christian Body*, esp. 180–91).

always with the intent of bringing all persons and things into the service of its own ends (229–31)—an "I" preoccupied with "getting even as I give," who approaches others with the question of how they will impact, impinge on, or benefit itself (230).[14]

Evoking Nietzsche's Zarathustra, Barth stages a scene of encounter between this self-loving, self-aggrandizing "I" and Christ:

> Christianity places before the superman [*Übermensch*] the Crucified, Jesus, as the Neighbour, and in the person of Jesus a whole host of others who are

---

From the vantage point of §45.3, my analysis agrees with Rogers's criticism of the dyadic emphasis Barth gives to his I/Thou exchange, insofar as it lends itself to Barth's fixing of marriage as the central site for the realization of human fellowship. However, I contend that §45.2 is in truth carefully patterned after Christ's relationship with a community of near and distant fellows (§45.1); furthermore, within the framework of §45.2 Barth's emphasis on the singularity of the "Thou" aims to secure the irreducible character of the "Thou": the "I" must allow the self-interpretation of the "Thou" to unsettle and correct precisely the sort of assumptions that arise from reducing the other to a collective. In this respect, the singularity of the "Thou" serves the ethical dimensions of human responsibility. I would argue that the problem that troubles Rogers most actually resides in §45.3 and its discontinuities with §45.2: I find that the communal dimension is lost in §45.3, when the "Thou" is restricted to the site of the sexually differentiated other and the paradigmatic ethical relationship becomes a heterosexual marriage. I would suggest then that it is specifically in this shift to sexual difference and to marriage in particular that Barth surrenders the commitments to which Rogers points.

On this front, I am in agreement with Jason Springs, "Gender, Equality, and Freedom in Karl Barth's Theological Anthropology," who argues that Barth uses I/Thou categories to expose the enabling effects of the constraints that others reciprocally place on the "I" in mutual recognition. Barth's configuration of human responsibility provides the social critic, protestor, visionary, or prophet critical leverage with which to resist prevailing consensus. The singularity of "I" and "Thou" resists the reduction or dissolution of individual identity and agency into social relations: they remain concretely particular, embodied, and responsible (447–77).

14. The ethical implications of Barth's account are close to the surface here, along with the indication that Barth has in view a far wider scope of relationships than those that cross the sexual divide. For Barth gestures at this point to the previous war in which political, social, and economic contingencies have raised the question of the rights, dignity, and sanctity of fellow human beings, and he claims that only an anthropology built on the gracious aid-lending Christ can adequately address these problems. He believes this is the case because the figure of Christ refuses any "hostility, neutrality and antithesis between man and man" (228); the burdens and needs of the human other are the object and focus of human agency. The christological "supreme I" that funds his anthropology is the Christ who suffers for the needs of his suffering fellows, and this divine-human gift demands of the beneficiary the recognition of what she or he owes to these same others.

wholly and utterly ignoble and despised in the eyes of the world (of the world of Zarathustra, the true world of men), the hungry and thirsty and naked and sick and captive, a whole ocean of human meanness and painfulness. Nor does it merely place the Crucified and His host before his eyes. It does not merely will that he see Him and them. It wills that he should recognise in them his neighbours and himself. It aims to bring him down from his height, to put him in the ranks which begin with the Crucified, in the midst of His host … Here are his brothers and sisters who belong to him and to whom he belongs. In this Crucified, and therefore in fellowship with this mean and painful host of His people, he has thus to see his salvation, and his true humanity in the fact that he belongs to Him and therefore to them. (241 [288])

Barth's redirection of the *Übermensch* rhetorically re-enacts his reading of the parable of the Good Samaritan, for Barth holds up to his readers (who may well recognize themselves in this superman) the mirror of their suffering neighbor, Christ, in a vast sea of fellow sufferers, among whom they belong, sharing the same need and benefiting from the same aid. Recognizing himself, among this humbling company, the reader will hear the ethical imperative and be redirected to his fellow sufferers.

The distorted pattern of activity that Barth locates in Nietzsche's *Übermensch* will reappear later in Barth's account of sexual difference, under the guise of the tyrannical self-asserting male and also under the guise of the modern feminist movement's supposed imitation of self-asserting male tyranny. But in the above quote, Barth's corrective is the figure of the crucified Christ in a host of fellow human sufferers: the hungry, thirsty, naked, sick, and captive. Seeing themselves in this mirror, his readers are not asked to line up on either side of a structural divide, but rather to recognize their own suffering in that of Christ and his companions. Here again Barth is more interested in the degrees of proximity to Christ. He hears Christ calling those who despise him down from their lofty and arrogant vantage point, into humble proximity with himself and his fellow sufferers.

Barth now delivers a lengthy reflective dramatization of the properly oriented human agent in its movement toward its other. He narrates an encounter between two histories, "between two which are dynamic, which move out from themselves, which exist, and which meet or encounter each other in their existence" (248). His language echoes his earlier depiction of the self's ecstatic relation to Christ: that movement of history wherein the circular movement of the self's own possibilities is interrupted by the movement of Christ towards it and its corresponding, self-transcending movement toward Christ (158).

Barth inhabits the movement of the "I" toward its "Thou," as it sees its own movement, need, and responsibility reflected in the movement, need, and responsibility of the "Thou." I hear the claim of this other as it demands something of me: "It poses questions which must be answered. And there are answers for which it asks" (246). In this other, I recognize someone who is also claimed and affected by myself (247). My movement toward the other is self-revelatory and it requires the self-revelation of the other, for I share with the other the same ignorance, having assumptions and misperceptions that can only be corrected with the self-manifesting aid of the other. I owe the same self-manifesting aid to the other. Barth thus patterns this self-revealing, aid lending activity after Christ's self-disclosing, salvific incarnational movement toward humankind.

Barth breaks the question-posing, answer-giving meeting of two histories into its constitutive parts, and he secures tasks for the senses as they are put to work in the activity of self-disclosure and the reception of the other's self-disclosure. For the full realization of human fellowship, there must be a mutual seeing, a mutual speaking and hearing, and a mutual aid-lending, and this reciprocal movement must be performed with a glad freedom of the heart.

The eye, turning to look the other in the eye, depicts for Barth the receptivity and openness each must have for the other if true fellowship is to take place, as well as the vulnerability and dependency of the self upon the counter movement of the other. I cannot look you in the eye without allowing myself to be looked at by you, and only as I open myself to this two-way exchange, giving myself to be known as I move toward a knowledge of you, do I begin to move out of isolation and into fellowship (250–2).

The mouth and ears depict for Barth a deeper level of this vulnerable and spontaneous movement toward the other that requires "reciprocal expression and its reciprocal reception, reciprocal address and its reciprocal reception" (253). The perceptions and assumptions gained through mere looking are inadequate, because each is to the other "something new and strange and different" (256–7). What each requires from and owes to the other is a self-manifesting, self-interpreting, discursive activity, offered to aid the other in correcting any misperceptions or faulty assumptions and preconceptions (252).

Barth's depiction of the dispositions with which the agent is both to hear and to speak to the other subtly reflects the gratuitous pattern and character of Christ's existence: self-manifesting speech is to be delivered as a gift to aid the other. While this speech will offer a much-needed critical corrective to the other's assumptions it should not be performed as a self-justifying or defensive assertion of oneself to the other.

> That I express myself does not mean in the first instance – and from my standpoint it ought not to mean – that I aim to relieve, defend or justify myself against the wrong which I am done or might be done by the picture which the other has of me. *My self-expression may later acquire this sense. But this cannot be its primary intention on my part.* The real meaning of the fact that I express myself to the other is that I owe him this assistance. Thus my self-expression, if it is genuinely human, has nothing whatever to do with the fear of being misunderstood or the desire to give a better portrait of myself and vindicate myself before him ... *My word as self-declaration is human only when, in seizing the opportunity of making myself clear and understandable, I have before me the necessary concern of the other not only to see but also to understand me, to escape the uncertainty of the view which he has of me, and the embarrassment caused by*

> this uncertainty. *I can help him in this respect only as I tell him who I am, what I think of it, what my view is, with whom and what he has to do in me and my whole being* according to the insight gained according to the best of my own knowledge and conscience. (254; emphases added)

Barth thus characterizes this self-revelation as a generous, rather than self-defensive, movement. Defending oneself against misunderstanding or misrecognition should not be what drives the subject's speech, yet Barth does suppose that the other is very much in need of helpful critical correctives (which may well require an element of self-defense), and it is precisely this need that should drive the subject's readiness not only to reveal itself but also to hear the other in turn.

The same generosity with which the subject speaks should also be exhibited in hearing the other's speech—a readiness to accept what she or he offers as a gift, rather than a self-interested self-assertion. Barth writes:

> He, too, tries to represent himself, inviting me to compare my picture of him with what he himself has to contribute. He, too, aims to help me. For this reason and with this intention he speaks with me. To receive or accept him in this sense is to listen to him. *I do not hear him if I assume that he is only concerned about himself, either to commend himself to me or to gain my interest, and that he makes himself conspicuous and understandable, forcing himself and his being upon me, only for this reason. When he speaks to me, I must not be affected by the fact that in innumerable instances in which men express themselves to me this might actually be the case or appear to be so.* What matters now is *the humanity of my hearing*, and this is conditioned negatively by the fact that at least I do not hear this other with suspicion, and positively by the fact that I presuppose that he is trying to come to my help with his self-expression and self-declaration. (255; emphasis added)

This prescription of a generous disposition has a risk-taking aspect, for, as Barth notes, the subject is well aware that, more often than not, others are not worthy of this generous assumption, for they advance upon the self with only their own interests in view. It is by way of this generosity that "I" am truly human, truly conformed to the activity of Christ, whose assistance was met by many with rejection and crucifixion. In keeping with this christological connection, Barth stresses the obligation of the self to act, to come to the aid of the other, not to withhold this assistance, even when the other may or does not respond in kind:

> *Why I cannot be silent but am required to speak* is that I necessarily abandon him and leave him to his own devices if I spare myself what is perhaps the thankless venture, and him the unwelcome penetration of his sphere, and withhold from him that which he definitely ought to know, but cannot know until I tell him … *No matter what the results, I cannot refrain from knocking.* The humanity of the encounter between I and Thou demands that I *should not merely make a few tentative efforts in this direction, but do my utmost. Speaking on this*

presupposition, not for one's own sake but for that of the needy other, is human speaking. (257/307; emphases added)

We will need to recall these words when we later hear Barth's efforts to silence feminist critique and to restrain the ways in which women might go about doing for men precisely what he calls all human beings to do here.

The parallels to Christ's gratuitous activity are deepened when Barth explains the purpose of this mutual seeing, speaking and hearing: all is done to summon the other to come to the self's aid, and to hear the same summons from the other (260). I am not to leave you alone with the anxiety and burdens that you bear, for I must be present to lend support and help (262–3). In turn I must not, with delusional self-sufficiency, attempt to carry my own anxieties and burdens alone, but I must instead summon and receive support from you. We must let ourselves be helped by others as readily as we hasten to lend aid to them (263).

This movement toward the other is, finally, to be performed with a gladness of heart that discovers in the other what it has always sought and needed. Barth here captures the disposition proper to the agential embrace of the divine gift mediated through the human other: "I have waited for Thee. I sought Thee before Thou didst encounter me. I had Thee in view even before I knew Thee. The encounter with Thee is not, therefore, the encounter with something strange which disturbs me, but with a counterpart which I have lacked and without which I would be empty and futile" (269). In these words we hear echoes of Adam's failed search and eventual glad recognition of Eve in §41. This glad embrace of the "Thou" expresses the same features of human freedom that Adam performed for Barth in his joyful election and affirmation of the only option God had chosen for him (272).

The sexually differentiated neighbor

Sexual difference and its order

Having described the subject's encounter with the human other in broad enough terms to embrace a wide range of inter-human encounters, in §45.3 Barth declares that this fellowship finds the occasion for its fullest realization and performance in the interaction between the sexes. It is most fully actualized in a lifelong monogamous marital relationship, wherein the free decision for fellowship with the other has the sort of exclusive longevity and commitment and ordering that reflects Christ's unwavering election of his community (288).

With Barth's reading of Genesis 2 in mind, this announcement comes as no surprise, but the incongruity between his depiction of the I/Thou relationship and that of the sexual relationship is striking, as above all is his silence on how the one can be integrated with the other. Why should a relationship between two members of the opposite sexes afford this opportunity? After all, the parable of the Good Samaritan does not direct us specifically to the aid of someone of the opposite sex, let alone a lifelong monogamous marriage to that person. With this transition, Adam and Eve have supplanted the fallen Israelite and the Good Samaritan, without any explanation as to why a variety of other inter-human relationships might not afford the same opportunities.

Christ's sea of fellow sufferers is now divided by "the only structural differentiation" (*die einzige strukturelle Differenzierung*) in which human beings exists (286 [344]). This alterity is said to be analogous to the distinction between the incarnate Christ and his community of fellows (now reduced to a simple collective), an unparalleled polarity persisting through every other difference that we might draw between groups of human beings, and expressing itself within these other differences. Of this sexual difference Barth writes,

> the antitheses between man and man are so great and estranging and yet stimulating that the encounter between them carries with it the possibility of a supreme difficulty otherwise absent, and yet in all these antitheses their relatedness, their power of mutual attraction and their reciprocal reference the one to the other are so great and illuminating and imperative that the possibility also emerges at least of a supreme interest otherwise absent. (288)

Barth does not attempt to describe what the difference between the sexes entails, such that it should acquire a status and exemplify an antithesis analogous to that which divides the incarnate Christ from his company of fellows, nor does he make explicit what he has in mind about the attraction existing between men and women. He assumes an obvious givenness of the antithesis between the sexes, and he is quite certain that no one can be fully human without participating in some capacity in this encounter with the opposite sex. The likes of Nietzsche and Goethe are Barth's philosophical foils here, with their desire to emancipate themselves from any dependence on women, a fault of which Barth suspects monks in their cloisters may also be guilty (290). But with respect to this latter point he makes no mention of the unmarried Christ in his close circle of twelve men, for with the introduction of sexual difference he also genders all Christ's others as a singular feminine collective.

Barth now imposes order (along with sexual difference) retrospectively on the "I" and its "Thou" of §45.2. The male subject acquires an agential precedence over the female that grants him a heavier stake in imitating the pattern of Christ's activity for and on behalf of his community. Yet again Barth is reticent on details, for he does not explain how the interpersonal exchange of §45.2 could possibly be performed successfully if only one party is to appropriate fully the gratuitous, self-risking movement of his christocentric model of human agency. The I/Thou relation described in §45.2 requires this very movement of *both* partners, each toward the other, in order for human fellowship to be fully realized. Yet Barth's ordering, in effect, requires women to refrain from conforming themselves to this pattern of Christ's activity. Barth does not attempt to address this implication of his ordering for the reciprocity of the I/Thou relation. He simply asserts both the difference and its ordering in the most general of terms, excusing himself from the task of further explanation:

> It cannot be contested that both physiologically and biblically a certain strength and corresponding precedence are a very general characteristic of man, and a weakness and corresponding subsequence of woman. But in what the strength (*Stärke*) and precedence (*Vorangehen*) consists on the one side, and the weakness (*Schwäche*) and subsequence (*Nachfolge*) on the other, what it means that man is the head of woman and not vice versa, is something which is better left unresolved in a general statement, and value-judgments must certainly be resisted ... What distinguishes man from woman and woman from man even in this relationship of super- and subordination is more easily discovered, perceived, respected and valued in the encounter between them than it is defined. It is to be constantly experienced in their mutual exchanges and co-existence. (287 [346–7])

I will return to Barth's uncharacteristic loss of words on the specifics of sexual difference and its ordering in my final chapter.

Barth prefers simply to construe sexual difference as a given distinction persisting and manifesting itself in ever-changing cultural mores, social customs and practices, all of which concretize and express an alterity not reducible to any of these features (309–12). He consistently avoids drawing from biological, reproductive, psychological, or sociological discourses for depicting the difference. His assertions express assumptions he does not anticipate his readers will contest, and so these unexamined assumptions, deeply embedded in social conventions, must do the heavy lifting. To say any more about this difference and its order would risk the legitimization of a natural theology—the confusion of the divine order with human orders. Barth does not consider that the very assumption of a deeply pervasive difference and antithesis between the sexes might itself by just as culturally conditioned as efforts to give it descriptive flesh.

Scriptural manifestations of the difference and its order

Rather than appealing to psychology, sociology, or philosophical typologies to support his assertions about sexual difference, Barth performs his familiar dogmatic task of discovering the givenness of this privileged alterity in Scripture. He summarily repeats the inter-testamental interpretative work he undertook in *Church Dogmatics* III/1. Linking Genesis 2, Song of Songs and Ephesians 5, he argues that the fellowship and special dignity of the relationship between the sexes lies in "the freedom of the heart for the other," and not in fatherhood, motherhood, or the establishment of family (293). In the context of the Old Testament, Genesis 2 and the Songs give us a marginalized view of the dignity of the relationship between the sexes. In the Old Testament, Barth reminds us, messianic anticipation drives the dominant tendency to define the relationship between the sexes (marriage in particular) in terms of sexual reproduction and patrilineage. With the advent of the long-awaited Messiah-Son, sexual reproduction and patrilineage fall to the wayside. In the New Testament picture of human fellowship, marriage is now understood as the free decision and love for a member of the opposite sex—an act that is to signify the love of Christ for his church, thanks to Paul's use of this bridal metaphor to order marital relationships (Eph. 5) (291–301).

But Barth's material here leaves in its wake a series of unanswered questions. If marriage has this role, why does the long-awaited Messiah not acquire an actual wife (rather than a metaphorical bride), considering the central place he occupies in delineating a theological anthropology? Why does the unmarried state of the long-awaited Messiah *not* have the same effect on marriage itself that his advent as son of Adam, Abraham, and David has on sexual reproduction? In this inter-testamental meta-narrative, should not marriage tread the same path as the patrilineage to which it has been so closely tethered? We receive no answer to these questions from Barth. Without explanation, he merely notes, and dismisses as irrelevant, the texts where Paul discusses and indicates his preference for celibacy (1 Cor. 2:8-12; 7:1-17; 7:25-40; 14:33-38) (309). We will have to wait until *Church Dogmatics* III/4—to be explored in the next chapter—to hear Barth's feeble attempts to account for Paul's statements and to come to terms with Christ's own unmarried state and Christ's words privileging celibacy over marriage. Yet Barth must find a way to secure a celibate Christ as the governing criterion for the central role he gives to marriage if he is to stay true to his methodological commitment of building anthropology on Christology. Thus, with the aid of the (unmarried) Paul's fondness for marital metaphors, Barth secures the Church as Christ's bride, and in a long section of fine print, he argues, once again, that the relationship of Christ to the Church is *the* paradigmatic human relationship prefigured in Adam and Eve.

Working through a list of Pauline texts on sex and marriage, the most important of which are Ephesians 5 and 1 Corinthians 11 (but including also Rom 7:16, 1 Cor. 6:12-20, and 2 Cor. 11:2-3), Barth rediscovers between men and women the same model of agency that Adam and Eve exemplified for him in Genesis 2, a model which serves for Barth as the defining feature of the relationship between the sexes. The relationship between the sexes is an agential exercise in freely choosing the only choice given to you by God—to freely be and enact the sexed person that you are, and to do so by directing your activity toward the opposite sex (301–16). In his exposition of these Pauline texts Barth evokes the primordial first couple of Genesis 2, now allowing his earlier image of the suffering Christ among his host of fellow sufferers to be displaced by New Testament references to harlots and wives.

In his reading of 1 Corinthians 6:12-20, it is especially clear that Barth is not appealing to a grid of hierarchically ordered binaries in order to support his account of the central place of the ordered sexual relationship, as he has often been read as doing. Here Paul compares the relationship of a man to a harlot with the relationship of a man to Christ—the harlot and Christ occupy analogous positions in relation to the human agent in view. Barth's interpretation of this and other passages focuses not on the question of order at all, but on the freedom of the human agent to choose the one thing given to him. The agent's use of a woman purely as an occasion to satisfy his sexual needs is discontinuous with and does not reflect his free decision to choose Christ (305). Barth writes:

> That the Christian is one body with his wife can take place only in correspondence with the fact that he himself is one spirit with the Lord. But in the kind of sexual intercourse referred to there is no such correspondence and therefore it is impossible ... *Belonging to a woman, he cannot contradict but must correspond to the fact that he belongs to Christ.* But he would contradict this if he belonged to a harlot and became one body with her ... What is intrinsically possible to the man who is one spirit with Christ in the relationship of man and woman and therefore in the completion of this relationship can only be, as *an exercise of his freedom and therefore his participation in the lordship of Christ, and in his obedience to "the law of the Spirit of life,"* the intercourse which beyond all need and its satisfaction is the completion of the encounter of man and fellow-man and the fulfilment of full and serious and genuine fellowship. (305–8; emphasis added)

Barth's problematic ordering of the sexes comes from the privileged place the male occupies in imitating Christ, and not from a grid of ordered dyads that relate neatly to each other (i.e., Father-Son, Christ-Church, man-woman, soul-body, heaven-earth, etc.). This becomes particularly clear in Barth's interpretation of Ephesians 5:22-23 (his dominant interpretive text), where Barth presents the order between the sexes (with husband and wife at the normative center) as a copy modeled on the pattern of Christ's relationship to the Church, and as such, one that follows the ordered pattern of Adam's recognition and naming of Eve in Genesis 2. It is specifically the agential initiative of the eternally electing Christ (and Adam, his prefiguration) that husbands are to imitate:

> They may and should and must precede women by accepting and affirming them in such a way that they do what man did at the climax of his creation in Gen. 2 ... as the love of Christ precedes the answering love of the community, so the love of the husband precedes that of the wife. In imitation of the attitude of Christ the husband may and should precede at this point as the wife may and should precede him in representing the community in its absolute subordination to Christ. (315–16)

Order now renders the agent of §45.2 paradigmatically masculine, just as it did in Genesis 2. The spontaneous self-risking movement toward the other, the imitation of Christ himself, is an activity to be appropriated by men alone.

Let us not forget that the Adamic affirmation in Genesis 2 required of Eve only the decision to refrain from decision, affirmation, or counter-election. Barth is not troubled by this abstention, assuring his readers that this male prerogative "does not give one control over the other, or put anyone under the dominion of the other" (313). Once again, he seizes upon his self-bestowed Adamic prerogative, which need fear no dissent (vocalized or otherwise) from female readers; their role is only to be gladly that which he has benevolently chosen and declared them to be. And so Barth is confident that the pattern of Christ's electing, self-giving incarnational descent on behalf of the needs of his creatures undermines any place for self-serving dominion, command-giving, and control. All is to be done with the needs of the other in view, and Barth is confident his female readers will have reason only to rejoice in so magnanimous an account of masculine responsibility and care.

Barth neglects to consider what is left to female agency now that his model of full human agency is unveiled as a male prerogative. And why should he trouble himself with such a question if it is not his task to attempt to enact the agential reticence that is here implied for woman? If she is not to imitate Christ in this respect, what other mode of agency does Barth leave to her? The answer is—none other than the image of the silent motionless Eve, for it is precisely her restraint that enables the male to assume the prerogative of playing Christ—a peculiarly passive and passionless requirement in an actualistic ontology, which supposes that human agents are always in motion. Eve's restraint secures Adam's prerogative insofar as she simply consents to be that which he has chosen and declared her to be.

What has become of the spontaneous, self-disclosing corrective declaration of the "Thou," so necessary to the inter-personal relationship of §45.2? Playing Adam, Barth has no need of it here. Between §45.2's discussion of a mutual exchange and §45.3's discussion of order we find two irreconcilable accounts of human agency, parallel to the discontinuity between the speaking Bride of the Songs and the silent Eve. The disconnection between §45.2 and §45.3 is exacerbated by the fact that Barth makes no attempt to articulate §45.3's order using the language and framework of mutual seeing, hearing, speaking and aid-lending that fleshed out his earlier depiction of the movement of "I" toward "Thou." He does not tell us how a relationship that begins with two people (necessarily simultaneously) looking each other in the eye can have a first actor or initiator. Nor does he tell us how the male is to preempt his female other as both first to speak (revealing himself to the other) and first to hear the self-revelation of that other. His depiction of order is as loosely tethered to his model human agent of §45.2 as his depiction of sexual difference is to his depiction of Christ in §45.1.

Barth's interpretation of 1 Corinthians 11:1-6, where Paul instructs women to wear veils to signify their subordination to men, betrays his awareness of the criticism that these two sets of claims about the relationship between the sexes are irreconcilable (309–12), and once again he attempts to pre-empt and silence feminist criticism of his dogmatic declaration. Here he evades the dogmatic task of reconciling his two contrary claims about the status of women by discovering that similar contrary assertions are made by Paul in two different epistles. Galatians 3:28 ("There is neither Jew nor Greek, there is neither slave nor free, there is neither male nor female; for you are all one in Christ Jesus") speaks of the mutuality of the relationship, while 1 Corinthians 11 supports a sexual ordering. Barth writes:

An enthusiastic attempt was being made to introduce equality where previously the custom had been both at Corinth and in other Christian communities that in their gatherings for worship the men should be uncovered and the women covered. We may well imagine that Gal. 3:28 ("neither male nor female") provided either verbally or materially the main argument in favour of abolishing this outward distinction and therefore against Paul, who had given this dictum but now favoured the keeping of the tradition (v. 2) ... Yet only an inattentive enthusiasm could deduce from this that man and woman are absolutely alike, that there can be no question of super-and subordination between them, and that it is both legitimate and obligatory to abolish the distinction between the uncovered and the covered head in divine service. (309–10)

Paul's voice now serves as the vehicle in which Barth indirectly deflects the arguments and claims of his contemporary feminists, who would find egalitarian implications in Galatians 3:28 to contradict any privileged position secured for men. If Paul sees no contradiction between the mutuality to which Galatians 3 gestures and the female subordination of 1 Corinthians 11, then Barth need not trouble himself with reconciling his own assertions:

It is the life of this new creature which Paul describes with the saying that the head of the woman is the man. Gal. 3:28 is still valid, in spite of shortsighted exegetes, like the Corinthians themselves, who shake their heads and think they can claim a contradiction. The mutuality of the relationship still obtains, as described [in 1 Cor. 11:11-12]. (312)

Barth continues, "It is only in the world of the old aeon that the feminist question can arise" (312).[15] And so he assumes his Adamic prerogative of silencing feminist criticism by answering the question regarding the possibility of a contradiction for and on their behalf.

Contemporary feminists will not find Barth practicing that generous hearing he prescribed for his readers in §45.2. He will not allow their voices to put his own assumptions and interpretive framework into question, nor will he even directly respond to their challenges. Paul must stand in for him. He thus performs the privileged place that his ordering of §45.3 has afforded him: he sets the terms of the exchange and the place of each partner in it, and he preemptively dismisses any questions, objection, or counter-arguments that critics might raise in respect of the matter. Like Adam, he does not need to hear and be unsettled and corrected by

---

15. See also III/2, 294–6 for Barth's efforts to fend off feminist appropriation of Galatians 3:28. Barth was confronted some years earlier by the feminist argument that used Galatians 3:28 to counter the ordering of 1 Corinthians 11 and to contest the privileged place granted men in church. His expositions of these two biblical texts indicate that he still has this challenge in mind in III/2. See Gary Dorrien, *The Barthian Revolt in Modern Theology: Theology without Weapons* (Louisville: Westminster, 2000), 165–6, 227 fn. 122, 123.

the voice of his female other in order to name her and speak for and on her behalf, and he certainly does not require her consent to the relation he has described. But the ethical obligation of the "I" that Barth describes in §45.2 demands much more of him than he here gives. His own performance here speaks further to the difficulty he has in reconciling the mutuality of §45.2 with the order of §45.3.[16]

Conclusion

Barth's theological anthropology provides a more fully developed picture of the human agent than that agent I identified in §18 and §41. In this chapter I have followed this agent as it comes first to know itself as a response to the gratuitous, revelatory and saving address of Christ, and then as it plays Christ in lending aid to its neighbor, from whom it must seek the same help. I have continued to foreground the ways in which Barth carefully patterns the human agent after his christological norm. Barth sets his human agent in motion, on the way to a fresh encounter with God's address in Christ, and on the way toward its human others. The properly oriented and moving agent is open to the interruption and critical corrections imposed on it by these divine and human others. It must reconfigure its interpretive framework in order to accommodate the self-revealing imposition of the other, and it is to offer this same self-revealing, corrective aid to the other.

In following this human agent, my intention has been to expose the distorting effects of Barth's intransigent sexism and heterosexism on his construal of human

---

16. Christopher Roberts (*Creation and Covenant: The Significance of Sexual Difference in the Moral Theology of Marriage* [London: T&T Clark, 2007]) praises Barth's reticence on the nature of sexual difference as an indication of epistemic restraint (145). He also attempts to soften Barth's language of male precedence, suggesting it be understood in terms of a primacy of service (as Barth himself says) (161). Roberts remains silent on Barth's more problematic language in III/2 and III/4, where male precedence is a leading, commanding, inspiring initiative that women are to follow and obey. Like many defenders of Barth who are not entirely comfortable with (or clear about) the implications of Barth's version of male privilege, Roberts reverts to Barth's own strategy for avoiding any clear explanation of what male precedence entails when he declares, with satisfaction, that for Barth, "what the content of this relationship will be, what men and women should do as they confront one another and live together, is left up to actual men and women to discover and unfold from what God has given" (144). In Barth's own words this evasive strategy is stated as follows: "What distinguishes man from woman and woman from man even in this relationship of super- and subordination is more easily discovered, perceived, respected and valued in the encounter between them than it is defined" (III/2, 287). I have suggested that this reticence is not a result of an epistemic humility, so much as it is an attempt to avoid recourse to a natural theology that would read theological meaning into the scientific discourse on the difference between the sexes.

agency. I have used the christological anchorage of this pattern of activity to trouble Barth's account of sexual difference and its ordering, and to highlight its tenuous attachment to the supreme christological "I," on whom Barth's gaze is always fixed and in whom he instructs all to see themselves indirectly reflected.

I have exposed the trouble Barth has in providing a coherent picture of women's agency. He wants them to do all that the agent of §45.2 does. Yet he wants them also to restrain this "doing" in order to secure a Christ-like male prerogative. His ordering eviscerates the agency of women by setting constraints on what otherwise is an agent who is always in motion, seeking, speaking and hearing, and helping the other. As in his reading of Genesis 2, when he introduces order into the relationship between the sexes, his model agent becomes paradigmatically male. In spite of Barth's best efforts to secure the full humanity of woman, woman turns out to be man minus his most important attribute—his ethical impulse. But if she is *to do* all that Barth's model agent does, this talk of ordering becomes unintelligible in the conceptual framework that Barth uses to describe his agent in §45.2. If she is to play the "I" of §45.2, then her self-revealing move toward the other must include the critical correction of and resistance to precisely such efforts to restrain and control her. In this sense, Barth's account of agency in §45.2 can be mobilized to expose and correct some of the most problematic aspects of his depiction of women.

With regard to sexual difference, I have aimed to show that this particular difference does not permeate Barth's depiction of human agency. It is not in play in Barth's reading of the parable of the Good Samaritan (§18); it is not in play in his depiction of Christ's relationship to his fellows (§45.1); nor is it in play in his construal of the "I" (§45.2). Whenever Barth describes the relationship between the sexes, he imports his non-gendered and reciprocal pattern of agency into a gendered and heteronormative framework, wherein the agent most fully performs its part in a relationship to one member of the opposite sex. The result is a restrictive, dyadic, and oppositional construal of ethical agency which is at odds with the agent of §45.2, who is summoned to recognize his place among a company of fellow sufferers. It is also at odds with Christ, whose saving activity is directed to this diverse host of needy people, for sexual difference cuts a dividing line into this community of the suffering beneficiaries of Christ's grace.

I have aimed to decenter this particular difference (to which Barth devotes little descriptive attention) using his more robustly developed depictions of christological and human agency. First, I have shown that this dividing line rests on an unsupported and unexplained appeal to the self-evident alterity between the sexes. Rather than sinking this difference into every feature of his theological anthropology, Barth simply tacks it on after his rich picture of human agency in §45.2, and he makes no efforts to integrate sexual difference and its ordering into that picture.[17] He relies on his reader's assumptions to do that heavy lifting

---

17. Suzanne Selinger argues that there is an interweaving and cross-fertilizing of ideas between Barth and his assistant, Charlotte von Kirschbaum, regarding sexual difference

for him. Second, I have shown that Barth tethers sexual difference very loosely to Jesus Christ, because he does not consider Jesus's male identity or his actual relationships with women to be significant for the christological grounding of his theological anthropology. The Ephesians 5 bridal metaphor must supply the wife that Christ never had, with the consequence of further exposing the disconnection of sexual difference from the life that Christ lived among human beings, and further mystifying the nature of that difference.

and relationship between the sexes. They shared overarching agreement with only minor divergences. Selinger notes von Kirschbaum's dependency on Barth's biblical exegesis and her appropriation of and reliance on Barth's writings in her published lectures, and she points to subtleties and divergences between von Kirschbaum and Barth, none of which amount to significant departures with respect to the problems I am exposing in Barth's account. Selinger observes that in the few writings we have of von Kirschbaum she makes the discussion of sexual difference, its ordering, and its connection to the *imago dei* central to her theological writing, whereas by contrast Barth's discussion of sexual difference and its ordering is insulated from the rest of his writing (*Charlotte von Kirschbaum and Karl Barth: A Study in Biography and the History of Theology* [University Park, PA: Pennsylvania State University Press, 1998], 177).

Selinger's work might offer a further clue as to why Barth's account of sexual difference is so poorly integrated into his theological anthropology, in spite of its pretensions to expose the heart of human existence—its very affinity with the *imago dei*. Carefully tracking the evolving views of both von Kirschbaum and Barth on the *imago dei* and on the difference and relationship between the sexes, Selinger argues that Barth's account was worked out through a long-term collaboration with von Kirschbaum. She ventures that the idea of connecting the relationship between the sexes to the *imago dei* may have been von Kirschbaum's, and she argues that his account of sexual difference developed in close collaboration with von Kirschbaum's thinking on the topic—a long-term preoccupation for von Kirschbaum, but not for Barth. If Selinger is correct, then this might help to explain why Barth will claim that the relationship between the sexes is the central human relationship and yet why his §45.3 discussion is so readily detachable from what precedes, so minimally developed, and so poorly integrated with it. It would explain also why Barth can give us figures of Jesus's relationship to others, and of human agency itself, that do not require or even refer to the importance of the opposite sex. By contrast, von Kirschbaum's lectures on women (*The Question of Woman*) indicate that she is thoroughly preoccupied with the question of the relationship between women and men, the subordination of women and what it means for their roles in family life and church.

Selinger's assessment might also explain why literature that begins by focusing on Barth's interpretation of the *imago dei* in III/1 leads to a distorting interpretation of the rest of his theology and human agency. If Barth's construal of the centrality and the ordering of the relationship between the sexes is not as significant for or as carefully integrated with his theological anthropology as his discussion of sexual difference would require it to be, then it is not surprising that the use of this ordering would lead to problematic interpretations of his doctrines of the Trinity and Christology.

I have drawn attention to Barth's use (in §45.2) of the Gospels' non-marital images to depict Christ's relationship to other human beings. If his reliance on the Gospels' image of Christ (at the center of an ever-widening circle of fellows) is allowed to overshadow Paul's fondness for bridal metaphors, we have a more sustainable christological framing for inter-human alterity than the one Barth attempts to secure in §45.3. Barth's depiction of Christ's location among this diverse circle of human beings does not lend itself readily to the heteronormative constraints of §45.3, which require him to settle down with a single metaphorical wife. Instead it suggests a framework in which multiple sites of alterity might provide occasions for the agent to seek and find its neighbors. In such a framework, sexual difference might then acquire the secondary and fluid status that Barth gives to other differences.

Chapter 6

AN ETHIC FOR THE SEXUALLY DIFFERENTIATED SELF

Introduction

Barth's final extended discussion of sexual difference, *Church Dogmatics* III/4, §54 ("Freedom in Fellowship"), belongs to the part-volume that develops the ethics of the doctrine of creation. In this particular paragraph, Barth develops an ethic for living out one's sexed specificity. It is located within a broader discussion of the divine command that directs the self in relation to other human beings. Barth divides his discussion of the full spectrum of possible human relationships into three spheres: the relationship between "man and woman" (§54.1), "parents and children" (§54.2), and "near and distant neighbours" (§54.3). Here he makes explicit what was implicit in §45.3: sexual difference (and with it the relation between the sexes) is the gift of the Creator, and, as such, it imposes obligations that the agent is to enact in obedience to the divine command. Through a set of guidelines, readers are encouraged to embrace their sexed specificity in a relational orientation to the opposite sex that plays out in an intersubjective exchange wherein men lead, initiate, and assume responsibility for their shared life and fellowship with women. The relational orientation and ordering are not limited to married couples but prevail at every level at which the sexes relate to each other, although marriage remains the normative center in which these guidelines are most fully realizable.

For the agent who is ever on the move toward a fresh hearing of the divine address, sexual difference is a "doing." It is a persistent performance, undertaken in obedience to the divine command and in constant negotiation of the culturally contingent conventions of a rigid two-sex framework that constrains and delimits the ways in which norms are appropriated, inhabited, and contested.[1]

---

1. As I explained in the book's Introduction, my reading of Barth's ethic for a sexually differentiated self draws upon Judith Butler's account of gender as a performance, a stylized sustained practice of repeated acts (including bodily gestures, postures, movements, dress, and styles) that do not express but rather constitute an intelligible sexed identity within a regulatory framework of social norms and constraints (*Gender Trouble: Feminism and the Subversion of Identity* [New York: Routledge, 1999], esp. 178–9).

In this chapter I continue to interrogate and decenter the place that sexual difference occupies in the regulation and ordering of inter-human fellowship. Sexual difference remains, for Barth, the structural divider of humankind, and it continues to elude reduction to biological, sociological, philosophical, or psychological discourses. In his efforts to resist a natural theology that conflates the divine command with social conventions, he will call his readers to a critical relationship to constantly changing cultural norms, mores, and conventions. In so doing, he unwittingly opens up the possibility of interrogating, subverting, and transgressing the reputedly unambiguous dividing line between the sexes which these very norms instantiate.

In §54 Barth at last finds a place for the celibate Christ in his heteronormative sphere of human relationality, but only at the boundary of that sphere. We shall see that the relational life that Christ lived among his fellows is not always a mirror in which Barth wants his readers to learn something of themselves, and certainly not when it comes to sexual relations. I argue that Christ's exile to the margin of the sphere of sexual relations betrays the nebulous grounds upon which Barth installs this particular difference at the center of human relationality. I will suggest that if this image of Christ is returned to the center, as Barth's method otherwise requires, it demotes sexual difference from its supreme status, allowing this one difference to fall in alongside the many other modes of difference that Barth renders fluid by reference to Christ.

The agent in a divine command ethic

The rehearsal of some key features of Barth's command ethics will help orient my analysis of Barth's guidelines for maintaining sexual difference and its ordering.[2]

---

[2]. My reading of §54 benefits from a number of recent books on Barth's special ethics, in particular Gerald McKenny, *The Analogy of Grace: Karl Barth's Moral Theology* (Oxford: Oxford University Press, 2010), Paul T. Nimmo, *Being in Action: The Theological Shape of Barth's Ethical Vision* (London: T&T Clark, 2007), William Werpehowski, *Karl Barth and Christian Ethics: Living in Truth* (Burlington, VT: Ashgate, 2014), as well as John Webster, *Barth's Ethics of Reconciliation* (Cambridge: Cambridge University Press, 1995), and Webster, *Barth's Moral Theology : Human Action in Barth's Thought* (Edinburgh: T&T Clark, 1998). While these books do not undertake a close analysis of the man–woman relationship of §54, they have shaped my understanding of the place and function of Barth's account within his special ethics. McKenny's book has been an especially helpful resource in my description of Barth's special ethics, and I find that the analogy McKenny continually draws between human ethical activity and God's gracious activity resonates with my own interest in tracking the ways in which the relationship between the sexes (and particularly the ethical impulse of §45.2) is to conform itself to Christ's gracious movement toward the other. Along these lines, McKenny studies human ethical activity as an analogy to God's gracious activity revealed and accomplished in the saving work of Christ, activity that interrupts our own

Barth incorporates ethics into dogmatics, and dogmatics into ethics, subjecting each to the same methodological restraints, rather than treating them as independent inquiries.³ Barth's agent is constituted as answerable to a divine command imposed from without. This command is tailored to the highly specific context in which the agent finds itself, and is a command that distinguishes the good—the prohibition imposed upon Adam to refrain from the fruit of one particular tree in the Edenic garden, for example. The agent has only to assent and conform him- or herself gladly to this command—as does Adam in his recognition and naming of Eve.⁴

Scripture plays an authoritative and normative role for Barth's ethics, as it does also for his dogmatics, and so the biblical expositions undertaken in §41 and §45 underwrite his discussion of sexual difference in *Church Dogmatics* III/4. However, as Barth makes clear in his doctrine of revelation, Scripture is not identical with the Word's address to human beings, for the Word is irreducible to the contextual, concrete, and culturally specific media in which it is veiled and through which it is heard. Accordingly, Barth refuses to identify the various biblical prescriptions and legal codes (i.e., the Ten Commandments, the Sermon on the Mount) with the divine command to which the agent is to conform him- or herself. However, these texts do provide the normative resources with which Barth attempts to guide his readers' moral reflection, just as they provide criteria for his dogmatic critical and constructive engagement with the Reformed tradition.

Barth objects to a casuistry that treats the command of God as a set of general laws (whether biblical laws, natural laws, or traditional precepts), for such would fix the command in a legal text that the human agent must then interpret and apply or make specific to a particular occasion, context, or question. The divine command is not a general norm which the human agent evaluates and then applies; rather, the command of God comes to particular people and individuals already fully specified to address a particular context and occasion, confronting them with the

---

moral striving, calling us into question while summoning us to pattern our activity after God's gracious activity (*Analogy of Grace*, 21). My reading of §54 is especially indebted to McKenny's lucid account of Barth's efforts to secure a place for the deliberation, judgment, and decision of moral agents as they discern and identify a particular course of action that corresponds to the gracious action of God. He looks at the role that a practice of ethical reflection and ethical inquiry finds in Barth's special ethics. While he does not directly address the problems in Barth's ethics of sexual difference, his study is especially informative for understanding the role Barth is attempting to play when he sets guidelines for the relation between the sexes in his special ethics of creation in *CD* III/4, §54, and when he calls for a critical relationship to the social customs and mores through which sexual difference is expressed.

3. For a helpful description of the relationship between ethics and dogmatics, see McKenny, *Analogy of Grace*, 122–65, and Nimmo, *Being in Action*, 41–62.

4. For an analysis of the ethical undercurrent in Barth's reading of Genesis 2, see Mckenny, *Analogy of Grace*, 96–106. His reading resonates with my own in Chapter 4; however, he does not address the gender dynamics that arise with the arrival of Eve.

choice of whether or not they will conform themselves to it. As Gerald McKenny puts it, the command of God is both the norm and its specification; it is both the law and the judge who applies it.[5]

In *Church Dogmatics* III/4 Barth distinguishes spheres [*Bereiche*] that delineate the boundaries within which agents can anticipate that the fully specified divine commands will come to them. These spheres refer to certain relationships and forms of activity that appear within broader modes of encounter and include the relationship of the worshipper to God, the relationship between men and women, and the relationship between parents and children. He distinguishes the spheres by reference to dimensions or lines of continuity that he finds in the specified commands of God as witnessed to in various biblical texts.[6] His figural, interscriptural connections between Genesis 2, the Song of Songs, and a select set of Pauline texts therefore play the dominant role we have come to expect in securing the relationship between man and woman as one such sphere, and he summarily recalls his earlier exegetical work on these texts.

If Barth refuses to identify the divine command with legal codes of the sort we find in the Decalogue, he does identify it with numerous biblical instances of highly specific orders and directions concerning particular deeds, activities, and modes of conduct given by God to Israel, by Jesus to his disciples, by the Holy Spirit to the apostles, and by Paul to the women of Corinth. The ethicist's access to the command of God is subjected to the same epistemological constraints as is that of the dogmatician: the command is always mediated in creaturely media. It is not immediately transparent. It therefore cannot be confidently possessed and wielded against others. Thus a persistent practice of ethical deliberation and reflection is required of all agents. We must examine and test our own conduct and test the possibilities before us in a process that culminates in a decision, but one made and acted on with the awareness that this activity is answerable to God's examination, judgment, mercy, and forgiveness.

In *Church Dogmatics* III/4 Barth offers a moral pedagogy aimed at instructing and guiding his readers' own ethical reflection.[7] Accordingly, we will see that if Barth does not expect his female readers to wear a veil just because Paul told his (quasi-feminist egalitarian) readers to do so, neither does Barth want to specify what the command of God is to the women of his own day with regard to dress

---

5. McKenny, *Analogy of Grace*, 239. For a discussion of the relationship of the divine command to Scripture, and of Barth's reservations regarding casuistry and his practical use of it in providing ethical instruction, see McKenny, *Analogy of Grace*, 57–61, 238–74; see also Werpehowski, *Karl Barth and Christian Ethics*, 15–16, 23–32, 37–55, 57–69, and Nimmo, *Being in Action*, 17–40, 41–61, 83–4.

6. See McKenny, *Analogy of Grace*, 249–62 on the function of these spheres (or "domains" as he prefers to call them) in Barth's moral theology; see also Werpehowski, *Karl Barth and Christian Ethics*, 23–32.

7. All parenthetical references inline are to *Church Dogmatics* III/4, while page references to *Die kirchliche Dogmatik* appear within brackets inside the parenthetical references.

and comportment. He wants instead to set his readers on a path of inquiry into what the command of God is for them, and thus on a deliberative and critical path in relation to external biblical norms and customs, and to contemporary social norms and customs, and in the process to discern the command of God as it comes specified with respect to the decisions they must make. Toward these ends he offers some guidelines in §54.1, developed out of his previous exegetical and dogmatic work on sexual difference, that aim to delineate the broad parameters within which the readers can expect the command of God to be heard.[8]

The methodological commitments I have just described have much to do with Barth's reticence to provide details for what sexual difference and its order entail. Nevertheless, these very commitments will give us reason to question the grounds upon which he installs sexual difference as the site of inter-human alterity, if that difference is indeed so unspeakable. For he will continue to show himself far readier to supply descriptive detail for other relational distinctions, not least of which is the distinction between creatures and their Creator, for which he has no shortage of words (in spite of the risk of conflating divine difference with the medium through which it is revealed).

While §54 identifies three spheres of inter-human fellowship (man and woman, child and parent, near and distant neighbors), Barth argues that only the first two are secured by a biblical precedence indicative of fixed and irreversible relationships. The distinction between near and distant neighbors proves to be a fluid and reversible relationship, for only the spheres of man and woman, parent and child entail "a constant determination of man whether in terms of creation, salvation or eschatology" (304). A human being is always either male or female, and she or he is always the child of two parents in an irreversible and fixed relation, with each sphere having a subordinate agent (woman and child) who is to enact a distinctive form of deference to the other partner(s) (298–305). The subordination of [male] children to parents is an ordering they outgrow, and therefore not a deference with

---

8. Here I follow McKenny's nuanced distinction between ethical reflection and the ethicist's role in offering ethical instruction. McKenny argues that Barth's moral theology, as we find it in *CD* III/4, is ethical instruction, and it functions as the first stage of ethical reflection, insofar as it aims to prepare and guide the reader's own ethical deliberation; yet it does not take the place of that deliberation that seeks to discern the specified command of God. Barth offers his readers moral guidance, yet he wants to avoid deciding right action for them in advance of their own ethical reflection; his aim is to prepare them for an encounter with the divine decision, to encourage and equip them with resources as they move toward this event (McKenny, *Analogy of Grace*, 238, fn. 35; 262–4). Barth's instructions regarding birth control and the decision-making involved in the question of whether or not to have a child exemplify the deliberative and discerning character of the testing that is ethical reflection, where one weighs the options and makes the best decision one can, well aware that one's decision may not be the response of a right hearing of the divine command (III/4, 268–76). This deliberative activity extends to more mundane matters as well (McKenny, *Analogy of Grace*, 229–66).

which our adult male dogmatician has himself permanently to contend, unlike the women (and feminists) that he will continually call to order. Yet Christ fails to align with the normative center of these two spheres, being technically the child of one human parent who selects twelve men for his closest companions rather than a wife. We might expect such a Christ would do more to unsettle Barth's retreat to rather conventional, contemporary, construals of social organization. Before Barth's discussion of either sphere begins in earnest, he signals the (necessary) exile of Christ to the boundary of his heterosexual framework and its intertwined reproductive logic.

Finally acknowledging the celibacy of Christ and of Paul, and their words in praise of celibacy (Mk. 10:1-12; Mt. 5:27-31; 1 Cor. 7), Barth finds a place for these two men (and the host of unmarried people with them) in the sphere of the relationship between the sexes (142–8). While Paul and Christ were both celibate and both praised the celibate state, he argues, neither meant any denigration of marriage itself. Rather, Christ and Paul show us that there are different ways of reflecting the relationship of Christ to the community. Both marriage and celibacy are spiritual gifts and vocations to which God calls some but not others. Marriage and celibacy are two types of calling to obedience of the one command, and neither has any inherent special dignity, although celibacy is a "direct imitation of the pattern set by Jesus Himself" (144). Of course, this admission raises the question of why the celibate state would not, then, occupy the normative center, considering Barth's christocentric methodology. Nevertheless, Barth can now finally admit that marriage is relativized with the advent of Christ, even if it does not follow the path Barth has procreation take in his figural reading of Genesis 2. At last, "the clamp which made marriage a necessity for man and woman from their creation is not removed but it is certainly loosened. Marriage is no longer an absolute but a relative necessity. It is now one possibility among others" (144). This is an admission Barth did not make in his figural reading and use of Genesis 2, where Christ's and Paul's preferred celibate state were discreetly ignored. Now Barth announces the need for a corrective to a Protestant ethic that, since the Reformation, has responded to a Roman Catholic privileging of celibacy by presenting marriage (with an end in procreation) as the superior state (140–1). He wants to relativize the place marriage has occupied and the exclusive attention it has received in traditional Protestant ethics, yet without denigrating its dignity.

Marriage may be relativized by the possibility of the celibate life, but Barth's depiction of inter-human fellowship remains heteronormative and complementarian. The distinction between the sexes remains the primary distinguishing marker among human beings, even if Barth still cannot tell us what it entails. The relationship between the sexes, with marriage at its normative center, continues to provide the opportunity for the fullest realization of inter-human fellowship (140), even if Christ and Paul did not require it.

Now that the celibate state of Christ and Paul is explicitly addressed, the relationship Christ had with his disciples must be carefully secured at the boundaries of Barth's normative framework, so that the disembodied abstraction of the Christ-groom and the ecclesial bride can retain their central place. Barth integrates celibacy into this heteronormative framework by securing celibacy (and thus also the unmarried Christ, the unmarried Paul, and their prescriptions on the topic) as boundary cases (*Grenzfälle*): such cases reside on the periphery of the relationship between the sexes yet belong to that sphere and legitimize marriage as that sphere's center. As McKenny explains, for Barth a "boundary case" is no lesser or greater state, but rather an obedience to a special situation. Boundary cases function not as exceptions to the fundamental principle and its specifications, but rather as highly unusual, strange, or paradoxical instances of the latter.[9] Thus for Barth, Christ's specific and unique ontological existence requires his singular whole-hearted devotion to all of humankind, and this calls for a relational orientation to multiple sites of alterity rather than to one particular member of the opposite sex. Paul answers a calling to a celibate state in response to the special set of ecclesial and missional contingencies that demand his attention and do not permit him the distractions inevitably arising in an intimate life-long fellowship with a wife (142–8). So, Barth writes, Paul and Christ teach us that "there are special situations which make decisions of this kind possible and necessary, and that to this extent there are those for whom entrance into the married state is not only not commanded but temporarily or even permanently forbidden" (144). Yet the question remains, considering Barth's christocentric methodology and christocentric figural reading of Genesis 2: Should it not be the celibate Christ who occupies the position at the center of sexual relationships (along with Paul his faithful imitator), while those who marry stand in the widely populated margins as boundary cases, as Paul's words might just as readily suggest: "for it is better to marry than to be aflame with passion" (I Cor. 7:9 [NRSV]). When it comes to domestic relations, Barth sets constraints on how far he will allow the New Testament depictions of Christ, together with his prescriptions—as well as Paul with his instructions—to destabilize conventional social arrangements, and so the celibate Paul himself must provide for Barth an obedient ecclesial wife for the celibate Christ, a wife who absorbs and elides the sex of his twelve disciples, along with all human beings. Yet precisely along these lines, the pervasive structural difference is rendered by Barth all the more mystifying, even as it effaces the agency of all women while preserving that of men.

Ethical guidelines for securing sexual difference

Before developing his guidelines on sexual difference and its order, Barth carefully demarcates his own ethic from those of his contemporaries by noting his intent to cast as broad a net as possible around the sphere of sexual difference. He will not reduce his discussion of the relationship between man and woman to the regulation of sexual activity any more than he will reduce sexual difference to physiology or sexual functions. He has in view the spirit-impelled body to whom the divine

---

9. McKenny, *Analogy of Grace*, 258–61.

command is addressed, and so his account will aim to encompass the whole agent—the would-be hearer of the divine address who hopes to conform him- or herself to its requirements. Barth's guidelines thus aim to have a broad reach, and so his extensive discussion of marriage is not integrated into his guidelines, but follows after them, as the occasion for the most concrete realization of the sexual relationship thus delineated.

The command of God will address and situate the self as: (1) either male or female, calling the self gladly and gratefully to embrace this identity and with it those culturally contingent features that differentiate it from its opposite; (2) as male and female together in an interpersonal relationship, with each person oriented in sexual specificity toward the opposite sex; (3) as male and female in subordination to an agential ordering in which the male assumes precedence and gives direction to the relational interactions and common life of men and women. It is specifically with these three features that my reading is concerned, for it is here that the most problematic aspects of Barth's account of sexual difference and its ordering are developed.

"Male or female": The difference between the sexes

Barth tells his readers to expect a command that will address them in their fixed sexed identity, as either male or female, and so they are to embrace and enact gladly this distinctive identity (149). This requires a somewhat ambivalent, even critical, relation to the social norms and conventions that mediate the expression of this identity. Barth criticizes systematizations of sexual difference that add descriptive flesh to the bare bones of the difference between the sexes, and he indicates his intent not to offer any such systematizations of his own. Brunner provides him an example of what is problematic in such caricatures. He quotes Brunner: "The man must be objective and universalise, woman must be subjective and individualise; the man must build, the woman adorns; the man must conquer, the woman must tend" (at 152). Not only do such systematizations hold up a descriptive picture (a caricature) in which few, if any, will recognize themselves, Barth complains, they also impose an absurd "ought."[10] In reference to the words of Brunner, he writes:

10. The significance of not being able to recognize oneself in such normative pictures of sexual difference is a concern Barth mentions more than once in §54 (153, 127). He says of Brunner's quote: "These things obviously cannot be said or heard in all seriousness. For they cannot be stated with real security. They cannot be stated in such a way that probably every third man and certainly every second woman does not become agitated and protest sharply against the very idea of seeing themselves in these sketches. Nor can they be stated in such a way that they will wholeheartedly accept the idea that this is what they, true man and true woman, ought to be, that here they see their true nature portrayed" (153). Some pages earlier, when criticizing another's description of the relationship between the sexes he says: "Has there ever been a couple that would seriously and sincerely recognise themselves in these ideal pictures, which, whether we call them frivolous or playful, are in any case quite intolerable because docetic?" (127).

> I quote this passage because over and above the characterisation it brings us into the sphere of an "ought" or "must," of definite tasks supposedly set the sexes in virtue of their inherent characteristics ... And how are these rather contingent, schematic, conventional, literary and half-true indicatives to be transformed into imperatives? Real man and real woman would then have to let themselves be told: Thou shalt be concerned with things (preferably machines) and thou with persons! Thou shalt cherish the mind, thou the soul! Thou shalt follow thy reason and thou thy instinct! Thou shalt be objective and thou subjective! Thou shalt build and thou merely adorn; thou shalt conquer and thou cherish etc.! Thou shalt! This is commanded thee! This is thy task! By exercising the one or the other function, thou shalt be faithful to thyself as man or woman! [152–3]

I will recall these words below when Barth, forgetting them, later evokes the relationship between the letters A and B as a model in which his readers might recognize their own place in a properly ordered relationship with the opposite sex (169–70).

At this point Barth insists on the freedom of the divine command from such culturally contingent systematization, and thus on the freedom of men and women from "the self-imposed compulsion of such systematization" (153). He would have men and women instead persistently pursue a fresh hearing of God's specific commands to them, which he is confident they can discover for themselves "without being enslaved to any preconceived opinions" (153). Barth imagines, then, a (somewhat) critical relationship to the culturally contingent norms and customs available for enacting one's specific sexed identity. Yet at the same time the appropriation and performance of these norms and customs must not transgress the boundary that distinguishes one sex from the other.

In order to preserve this freedom of the divine command, Barth declines to describe what he imagines to distinguish one sex from the other. Instead he limits himself to simply asserting the alterity between the sexes, the "structural and functional distinction" (*strukturellen und funktionellen Unterscheidung*) unique to this one relationship (117 [128]). The distinction is not reducible to psychology, biology, physiology, or sexual function, and so while all of these seem to have some part in the obedient living out of one's sexed existence, Barth does not attempt to explain in what way they do so. He simply assumes his readers will recognize with him the givenness of this primal alterity. Thus:

> No other distinction between man and man goes so deep as that in which the human male and the human female are so utterly different from each other. And no other relationship is so obvious, self-explanatory and universally valid as that whose force resides precisely in the presupposed underlying otherness. The female is to the male, and the male to the female, the other man and as such the fellow-man. It is with reason, therefore, that we first enquire what the divine command has to say in this sphere of fellow-humanity. (118)[11]

---

11. At points he echoes the rhetoric of romantic love, as he sympathizes with but faults those who deify the sexual relationship (121–9).

Hence, while Barth is eager to unsettle and relativize the assumed givenness of an alterity between the races (as he does in §18, §41, and §54.3), he will depend on shared cultural assumptions to support his assertions about the givenness and primacy of sexual difference. Since he dares not venture descriptive exercises of his own, he must instead make an appeal to its mystery:

> We can call man and woman "he" and "she." We can describe individual men and women by their Christian names and surnames, their date of birth, family, birthplace or titles. But we have to realise that when we say all this we merely point to something which cannot be expressed, to the mystery in which man stands revealed to God and to Him alone. It is at the point where he is indefinable that he is sought and found by the divine command, that the decision is made, that he is obedient or disobedient, good or bad ... We have no right, especially if we ask concerning the command of God, to define or describe this differentiation. (150–1)

Barth is far more forthcoming when describing other inter-human differences in §54. In §54.2 he locates the difference between child and parent in the wisdom and knowledge upon which children depend, albeit in changing degrees, as they age (253–5). In §54.3 he offers a detailed discussion of how language, geography, and history locate the self among near neighbors and on a journey toward more distant neighbors (289–98). Only before the mystery of sexual difference does Barth bow in silence. He can only recall God's creation of man and woman in the Genesis 1–2, assert an alterity between the sexes, and rely on his reader's shared assumptions to do the heavy lifting for him. However, the unspeakable, performative, character of this supposedly self-evident "structural difference" may in actual fact invite a critique of the unnamed assumptions supporting Barth's assertion, while at the same time making possible a proliferation of performances exceeding his unspeakable—or at least unspoken—constraints.

Barth encourages his readers to seek to discern for themselves what the command of God demands of each of them (153). He assures them that they should anticipate from the start that it will entail the concretization of two important prohibitions. First, they should not seek to exchange the (undefined and undefinable) features of their own sex for that of the other, an envious "grasping" that Barth associates more often with women than with men. Second, they should not attempt to occupy a midway position that is neither one sex nor the other, and that views the distinguishing features of the sexes as external and incidental to a sexless third thing (144–56). If we pause to consider that the features of each sex remain undefined and undefinable, and thus open to constant negotiation, contestation, and individual discernment, these prohibitions are far less restrictive than Barth appears to realize. In any event, for Barth, in resisting these two errors, his readers should aspire to a deliberative, thoughtful, exhaustive, and all-embracing performance of their God-assigned sex, one that adheres resolutely to the appropriate side of the dividing line (wherever that may be drawn) by way of available cultural conventions. The reader should expect the divine command to extend to and have relevance for every aspect of the enactment of his or her sexual identity.

On the one hand, obedience to the divine command will require some sort of adherence to available conventions. Barth makes this point clear when once again he names his proto-feminists at Corinth as examples of those who would flee their sex, first by refusing the custom of donning veils (1 Cor. 11) and second by refusing to respect the convention that women keep silent in church (1 Cor. 14) (156). Barth lumps the modern feminist movement into this same category of those who would flee their sex, for here he finds "a more or less express and definite desire on the part of women to occupy the position and fulfil the function of men" (155). Indeed, the very desire of feminists for revolution is itself an attempt to appropriate the dubious project of the male sex, and the entire movement betrays "an element of theoretical and emotional pathos in the direction of an exchange of one's own sex for the other which cannot be explained merely by this revolution and in regard to which further clarification is necessary" (155). Rather than hear in the voice of feminists the self-revealing corrective of the "Thou" (that generous hearing prescribed in §45.2), Barth dismisses their claims as a self-asserting reach for the prerogatives of his sex—envy, once again, is a characteristic especially peculiar to women, or so Barth readily (and rather ungenerously) assumes.

On the other hand, Barth's command ethics requires a critical relationship to conventional categories and norms and so he adds an important qualification:

> Of course, it is not a question of keeping any special masculine or feminine standard. We have just seen that the systematisations to which we might be tempted in this connexion do not yield any practicable imperatives. Different ages, peoples and cultures have had very different ideas of what is concretely appropriate, salutary and necessary in man and woman as such. (154)

He goes on to instruct women (especially would-be feminists) to occupy a critical relationship to the conventions that enable them to distinguish themselves from the opposite sex, and to discern for themselves how they shall express and enact their sexual specificity:

> The question what specific activity woman will claim and make her own as woman ought certainly to be posed in each particular case as it arises, not in the light of traditional preconceptions, but honestly in relation to what is aimed at in the future. Above all, woman herself ought not to allow the uncalled-for illusions of man, and his attempts to dictate what is suitable for her and what is not, to deter her from continually and seriously putting this question to herself. (155)

These are encouraging words, until we recall Barth's categorization of the activities of the proto-feminists of Corinth and the modern feminist movement. It would seem, then, that women are free critically to renegotiate and inhabit the conventions of their time (discerning for themselves the command of God to them), as long as they do not encroach on the activities, conventions, and prerogatives that men, having a higher place in the order, have already carved out for themselves. Should women's efforts transgress these boundaries, they are not entitled to the generous hearing that Barth described in §45.2 and will again describe shortly: a hearing that does not dismiss the other's speech as self-assertion but instead receives it as an aid-lending critical corrective to one's own assumptions. In his words here to women and to the modern feminist movement, then, Barth assumes his rightful place of superiority in the order, by setting the terms for any interaction between the sexes. He diagnoses, describes, and dismisses the activity of these women as an envious, self-assertive power-grab—and not for the last time.

Precisely because these agents are to occupy a critical relationship to cultural conventions while at the same time appropriating them in order to stay true to their own specificity, Barth calls his readers to the exhaustive (and exhausting) task of holding themselves accountable to what the command of God might be in every moment and decision, for:

> there is hardly a possibility of everyday life which is ethically irrelevant in this respect or falls outside the scope of this distinction, even down to the problems of dress and outward bearing. Nothing is indifferent in this connexion. The decision with regard to this requirement of faithfulness to sex is made at every point by both man and woman. (155)

Barth anticipates the need for a continuous self-policing that resists the temptation of intruding on the distinctive features and characteristics of the opposite sex, whatever they might be. In regard to the relativity of social mores, norms, and conventions, he writes:

> But this does not mean that the distinction between masculine and non-masculine or feminine and unfeminine being, attitude and action is illusory. Just because the command of God is not bound to any standard it makes this distinction all the more sharply and clearly. This distinction insists upon being observed. It must not be blurred on either side. The command of God will always point man to his position and woman to hers. *In every situation, in face of every task and in every conversation, their functions and possibilities, when they are obedient to the command, will be distinctive and diverse, and will never be interchangeable.* (154; emphasis added)

With his first guideline, then, we see that Barth takes care not to conflate the divine command with any of the norms and conventions through which obedience to the command is mediated. Yet he nevertheless abstracts the binary of sexual difference from its instantiation in such conventions and renders it an unassailable law, detached from the social sphere of conventions and mores, but always to be expressed, enacted, and shored up within that sphere. In this way, then, he unwittingly makes recourse to a natural theology by transforming cultural assumptions into a divinely imposed ought. The perpetual enactment of one's sex therefore proves to be the mechanism by which sexual difference is continually reproduced and stabilized, and yet it might also be the mechanism by which this difference is undermined and destabilized. This very susceptibility of sexual difference to such subversive and transgressive performances is perhaps what drives Barth's words here and his concern with the securing and stabilizing of the distinction.[12]

"Male and female": The relationship between the sexes

Barth's second pedagogical insight now takes up the ethical dimensions of the I/Thou intersubjective encounter described in *Church Dogmatics* III/2, §45.2. Only here, he has the alterity between the sexes in view, and he further specifies the critical character of their interaction, specifically with respect to the norms which distinguish one sex from the other. As we saw in §18 and §45.2, the unsettling effects of the other on the self require a critique of one's own assumptions. Confrontation with the mystery that is the opposite sex now provides the primary occasion for this sort of work on the self, for "among the immediate data of existence there is certainly no greater riddle for man than the fact of the existence of woman and the question as to her nature" (and vice versa). Hence "to live humanly means never to escape the astonishment of one's own sex at the other, and the desire of one's sex to understand the other" (167). Unfortunately, this desire eludes Barth when he encounters feminist critique, as I noted earlier.

As we saw in the I/Thou encounter of §45.2, the quest for knowledge of the other entails putting questions to the other. The two sexes are to pursue a knowledge of each other, "not, then, as if they already knew about one another; not on the basis of a preconceived general or even personal judgment of men about women or of women about men; but with unprejudiced eyes and generous hearts, always ready to learn something new, to turn the corner and see something better" (167). Thus, the faithful enactment of one's sexed identity is answerable not only to the divine judgment, but also (and as such) to the critical questions the opposite sex puts to one's own sex. One must allow oneself to be put into question by the other's norms, and must respond by way of the terms of the other's questions, with the intent of making oneself intelligible to the other. That is to say, each sex is answerable to the other's inquiries, and must give an account of itself to the other. The faithful living out of one's sexed identity and the careful maintenance of its specificity are to unfold in this dynamic and critical exchange with the sexually differentiated other.

> As they consider one another and necessarily realise that they question each other, they become mutually, not the law of each other's being (for each must be true to his particularity), but the measure or criterion of their inner right

---

12. My analysis and critique of the relationship Barth establishes between sexual difference and the culturally contingent norms and customs that mediate its performance is indebted to Judith Butler's *Undoing Gender* (New York: Routledge, 2004), esp. 40–56, 174–203.

to live in their sexual distinctiveness ... They are not to elude their mutual responsibility, but to fulfil it. And, of course, they must fulfil it even when no representative of the opposite sex is present. *As a norm and criterion the opposite sex is always and everywhere invisibly present.* (167–8; emphasis added)

The performance of one's sexed identity is not, then, an isolated quest to discern and enact the will of God, but an activity that seeks to hear the voice of God in the critique that the sexually differentiated other directs at the self. The unsettling effects that the other has on the self, the many ways in which the other puts the self into question, opens up opportunity for self-critique—for evaluating one's own norms, values, and activities specifically as a sexed self, and for correcting one's assumptions about the other through inquiries into who the other is (167). Furthermore, it is only through this critical interaction with the norms of the opposite sex that one can properly police and maintain one's own sexual distinctiveness.

However, the above quotation further suggests that this critical interaction is, in some respect, with and within culturally contingent norms and conventions, if indeed the "norm and criterion" of the opposite sex is "always and everywhere invisibly present," even when a member of the opposite sex is not present as a reminder. Irreducible to the speech, address, or questioning of specific individuals that appropriate them, these norms of sexual difference seem for Barth to mediate the exchange between "I" and "Thou." The enactment of one's sexed specificity is then in some sense always to be undertaken in a critical and reflective relationship to the norms and conventions through which sexual difference is expressed.[13] These norms and conventions are open to renegotiation, resistance, and subversion, and yet any such activity must resist transcending the dividing line of sexual difference itself—unless, of course, we are to question the binary itself as a culturally contingent norm.

It is not surprising that Barth's only discussion of homosexuality is found (in a brief excursus) in this particular section of §54 (165–7). He broaches the topic as he casts suspicion on men and women who segregate themselves from the opposite sex, whether in same-sex social groups or religious orders. The decision

---

13. Barth's account here of the critical relationship of the self with the opposite sex resonates with what Judith Butler explores and appropriates in post-Hegelian accounts of recognition. Like Barth here, she interrogates the ethical dimensions of the direct address "Who are you?", but she does so by foregrounding the social dimensions of normativity that precede and condition the dyadic exchanges, constituting the intelligibility of the subject and mediating the scene of recognition and address wherein one gives account of oneself, attempting to make oneself intelligible to the other (Judith Butler, *Giving an Account of Oneself* [New York: Fordham, 2005], 3–40). Butler's appropriation of post-Hegelian accounts of recognition is a helpful resource in exposing not only the role that social conventions play for Barth in mediating the relationship of the self to the other but also their susceptibility to critique and renegotiation.

to live in same-sex communities or groups is, more often than not, expressive of a flight from human fellowship, a preference for isolation and self-love, he declares. But what epistemic vantage point does Barth assume in order to dare such an assertion? Such a question does not seem to trouble him, for he already knows that human fellowship must have the riddle of the opposite sex driving and directing it in some capacity. If this is not the case, Barth fears that such a preference for the company of the same sex will lead to same-sex attraction. With a side glance to the sciences, whose authority he now requires to dare a hasty diagnosis (which includes a recourse to natural theology), he issues his warning:

> These first steps may well be *symptoms of the malady* called homosexuality. This is the *physical, psychological and social sickness*, the phenomenon of perversion, decadence and decay, which can emerge when man refuses to admit the validity of the divine command in the sense in which we are now considering it. (166; emphasis added)

Wielding Romans 1, Barth situates homosexuals in a circle of isolated self-love. Refusing to recognize God, they refuse also to appreciate and embrace the fellow-human being. But this despised fellow (the sexually differentiated other) remains the desirable subject to which God directs the self, and so desire for the opposite must find its substitute in desire for the same. Hence, Barth writes, "there follows the corrupt emotional and finally physical desire in which—in a sexual union which is not and cannot be genuine—man thinks that he must seek and can find in man, and woman in woman, a substitute for the despised partner" (166). His warning continues:

> the real perversion takes place, the original decadence and disintegration begins, where man will not see his partner of the opposite sex and therefore the primal form of fellow-man, refusing to hear his question and to make a responsible answer, but trying to be human in himself as sovereign man or woman, rejoicing in himself in self-satisfaction and self-sufficiency. (166)

Yet considering that Barth refuses to explain what makes up the difference between sexes (or how copulation itself plays a part), it is not at all clear why a relationship with a person of the same sex should be dismissed here as self-satisfaction and self-sufficiency, a claim especially puzzling if we recall that the lengthy description of the I/Thou relationship in III/2 was inclusive of all inter-human relationships.

The gospels' pictures of the unmarried Jesus and his intimate inner circle of twelve men are not mentioned here. Barth makes only a passing reference to "an emergency measure" that might justify a decision to live in same-sex groups—a backward glance to his earlier discussion on celibacy, although he does not actually name Christ or Paul here. With Paul and his higher way (1 Cor. 7:38) and Christ and his eunuchs (Mt. 19:11-12) safely confined to the boundaries of the sphere of the relationship between the sexes, Barth need not allow his suspicion of same-sex communities to cast a shadow on the examples of Christ and Paul, nor need he allow their examples to put into question his own assumptions about the necessity of the opposite sex for human fellowship.[14]

At this juncture I must pause to consider briefly Barth's sphere of "near and distant neighbours" (§54.3). Here Barth can imagine a far more fluid boundary between the self and those others who are distinguished by geographical location, history of traditions, and customs (285–98). No dividing line cuts through this sphere, but rather one finds oneself among one's near neighbors, on a journey (out of isolation) toward a knowledge and interaction with more distant neighbors, in a dynamic movement that continually redraws the boundaries between "near" and "far" as one moves beyond the confines of one's own dialect, language, locale, customs, and history to understand and relate to the gradually less-distant other (299–305). Although language has a central role in mediating the relationship of the self to the other, language barriers and alien social customs do not produce an alterity as mystifying to Barth as that of a member of the opposite sex who shares his own language and customs. While the relationships in both spheres require a movement toward a deeper knowledge and understanding of the other, Barth intends the interaction with the sexually differentiated other to secure, maintain, and stabilize the distinction between the self and the opposite sex: the self can more securely enact its distinctive sexual identity through exposure to the norms of the other. By contrast one's interaction with more distant neighbors does not shore up the distinction between the self and the other but instead reduces the distance.[15]

This sphere of "near and distant neighbours" has recourse to christological imagery that can be used to correct the primacy of place Barth gives to sexual

---

14. In reference to Barth's brief discussion on homosexuality, Jaime Balboa ("A Constructivist-Gay Liberationist Reading of Barth," 771–89) argues that Barth's sexual difference rests, in spite of his intentions, on natural categories (i.e., the naturally sexed body desiring in a specific direction), and that in this respect he resorts to natural theology. See also Eugene Rogers (*Sexuality and the Christian Body*) for a book-length critique of Barth's heteronormative account of sexual difference, and Graham Ward ("The Erotics of Redemption: After Karl Barth," *Theology & Sexuality* 8 [March 1998]: 52–72) who argues that while Barth reifies naturalistic observations sexual difference remains a highly unstable site.

15. In a lengthy section of fine print in §54.3, Barth makes explicit the impact that the National Socialist ideology of the 1930s has on his construal of fluidity between near and distant neighbors, and I argued in Chapter 2 for the comparable impact it also had on his subversion of ethnic distinctions in §18. His aversion to an orders of creation framework that reifies racial differences and supports nationalistic fervor underlies his refusal to fix the distance between the self and the foreign other. It is this very aversion to the orders of creation that makes his reification of sexual difference so difficult for him to explain and describe (304–22). For Barth, the distinctions of ethnicity and race prove to be secondary features of human nature in a way that sexual difference is not.

difference. Consider again the sort of images Barth sources from the gospels in his discussion of the inter-human relational orientation in *Church Dogmatics* III/2—images displaced by the dyadic marital metaphor whenever sexual difference comes into view. In his discussion of Christ's relational orientation to his fellows, in §45.1, he writes, "if we see Him, we see with and around Him in ever widening circles His disciples, the people, His enemies and the countless millions who have not yet heard His name" (III/2, 216). In §45.2, using the image of the crucified Christ surrounded by a sea of fellow human suffers he holds up a mirror to Nietzsche (III/2, 241), redirecting him to his neighbors. But in §45.3 these images are elided by Paul's marital metaphor—the many others of the "I" collapsed into a singular, sexually differentiated "Thou." These collections of images, and the work they do for Barth, reveal how very tenuous is the hold of this marital metaphor (and the primacy it secures for sexual difference and the sexual relationship) in Barth's theological imaginary. It is a difference that is apparently so readily forgettable that it eludes discussion in precisely the places you might expect it to appear: in the discussion of parents and children, which proceeds as if the particular sex of the parent and of the child were completely inconsequential; in the discussion of the body in §46 ("Man as Soul and Body"), where Barth excuses himself of the need to consider the sexual specificity of Christ, positing that, in the New Testament, "an impenetrable veil of silence lies over the fact that He was a male (Jn. 4:27)" (III/2, 329–30); in images of Christ's relational life among his disciples and followers.

If we move the Christ of the Gospels' witness from the margins of Barth's heteronormative construal of inter-human fellowship back to the center where Barth would otherwise place him, we have a model of agency that situates the self in an ever widening circle of near and distant neighbors: a broad sphere encompassing multiple sites of alterity. In this sphere we can re-imagine sexual difference as one among other fluid and open-ended distinctions, rather than the overarching distinction that cuts through all others. The careful, yet critical, maintenance of one's sexual specificity might then instead become a subversive, transgressive activity that unsettles the presumed alterity by an appropriation of norms that crosses boundaries between one sex and the other. With sexual difference decentered, a wide range of relationships might become occasions for imitating Christ's relationship to others, including various types of friendships, homosexual relationships, communal arrangements, and monastic orders.

Ethical guidelines for ordering the sexual relationship

With his third pedagogical insight Barth now turns to the ordering of the sexes, which, once again, he does not attempt to integrate into the scene of mutual questioning described in the previous section. He now introduces his readers to his own peculiar caricatures for sexual difference, in which they might see themselves and their place in the order: "A" and "B." Barth writes:

> They [man and woman] stand in a sequence. It is in this that man has his allotted place and woman hers. It is in this that they are orientated on each other. It is in this that they are individually and together the human creature as created by God. Man and woman are not an A and a second A whose being and relationship can be described like the two halves of an hour glass, which are obviously two, but absolutely equal and therefore interchangeable. Man and woman are an A and a B, and cannot, therefore, be equated. In inner dignity and right, and therefore in human dignity and right, A has not the slightest advantage over B, nor does it suffer the slightest disadvantage. What is more, when we say A we must with equal emphasis say B also, and when we say B we must with equal emphasis have said A. (169)

This proposal comes with the now-familiar assurances that no offense need be taken on the part of woman, for as the letter A does not enjoy any advantage over the letter B as far as letters go, man should not think himself superior to woman or permitted to degrade her, nor should woman think herself entitled to envy or grasp at his prerogative. With letters now illuminating the interaction between self-revealing agents and modeling the appropriate dispositions (170–1), Barth is quick to enlist other (equally odd) metaphors, citing approvingly (without further elaboration) the words of another author: "Woman is related to man as the service corps to the fighting troops, as the laboratory to the factory, the lawgiver to the sheriff" (173)— though with the usual reservation applicable to any metaphor in mind, he notes that "it is as well to bear in mind the rich significance of the notion" (173).

How can such relations of sequence possibly shed light on all he has just said of this relationship of a mutual self-revelation, and critical correction? Why would his readers recognize themselves here if they cannot do so in Brunner's caricatures? What sort of livable "ought" can his readers find here? These are not questions Barth answers, but his own dismissal of Brunner's caricatures provides a fitting response *to his own musings* at this point:

> This is quite impossible. Obviously we cannot seriously address and bind any man or woman on these lines. They will justifiably refuse to be addressed in this way. On what authority are we told that these traits are masculine and these feminine? ... But if these descriptions fail us the moment we take them seriously and change them into imperatives, it is evident that we have moved onto ground which may be interesting but is extremely insecure. What, then, is the point of these typologies? [153]

When it comes to imperatives, Barth is, once again, at a loss of words: "Every word is dangerous and liable to be misunderstood when we try to characterise this order" (169–70). He gestures vaguely to a sequential precedence and initiative on the part of men who would pattern their activity after the letter A:

> A precedes B, and B follows A. Order means succession [*Folge*]. It means preceding and following [*Vorordnung und Nachordnung*]. It means super- and

sub-ordination [*Überordnung und Unterordnung*]. But when we say this we utter the very dangerous words which are unavoidable if we are to describe what is at issue in the being and fellowship of man and woman. (169 [189])

With such (unnamed) dangers restraining him, Barth can only tell us that the man bears the "primacy of service" and fulfills his role "in preceding her, taking the lead as the inspirer, leader and initiator in their common being and action." He does this "as he first enters into fellowship with her, as he first bows before the common law of humanity as fellow-humanity" (170–1). Christ's *sui generis* relationship to the Church must once again direct men to the part Adam played:

> In the light of that archetypal love, [man is] to love her as himself, to treat her as the fellow-creature without whom he himself could not be a man and could not be saved, in whose person he has in every respect to do with himself, in whom he does himself good or harm, honour or dishonour, glory or shame, with whom he stands or falls, whose existence first gives true humanity to his own. This is man's special responsibility in this order. He can and should precede woman by affirming and accepting and living with her in this way, by doing (v. 31 f.) exactly what man (Gen. 2) did at the climax of his creation: "Therefore shall a man leave his father and mother, and shall cleave unto his wife." (175)

Of course, the relation between Christ and the church does in fact entail a difference in "inner dignity and right" (169), and Christ does retain a significant ontological advantage, which is perhaps why Barth finds it necessary to introduce letters of the alphabet for further assurance about the undiminished dignity of women. But there is little assurance to be found when we recall that Barth's model human agent of §45.2 is patterned after Christ's love for his fellows, with its ethical obligation reflecting Christ's initiating and gracious incarnational descent to and on behalf of the needs of his fellows. From the vantage point of §45.2, the question remains: what is left for the female agent to "do" if not also to imitate Christ in precisely this way? Apparently nothing at all, for by recalling the image of a seeking, desiring, electing Adam, Barth evokes also the image of the silent, immobile Eve whose active inactivity (that "act" wherein she consents to let Adam act for and on her behalf) secures and reveals Adam's privileged place.

A quick side-glance at Barth's discussion of the sphere of parents and children will show that this permanent evisceration of the subordinated partner's agency is peculiar to women in Barth's sphere of human relations. Barth is not plagued by the same incapacity to speak of the distinction between parents and children and the nature of the authority the former have over the later. He describes the wisdom and experience that distinguishes parents from children and secures the direction they are to give to children; he delineates the different stages through which the child develops, before it finally becomes an agent in its own right (moving from heteronomy to autonomy). He secures for the growing child a developing and finally robust account of agency and ethical deliberation wherein the child gradually comes to depend less and less on the guidance of parents (243–55). But he provides no such detail when speaking of the given alterity between the sexes, nor does he attempt to explain how women remain fully functioning agents under male precedence. He will simply assert that they do so and prohibit any protest to the contrary.

His discussion of parent–child relations also neglects the question of whether and how the development toward autonomy differs for girls and boys or what the ordering of sexes means for the developing relationship between mothers and sons—both noteworthy omissions in view of the claim that sexual difference is a structural divider that permeates and has an impact on all other modes of difference. If the sexual specificity of the parent and the child has no bearing on this particular discussion, why does sexual difference (and its order) occupy a site of central importance for Barth's theological anthropology and special ethics of creation? Considering its centrality as the one structural divider, sexual difference has a surprising way of disappearing when it is not the direct object of discussion.

Barth next develops a sequence of highly generalized depictions of properly ordered and disordered relationships, resorting to caricatures that are even more troubling than his A and B. First he briefly describes what a model relationship looks like. He then gives a lengthier description of what a disordered relationship looks like and the trajectory it usually follows. He finally provides some general instructions as to how those who recognize themselves in the disordered model might return their relationship to its proper order: how they might become the "kind man" (*der gütigen Mann*) and the "self-restraining" or "modest" woman (*die bescheidende Frau*) (180 [201]).

Barth's model relationship features the "strong (*starke*) man" and the "mature (*mündige*) woman" (176 [197]). This man oversees the proper interaction and ordering between the sexes, for

> he will not leave it to chance whether the order subsists and prevails. Nor will he wait for woman to do her part in serving it. On the contrary, he will forestall her in this ... He will really be superior only in so far as he will primarily accept as his own a concern for the right communion of the sexes as secured by this order, and therefore for the order itself. He is strong to the extent that he accepts as his own affair service to this order and in this order. He is strong as he is vigilant for the interests of both sexes. (176)

Again Barth does not explain what this leaves for the mature woman to do, other than to leave to the men the ethical busy-work of discerning the proper communication and interaction between the sexes, and of assuming the greater burden of ethical deliberation itself, with respect to their co-existence.[16]

---

16. In this respect Barth participates in an idealistic trajectory of ethics in which men alone are fully formed ethical agents and women depend on the reasoning capacities

Furthermore, it would seem that women need not, after all, discern for themselves what actions they are to take in securing their sexed specificity, at least not without first allowing men to set the terms under which they proceed.

In describing woman's part, Barth is concerned less with what she might "do" and more with her appropriate dispositions, which, once again, he suspects are inclined toward an envious self-assertion:

> [her] only thought is to take up the position which falls to her in accordance with this order, desiring nothing better than that this order should be in force, and realising that her own independence, honour and dignity, her own special wishes and interests, are best secured within it. Thus in regard to the precedence which she sees man assume in this matter, *she will feel no sense of inferiority nor impulse of jealousy. She will not consider herself to be attacked by this, but promoted and protected.* She will see guarded by it just what she herself desires to see guarded. She has *no need to assert herself by throwing out a challenge to man.* She will perceive the opportunity which man places within her grasp. She will not merely accept his concern for the order and for herself, but make it her joy and pride as woman to be worthy of this concern, i.e., to be a free human being alongside man and in fellowship with him. (177)

Her position would seem to entail a dubious dignity indeed if it can be so readily confused with an assault, a slight, or inferiority, and if it can be expected to evoke jealousy and a need to challenge the male role. But we have seen Barth repeatedly offers such reassurances whenever he brings up the topic of women's subordination, reassurances that are aimed at preempting any challenge women might hurl at him. With these words Barth again plays his part in the order that he has assigned to his sex: discerning in advance the best interests of both; instructing and directing women to their proper place and to the appropriate dispositions that will ensure both a peaceful communion between the sexes and the role he has secured for himself in it; and, above all pre-emptively silencing any question-raising critique or protest from women with his vacuous reassurances.

Barth next describes a disordered relationship, one which he expects will be more familiar to his readers. It features the tyrannical (*tyrannisch*) man who attempts to make the order (and thus woman herself) serve his own interests and desires, and the compliant or submissive (*hörige*) woman who adapts herself to his manipulation. The latter plays her part in the disorder by conforming herself to what the tyrant expects from her: "She finds it convenient to make things as

---

and ethical deliberation of men. Masculine activity and spontaneity are contrasted with feminine passivity, and female activity is depicted as merely the development of that which has been received through the spontaneous active influence of the male (see Patricia E. Guenther-Gleason, *On Schleiermacher and Gender Politics* [Harrisburg, PA: Trinity Press, 1997], 138–9, 162–93, 277–9, 350).

convenient as possible for him. She also finds it attractive—and the clever tyrant will certainly support this view—to be his pliable kitten, his flattering mirror. In pleasing him, she thus pleases herself" (178).

Barth imagines this sort of relationship will follow an inevitable trajectory. It will prove to be unsustainable for both, but especially for the compliant woman, "for even when she co-operates she is in fact the one who is injured and suffers" (178). "The disorder will be avenged on her first" (178), and if she is to suffer the most, Barth informs her, it is because the order assigns to the male the ethical burden of securing her interest along with his own and thus overseeing the progress and communion between them; hence if he does not secure her interests, they will not be secured.

As the story unfolds, the compliant woman enables (even invites) male tyranny, but since her own interests cannot be secured in a relationship that man has designed to advance his own ends, she will eventually tire of this unsatisfactory game and seek to extricate herself from the abuse (178). She will do so by asserting her own needs and defending her own interests in an overt grab for power that can only mime the tyrant's will to mastery and thus deepen the disorder. But in doing so, the compliant has unveiled and exposed her true identity as the rebellious (*rebellische*) woman. Barth's disturbing caricature of the abused rebel resembles his earlier depiction of the power-grasping, envious feminist (155):

> For somewhere in the submissive [*hörigen*] woman there lies concealed—not merely crouching in readiness, but already active—the rebellious [*rebellische*] woman. In her own way even the submissive woman illegitimately exercises power over man. By her very compliance—she knows well enough what she is about—she grasps at control over man. She avenges herself for his tyranny by performing so exactly the part which he desires her to play. In her voluntary weakness and readiness to yield, she acquires authority over him and is secretly the stronger. But this secret state of affairs can and must break out and come into the open. The order which is only apparently respected, but in reality abused and perverted, can clearly be challenged and infringed openly. Where it is not really obeyed, it may one day occur to woman to question not only the claimed prerogatives and postured lordship but also the real primacy of man, openly abandoning her position and snatching power from his hands. This dramatic turn obviously demands a change of scenery. Claim is now met by counter-claim, power by power, tyrant by tyrant. What objection can man bring when he himself and primarily is a transgressor of the order? The conflict thus starts in real earnest. It is now to be seen which will prove the stronger party. But whatever the result, on neither side is there right in the true and Christian sense. (179 [199])

Barth's gaze pierces the veil of compliant woman's passive and malleable performance to discover that she is covertly far more active than she is entitled to be, engaged in a manipulative effort to secure her own interests. If this "pliable kitten" will finally expose herself as the rebel (feminist), then this can only mean that tyrannical man will eventually expose himself for the weakling he has been all along: unable to retain control over his rebel, he will eventually bow to her rebellion, which—as Barth admits—is somewhat justified, becoming even weaker, or he will attempt to reassert control, thereby beginning the vicious circle all over (178–80). But he is now in a weakened position, for "as the offended and humiliated party, woman does not have right on her side, but she has the appearance of right ... How can he now dare to assert his primacy over her?" (178–80). But her way out of this disorder and abuse is not, Barth instructs, "a question of woman attaining her rights as opposed to man," but rather of "man's understanding the order and sequence and therefore the obligation in which he is the first" (171). And so she is not to protest or rebel, apparently she is not to "do" anything at all to extricate herself, for the way back to order is for man, quite simply, to play his part.

Barth's final model prescribes the way back to that order in which man becomes "*der gütigen Mann*" and woman "*die bescheidende Frau.*" This sort of woman does not assert herself, demand her rights, and protest, rebel, or complain in the face of male tyranny, abuse, and exploitation. Rather she will incite the man to play his part by appealing to his inclination to do so. How so exactly? Barth does not say. Barth's "*bescheidende Frau*" is the picture of "quiet [*ruhend*] self-restriction," gentle resistance, and modest self-restraint: she knows who she is as a woman in her differentiation from men, she knows her place in the order, and keeps to it in the very act of refraining from asserting or defending her rights and needs. Barth seems to imagine that this pious, dignified, quiet, long-suffering disposition will evoke the best in self-serving, abusive tyrants, and he seems absurdly optimistic that the latter have the capacity to be so readily redirected. It is precisely in this self-restraint and self-limitation that Barth imagines woman's existence might serve as "an appeal to the kindness [*Gütig*] of men" (181 [201]). "Kindness belongs originally to his particular responsibility as a man" (180–1), Barth declares, and his description of it indicates, once again, that the male prerogative coincides with the ethical impulse itself:

> [Kindness] means the free impulse in which a man interests himself in his neighbour because he understands him and is aware of his obligation towards him. The self-restricting woman appeals to the kindness of man. She puts him under an obligation to be kind. The opposite is also true, but in this respect the advantage is perhaps with woman. She may win the respect of man. *If he is capable of this at all, it is in face of the mature and therefore self-restricting woman* ... If anything can disturb his male tyranny and therefore his male weakness, if anything can challenge him to goodness and therefore to the acceptance of woman, it is encounter with the self-restricting woman. Why? Because her maturity is displayed in her self-restriction. (181; emphasis added)

If kindness belongs originally and properly to man, then self-restraint belongs originally and properly to woman, for "she need not wait for the kind man to know and limit herself, as he need not wait for the modest woman to be kind" (181). But what if the man in question is not capable of being redirected by such restraint? This question does not trouble Barth; the woman's only way out of an abusive relationship is for the tyrant to reform his ways, and if she works keenly to restrain her inclination to protest, assert, or defend herself, he may eventually do just that.

Barth's antidote to feminist rebellion, male tyranny, and abusive domestic relations is, then, none other than the silent Eve of Genesis 2: she need say and do nothing at all for Adam to play his ordained part; she ought to say and do nothing if he fails to play his part; she should hasten to say and do nothing, regardless of his part. Oblivious to the unlivability of the "ought" he has here imposed on women, as he goes about his male prerogative of overseeing the best interests of both sexes, Barth directs women (the abused, the mistreated, rebellious feminists) back to their place in the order, assuring them that their interests are best served if they refrain from self-assertion (and from posing any challenge to his prerogative to do precisely this).

Under all these layers of restraint, there is no place in this narrative of tyranny for woman to enact that gratuitous, spontaneous, self-revealing, yet at the same time, critically corrective self-expression of the "I" of §45.2, without subverting the order. Barth gives no sense that such a self-revealing activity is even needed from her, for he can already see through the complainant's performance, and he already knows that what she is really after is his own privileged position. Not until she finds her way back to her own proper place, respecting his prerogative to direct her there, is he ready to hear what she might have to say of herself. After all, Adam had no need for the voice of Eve to name and label her.

Yet if Eve is to play the part of the "I" in §45.2, then her critique of and resistance to such tyrannical activities, misperceptions, and assumptions is all part of the act. The ethical impulse of that movement has no place for the sort of quiet restraint Barth here demands of woman. It has no place, because it is patterned after the gracious, self-revealing, critically corrective movement of the incarnate Word toward humankind, a Word that critiques, judges, discomfits, unsettles, and humbles the human recipients. Let us recall the divine analogue to what this sort of critique might be, using Barth's words from *Church Dogmatics* I/1 to depict the content of revelation to the human subject: "It will also be the limitation of his existence by the absolute 'out there' of his Creator, a limitation on the basis of which he can understand himself only as created out of nothing and upheld over nothing. It will also be a radical renewal and therewith an obviously radical criticism of the whole of his present existence" (I/1, 194). If women are to conform themselves to this christocentric pattern of activity, then they simply cannot keep silent nor can they hesitate to play their part. For they are to make haste to question, challenge, critique, and reject the distorted assumptions and normative constraints embedded in such dogmatic depictions of them.

Conclusion

Barth's final discussion of sexual difference completes the picture he began with his narrative re-description of Adam and Eve in *Church Dogmatics* III/1. Human beings encounter their divine other in the man Jesus Christ, and they encounter their human other paradigmatically in the opposite sex. Cutting through Christ's ever-widening circle of fellow-sufferers is the line that distinguishes one sex from the other. All other inter-human differences are permeable, fluid, and open to renegotiation. This one difference must be sustained and preserved through the faithful and discerning enactment of an array of culturally contingent customs, conventions, and norms. The command of God will be specified through the medium of these gender norms, and since that command is not readily transparent to the agent, ethical deliberation includes a discerning critical relationship to gender norms. While the command of God is not identical to sexual difference itself, Barth assures his readers it will not summon them to a transgression of this dividing line, and so the critical enactment of gender norms must faithfully instantiate the difference. While the burden is on each individual to discern the specified command of God for themselves, man's privileged place in the ordering of the sexes secures for him the role of overseeing the proper maintenance of the distinction itself and the interests of both parties. Woman is free to speak and enact her difference before him, as long as this speech and activity does not entail a grasping after privileges and activities he has already secured for himself—which include his oversight of how she engages their relationship.

Barth's order exerts a corrupting and distorting influence on Barth's ethical picture of an "I" that lets itself, its assumptions, and its categories be put into question by its "Thou" (as he depicted it in §18 and §45.2). This order sets restraints on the unsettling impact of the female other. Barth's male subject retains control of the terms under which he will permit the female other to question and unsettle him. In spite of his insistence to the contrary, this male prerogative reduces female agency to an atrophied version of the male. She keeps her place in the order by restraining her ethically oriented activity of seeking, speaking, and hearing the male other in order for him to act and speak *first* on her behalf. Male precedence thus costs her the central characteristics of Barth's seeking, speaking agent, who is always in motion towards its others, and it allows her no course of proactivity in the face of male tyranny and abuse.

Barth's depiction of human agency in §54 does, however, retain the resources and mechanisms for questioning and resisting these two problems—his truncation of female agency and his reification of sexual difference. First, with respect to Barth's truncated female agent, I have argued from the beginning that his construal of agency is one of ceaseless motion toward divine and creaturely others. There is no place in his account for the restraint and restrictions with which he burdens the would-be female agent. If she is to discern and speak her sexual specificity with the generous intent of correcting the misperceptions of male onlookers and tyrants, then there can be no talk of withholding this aid-lending activity. She cannot undertake such a correction if she must subordinate this activity to male hearers;

if she must grant them the privilege of discerning whether she is speaking her sexual specificity or enviously grasping after the characteristics, roles, and rights they have claimed for their own sex; and if she must concede to them the task of discerning for themselves the extent and reach of her specificity.

Second, in regard to sexual difference, Barth elevates this difference above other differences by abstracting this difference from its instantiation in cultural norms and conventions and rendering it immune to critique or questioning. I have shown how difficult this move proves to be for Barth if he is to continue to resist a natural theology that conflates the divine command with social conventions and orders. He wants to avoid any detailed description of what this difference entails because to provide such a description would be to conflate the divine command with constantly changing cultural norms and conventions; and yet Barth relies on shared cultural assumptions about the indisputable givenness of sexual difference to assert its privileged place as the structural divider pervading all other distinguishing features of human individuality. And because Barth refuses to reduce sexual difference to biological, psychological, and sociocultural definitions, he sets the agent in a critical relationship to all such discourses, and on a deliberative path of discerning, evaluating, and critically appropriating their norms and constraints. Barth's assumption of a fixed, oppositional alterity between the sexes is thus itself susceptible to this sort of critical exercise and to subversive performances.

I have argued that Barth's christological agent does not conform readily to Barth's heteronormative framework, and in §54 Christ finds a home only on the boundaries of this sphere. I have argued that if we return Christ to the center of inter-human fellowships, then his relationship to his ever-widening circle of fellows, his unmarried status, and the theological insignificance of his sexed identity together expose the instability of this binary and its pretensions to a mysterious, unassailable site above the social conventions in which it is said to be instantiated. Sexual difference then falls into place alongside other differences that are fluid and open to contestation and renegotiation. In the figure of Christ in an ever-widening circle of fellows, Barth provides a different model of human fellowship and ethical accountability, one that is not burdened, constrained, and distorted by his complementarian model of a heterosexual marriage.

CONCLUSION

In following Barth's agent into its entanglements in sexual difference and sexual hierarchies, I have focused on two central problems: Barth's heterosexism and androcentrism. First, Barth reifies sexual difference and with it a heteronormative structure for human relationships. He elevates sexual difference to a fixed, oppositional binary that transcends all other differences. It is a division that Barth considers to be immune to critique or renegotiation. The relationship between the sexes (and marriage in particular) occupies the center of Barth's theological anthropology insofar as it provides the occasion for the fullest realization of human existence.

Second, Barth's asymmetrical ordering of the relationship between the sexes ultimately produces a truncated model of female agency lacking any christological grounding. Men retain an agential precedence and initiative that eludes description, as Barth is dubiously reticent on developing its implications—and for good reason. I have argued that male precedence coincides with the ethical obligation of the human agent as he imitates the gracious activity of Christ by coming to the aid and need of his female other.

I have sought to reframe the ways in which the problems of sexual difference and order might be analyzed in Barth's *Church Dogmatics*, by focusing on the agent as constituted in a network of relations, rather than on the ordering of that network. I will now draw together the strands of the previous chapters to highlight those features of Barth's understanding of agency that make possible a critique and reconfiguration of his framework for sexual difference.

Disentangling the agent from a sexist order

As we have seen, many critics of Barth's complementarian account of the sexes suspect that these two problematic features (the sexual binary and its hierarchical ordering) are inevitable consequences of his dogmatic commitment to an all-powerful divine actor and a subordinate, obedient human agent. They find that this commitment produces a recurring pattern of hierarchically ordered, dyadic relationships, wherein one actor leads and directs another. I have shown that the ordering of sexual difference provides an inadequate interpretive lens from which to approach Barth's "analogy of relations," for it distorts his understanding of human agency in its relationship to multiple sites of alterity and it reduces his "analogy of relations" to a series of dyads comprising two types of actors: those who lead, command, and direct, and those who follow, obey, and respond.

I have argued that due to Barth's christocentric methodological commitments, his theological anthropology should be governed by only one model of human agency, based on a pattern of activity he finds manifested in Christ. In his theological anthropology Barth carefully conforms his human agent to a pattern of divine activity that is reiterated in trinitarian, incarnational, and anthropological registers. In each of these registers Barth focuses on the self-revealing, saving, relationship-constituting activity of the Word made flesh, which sets in motion an imitative human activity directed toward other human beings.

Human agents are always already constituted by this christological activity. They are constituted as recipients of an un-repayable gift that imposes on them an obligation to imitate this gratuitous activity in a turn toward other human beings, on whom they depend for the same sort of aid. That is, human beings are always already set in motion by their divine benefactor and directed toward their neighbors in a relationship of dependency and obligation that is analogous to their relationship to the divine benefactor. In this construal of human agency, "order" comes into view as a divine interruption of the agent's self-referential focus, a reorientation of the agent outward toward the other.

I have shown that Barth's ordering of the sexes assigns to the male the role of imitating Christ's grace by preempting and preceding the female in this aid-lending activity. For on Barth's own terms, to claim that it is a male prerogative to imitate Christ's relation to the Church *is* to claim that it is a male prerogative to imitate Christ's aid-lending gratuitous activity itself. Such a claim robs women of their very humanity by robbing them of the ethical gratuitous impulse that drives the human agent toward its other. Barth thus sets restraints on the ways women are to come to the aid of their male neighbors. They are *not* always-already set in motion toward their male others. Rather they are suspended in an unlivable state of passivity wherein they perpetually await the aid-lending initiative of men. Barth never troubles himself to explain how women are to "enact" this state of restraint—indeed, how could he? He gives us only the figure of the silent immobile Eve. Barth's ordering of the sexes thus distorts and truncates the model of agency he expects women to appropriate.

The super-/subordering of the relationship between the sexes does not, then, expose an insidious pattern of domination and submission permeating Barth's theology as many have suspected. Rather it is a one-sided, tangential, unsustainable departure that Barth tacks onto his account of interpersonal human relationships in §45 and §54 with corrupting and distorting consequences. The mutuality and reciprocity of the relation of "I" to "Thou," described in §45.2, is not an aberration in a series of hierarchal dyads. Rather it is an iteration of a pattern of aid-lending and aid-receiving human agency central to Barth's dogmatic project. In its orientation, vulnerability, and openness to its "Thou," Barth's agent maintains the critical and self-reflective mechanism to challenge and contest categories, boundaries, norms, and constraints that would silence or distort the speech and activity of the other—an openness to the challenge the other imposes upon its own assumptions and self-invested attachments.

In developing this argument, I have joined a growing number of interpreters who have worked to correct the long-held suspicion and widely voiced criticism that Barth's divine subject overwhelms and eviscerates Barth's human subject. My reading of Barth's construal of human agency has also resisted this suspicion. However, I have found instead that Barth's male agent overwhelms and eviscerates the female agent. I have shown that there is no place in Barth's account of human agency for the silence and restraint he imposes upon women. As benefactors of Christ's grace, they too are to hear the call of Christ to "go and do likewise," to play neighbor to the other. If, as Barth suggests in both §45.1 and §54.1, part of this movement of the self to the other entails a self-revealing corrective of the misperceptions of the other, then Barth's account of human agency actually secures a place for precisely the sort of feminist critique that he attempts to quash with his prescriptions of subordination and restraint: a critique that challenges the prerogatives and positions of power that Barth presumes are proper to men alone.

Disentangling the agent from a heteronormative framework

So much for the ordering of the sexes, but what of Barth's heteronormative construal of human relationships? Barth imagines the difference between the sexes as a fixed, permanent, structural difference—the only one of its sort among the many differences demarcating human beings from each other. A marital relationship between two people of opposite sex he finds is best suited to reflect the difference and thus the alterity-crossing relationship between Jesus Christ and his community. And so Barth casts homosexual relationships outside the sphere of human fellowship, depicting them as self-loving, self-isolating repudiations of the human "other" who is most properly embraced only in someone of the opposite sex. He marginalizes various patterns of communal living, same-sex organizations, and monastic orders, all of which he likewise deems suspect of an isolated rejection of fellowship with the "other."

I have drawn attention to the challenge that the gospel picture of the unmarried Christ presents for Barth's unreflective, dyadic construal of the relationship between the sexes, for it exposes the difficulty Barth has in securing a two-sex relational framework for an anthropology that purports to be built out of christology. Barth's initial response to this challenge, in §41 and §45, is to ignore Christ's celibacy, to efface the significance of Christ's sexed corporal existence, and to disregard Paul's words in praise of celibacy. He keeps Christ at the center of his two-sex framing of human fellowship through the use of Paul's marital metaphor of Christ's relationship to a bridal Church. However, this interpretive move only amplifies Barth's detachment of his christological reference point from the corporal and physiological dimensions of human existence, thereby further mystifying the nature of this intransigent "structural difference."

When, in §54, Barth does finally attempt to come to terms with Christ's and Paul's unmarried state and their praise of celibacy, he secures a place for their relational life *on the margins* of his framework for ordering human fellowship—as paradoxical, emergency iterations of the norm. He finally admits that celibacy is a more direct imitation of Christ's relationship to the opposite sex. Nevertheless, marriage retains its central normative status. Thus, while Barth finally acknowledges the significance of Christ's unmarried state, he fails to address the significance of Christ's life and ministry in the fellowship and company of twelve men.

Barth's determination to maintain a christological point of reference for theological anthropology flounders very obviously here. From the beginning I have drawn attention to the ways in which Barth's christological interpretive method uses biblical texts to challenge his contemporaries' dogmatic and cultural assumptions. Barth uses biblical characters (the Good Samaritan, Adam, Mary, Elizabeth) to prefigure and point to Christ. He uses these characters to challenge contemporary assumptions about the nature of human freedom, mastery, and power. Such challenges expose, for Barth, the need for a critical evaluation and reconfiguration of dominant theological assumptions, commitments, and categories. Barth's efforts to conform the figure of Christ to his complementary two-sex framing of human fellowship expose his own assumptions about the mystifying alterity between the sexes. For Barth does not allow the figure of Christ to put into question his own assumption about the fixed alterity between the sexes and their relational orientation toward each other. Instead he shifts Christ to the margins of this particular domain of human relationships. To return Christ to the methodological center of his christologically funded theological anthropology would call into question his assumption that sexual difference provides the greatest site of inter-human alterity and with it the most opportune occasion for the fullest realization of human fellowship, intimacy, and companionship.

The figure of Christ, in his relation to other human beings, thus calls for a critical intervention into Barth's account of sexual difference. Toward this end, I have drawn attention to some other images of Christ's relationship to his fellows, which Barth uses when he is not attempting to secure sexual difference and its order at the center of human fellowship. These images invite a decentralizing of sexual difference, and they suggest, furthermore, that Barth's understanding of inter-human fellowship is not as constrained by this two-sex framework as it appears within the confines of §41, §45.3, and §54.1.

In Chapter 5 I noted in particular the image of Jesus the crucified in a host of fellow sufferers, inviting those who despise him and his fellows into a fellowship of shared suffering. Barth invites his readers to recognize themselves among this company: to see in Christ and this host of people their own neighbors, on whom they must depend and for whom they are responsible. In Chapter 6, I drew attention to the image of Christ at the center of a series of ever-widening circles: disciples, the crowds following him, his enemies, and the countless number who have not yet heard of him. Barth uses this image to point to the fluidity of the boundaries by which we distinguish ourselves from others, such as language, geography, and shared history. He depicts these boundaries as open to constant renegotiation. The would-be imitator of Christ is to tread continually the path from near to distant neighbors in a movement toward an ever-increasing understanding of and intimacy with these others: a movement that constantly shifts the boundaries between the "near" and "far." This depiction of the fluidity of ethnic differences resonates with Barth's earlier reading of the parable of the Good Samaritan, discussed in Chapter 2. Barth uses the parable to detach the biblical concept of the neighbor, for whom one is responsible, from any association with contemporaneous appeals to societal institutions of shared blood and nationhood. Within the sphere of God's grace, there is no outside to the Christian's ethical obligation.

With these images, then, Barth sets his reader on a ceaseless movement toward an ever-widening circle of neighbors, ready for the redirection and reorientation that the neighbor imposes on the self. There is no fixed line dividing self from other. All human beings are called to recognize that they are already in the sphere of Jesus's fellows, and are invited to move into ever closer proximity with him and into ever closer degrees of fellowship, understanding, dependency, and obligation with other human beings. These images of shared fellowship do not require the policing and shoring up of a dividing line that distinguishes self from other—the sort of line that Barth would have distinguish the sexes. Rather, such images suggest a more open, fluid, and flexible way of thinking about the self's relationship to other human beings, inclusive of a wide variety of relationships and communal organizations, than does Barth's use of dyadic, oppositional marital figures (Adam and Eve, Yahweh and Israel, Christ and Church). They invite us to locate sexual difference on the same plane and with the same fluidity as other differences, such as ethnicity, age, and class. This wide range of relationships would allow more diverse occasions for imitating Christ's relationship to others, including various types of friendships, homosexual relationships, communal arrangements, and monastic orders.

In fact, with the aid of the figure of Adam from §41, we might expand this sphere of ethical obligation and cohabitation well beyond the boundaries of human actors, to incorporate the full range of creaturely others. If, like Elizabeth, Mary, and the Good Samaritan, Adam is read as another biblical model for readers to imitate regardless of sexual or ethnic identity, then in Adam we have the image of an agent in a network of non-human collaborators (animal life, plant life, water, mineral), on whom he depends and who likewise depend on him. Adam recognizes the gracious provision of God for him in the activities and functions of these many creaturely others, and he recognizes also his own obligation to come to their aid in playing his part of service to animals, garden, and earth. It is only upon the arrival of Eve that Barth loses sight of the broader network of creaturely neighbors in which Adam is embedded, just as, with the arrival of Paul's bridal church, Barth loses sight of Christ's ever-widening circle of fellows. Barth's marital dyad thus distorts and distracts from a far richer and open-ended account of human relatedness that he develops from his christocentric doctrine of creation.

Interrogating gender norms

Barth's account of the self's relationship to gender norms is, I have shown, a mixed bag. He refuses to naturalize sexual difference with reference to biological and reproductive functions, and his ethics of sexual difference calls for a critical, deliberative, self-reflective, and evaluative relationship to social conventions and normative constraints. At the same time, however, the agent is bound by Barth to the way those very constraints function to distinguish the sexes. For the agent is not permitted to contest the division itself nor the methods and means by which one is assigned one's sex. Sexual difference thus operates as an empty category that must pervade and govern every act that would concretize one's identity in a particular sociocultural framework. While Barth allows an openness and fluidity in how one might perform one's sex, part of the ethical exercise entails carefully discerning how to respect and honor the formal and material difference between the sexes and so to shore up one's sexual specificity in an oppositional framework.

I have argued that Barth's agent retains the critical and reflective mechanisms for contesting the normative constraints of his rigid two-sex regulatory framework. His ethics of sexual difference lends itself to an anti-essentialist, performative account of gender that subverts the gender binary and its compulsory oppositional ordering of identity and desire. The possibility thus arises for reimaging Barth's agent as not only freed from the ethical "oughts" of culturally contingent stereotypes regulating the differences between the sexes, but freed also from the compulsory oppositional binary instantiated in these stereotypes, which would require of individuals an exhaustive performance aimed at carefully shoring up their distinction from the opposite sex. The self's relation to gender conventions might then entail performances that subvert and contest the seeming givenness of the two-sex oppositional binary and its ordering of identity and desire. Barth's christocentric agent might then be reimagined as a relational site, open to a wide variety of relationships and communal organizations, and also as a critical site of resistance and liberative activity.

I have sought to free Barth's agent from its sexist and heterosexist entanglements in order to remove barriers to and clear space for constructive theological appropriations that engage and respond to contemporary conversations about sex, gender, and sexuality, and their intersection with race, class, and empire. The ethical imperative driving Barth's agent calls for the critical interrogation of ideological constructions and marginalizations of the "other." Barth's dialogical account of neighbor-love functions both to secure a site from which the "other" might speak its irreducible difference and to harness theological incentives for the agent to render itself vulnerable to the disruptive speech of the other.

The possibility, therefore, opens up for constructive ventures in which Barth's theological anthropology and accompanying ethics might be engaged from the vantage point of feminist theologies concerned with agency, freedom, and the ethical dimensions of critique in its relation to social and political transformation. Barth might, for instance, be read together with theorists like Adriana Cavarero, Luce Irigaray, Judith Butler, Saba Mahmood, Linda Zerilli, and Ellen Armour, with an eye to shared themes of vulnerability, exposure, interdependence, and embodiment as these relate to gender, race, class, religion, and physical ability. Such constructive exercises might entail not only exposing the hegemonizing impulses in Barth's theology; they might also put Barth's theological anthropology to service in configurations of the category of "woman" as an open, contestable, collaborative, and enunciative site from which to speak, act, and form alliances with the marginalized for liberative and transformative ends. I have sought to show that Barth's account of the sexed dimensions of human agency need not simply be bracketed as an irredeemably problematic aspect of his *Church Dogmatics*. Instead it might be harnessed and appropriated toward ends far exceeding the constraints he himself placed on the critical edge of the Word.

BIBLIOGRAPHY

Abrams, M. H. *Natural Supernaturalism: Tradition and Revolution in Romantic Literature.* New York: Norton, 1973.

Andrews, Isolde. *Deconstructing Barth: A Study of the Complementary Methods in Karl Barth and Jacques Derrida.* New York: Peter Lang, 1996.

Balboa, Jaime Ronaldo. "'Church Dogmatics,' Natural Theology, and the Slippery Slope of '*Geschlecht*': A Constructivist-Gay Liberationist Reading of Barth." *JAAR* 66, no. 4 (Winter 1998): 771–89.

Balthasar, Hans Urs von. *The Theology of Karl Barth: Exposition and Interpretation.* Translated by Edward T. Oakes. San Francisco: Ignatius Press, 1992.

Barth, Karl. *Anselm: Fides Quaerens Intellectum.* London: SCM Press, 1960.

Barth, Karl. "The Christian Community and the Civil Community." In *Community, State and Church.* Gloucester MA: Peter Smith, 1968.

Barth, Karl. *Church and State.* Translated by G. Ronald Howe. Greenville, SC: Smyth & Helwys Publishing, 1991.

Barth, Karl. *Church Dogmatics.* Edited by G. W. Bromiley and T. F. Torrance. 4 vols. in 13 parts. Edinburgh: T&T Clark, 1956–1975.

Barth, Karl. *Dogmatics in Outline.* Translated by G. T. Thomson. London: SCM, 1949.

Barth, Karl. *The Epistle to the Romans.* Translated by Edwyn C. Hoskyns. London: Oxford University Press, 1933.

Barth, Karl. *Evangelical Theology: An Introduction.* Translated by Grover Foley. Grand Rapids: Eerdmans, 1963.

Barth, Karl. "Fifteen Answers to Professor Adolf von Harnack." In *Adolf von Harnack: Liberal Theology at Its Height*, edited by Martin Rumscheidt, 87–90. Minneapolis: Fortress Press, 1991.

Barth, Karl. *The Göttingen Dogmatics: Instruction in the Christian Religion.* Vol. 1. Edited by Hannelotte Reiffen. Translated by Geoffrey W. Bromiley. Grand Rapids: Eerdmans, 1991.

Barth, Karl. *The Great Promise.* Translated by Hans Freund. New York: Philosophical Library, 1963.

Barth, Karl. *Die kirchliche Dogmatik.* 4 vols. in 13 parts. Zürich: TVZ, 1938–1965.

Barth, Karl. *Letters, 1961–1968.* Edited by Jürgen Fangmeier and Hinrich Stoevesandt. Translated and edited by Geoffrey W. Bromiley. Edinburgh: T&T Clark, 1981.

Barth, Karl. "Ludwig Feuerbach." In *Theology and Church: Shorter Writings, 1920–1928*, translated by Louise Pettibone, 217–37. London: SCM Press, 1962.

Barth, Karl. "Luther's Doctrine of the Eucharist: Its Basis and Purpose." In *Theology and Church: Shorter Writings, 1920–1928*, translated by Louise Pettibone, 74–111. London: SCM Press, 1962.

Barth, Karl. "No! Answer to Emil Brunner." In *Natural Theology: Comprising "Nature and Grace" by Professor Dr. Emil Brunner and the Reply "No!" by Dr. Karl Barth*, translated by Peter Fraenkel, 65–128. Eugene, OR: Wipf & Stock, 2002.

Barth, Karl. "The Principles of Dogmatics According to Wilhelm Herrmann." In *Theology and Church: Shorter Writings, 1920-1928*, translated by Louise Pettibone, 238-71. London: SCM Press, 1962.
Barth, Karl. *Protestant Theology in the Nineteenth Century: Its Background and History*. London: SCM Press, 1972.
Barth, Karl. "Schleiermacher's Celebration of Christmas." In *Theology and Church: Shorter Writings, 1920-1928*, translated by Louise Pettibone, 136-58. London: SCM Press, 1962.
Barth, Karl. "The Strange New World within the Bible." In *The Word of God and the Word of Man*, translated by Douglas Horton, 28-50. Gloucester, MA: Peter Smith, 1978.
Barth, Karl. *Theological Existence To-Day!: A Plea for Theological Freedom*. Translated by R. Birch Hoyle. Eugene, OR: Wipf & Stock, 2012.
Benhabib, Seyla, Judith Butler, Drucilla Cornell, and Nancy Fraser. *Feminist Contentions: A Philosophical Exchange*. Thinking Gender. New York: Routledge, 1995.
Bergen, Doris L. *Twisted Cross: The German Christian Movement in the Third Reich*. Chapel Hill: University of North Carolina Press, 1996.
Biggar, Nigel. *The Hastening that Waits: Karl Barth's Ethics*. Oxford: Clarendon, 1993.
Bliss, Kathleen. "Male and Female." *Theology* 55 (June 1952): 208-13.
Bonhoeffer, Dietrich. *Creation and Fall: A Theological Interpretation of Genesis 1-3*. New York: Macmillan, 1959.
Briggs, Sheila. "Images of Women and Jews in Nineteenth- and Twentieth-Century German Theology." In *Immaculate & Powerful: The Female in Sacred Image and Social Reality*, edited by Clarissa W. Atkinson, Constance H. Buchanan, and Margaret R. Miles. Boston: Beacon Press, 1985.
Bromiley, Geoffrey W. *An Introduction to the Theology of Karl Barth*. Grand Rapids: Eerdmans, 1979.
Brunner, Emil. *The Divine Imperative*. Translated by Olive Wyon. Philadelphia: Westminster, 1936.
Busch, Eberhard. *Karl Barth: His Life from Letters and Autobiographical Texts*. Translated by John Bowden. London: SCM Press, 1976.
Busch, Eberhard. *Unter dem Bogen des einen Bundes: Karl Barth und die Juden 1933-1945*. Neukirchen Vluyn: Neukirchner Verlag, 1996.
Butler, Judith. *Bodies That Matter: On the Discursive Limits of Sex*. New York: Routledge, 1993.
Butler, Judith. *Gender Trouble: Feminism and the Subversion of Identity*. New York: Routledge, 1999.
Butler, Judith. *Giving an Account of Oneself*. New York: Fordham University Press, 2005.
Butler, Judith. *Subjects of Desire: Hegelian Reflections in Twentieth-Century France*. New York: Columbia University Press, 1987.
Butler, Judith. *The Psychic Life of Power: Theories in Subjection*. Stanford, CA: Stanford University Press, 1997.
Butler, Judith. *Undoing Gender*. New York: Routledge, 2004.
Campbell, Cynthia M. "*Imago Trinitatis*: An Appraisal of Karl Barth's Doctrine of the *Imago Dei* in Light of His Doctrine of the Trinity." PhD diss., Southern Methodist University, 1981. ProQuest (8209230).
Charnley, Joy, Malcolm Pender, and Andrew Wilkin, eds. *25 Years of Emancipation? Women in Switzerland, 1971-1996*. Berne: Peter Lang, 1998.
Clark, E. and H. Richardson. "The Triumph of Patriarchalism in the Theology of Karl Barth: Selections from *Church Dogmatics* 3/4 ('the Doctrine of Creation')." In *Women

and Religion: 1972, edited by Judith Plaskow Goldenberg, 239–58. Missoula, MT: University of Montana, 1973.

Clough, David. *Ethics in Crisis; Interpreting Barth's Ethics*. Aldershot: Ashgate, 2005.

Congdon, David W. *The Mission of Demythologizing: Rudolf Bultmann's Dialectical Theology*. Minneapolis: Fortress, 2015.

Deddo, Gary W. *Karl Barth's Theology of Relations: Trinitarian, Christological, and Human: Towards an Ethic of the Family*. New York: Peter Lang, 1999.

DeFranza, Megan K. *Sex Difference in Christian Theology: Male, Female, and Intersex in the Image of God*. Grand Rapids: Eerdmans, 2015.

Dempsey, Michael T., ed. *Trinity and Election in Contemporary Theology*. Grand Rapids: Eerdmans, 2011.

Dorrien, Gary. *The Barthian Revolt in Modern Theology: Theology without Weapons*. Louisville: Westminster, 2000.

Dreyer, Yolanda. "Karl Barth's Male-Female Order as Asymmetrical Theoethics." *Hervormde Teologiese Studies* 63, no. 4 (November 2007): 1493–521.

Eller, Cynthia. "Matriarchy and the Volk." *JAAR* 81, no. 1 (March 2013): 188–221.

Ericksen, Robert P. *Theologians under Hitler: Gerhard Kittel, Paul Althaus and Emanuel Hirsch*. New Haven: Yale University Press, 1985.

Ericksen, Robert P. and Susannah Heschel, eds. *Betrayal: German Churches and the Holocaust*. Minneapolis: Augsburg Fortress Publishers, 1999.

Fiddes, Paul S. "Mary in the Theology of Karl Barth." In *Mary in Doctrine and Devotion: Papers of the Liverpool Congress, 1989, of the Ecumenical Society of the Blessed Virgin Mary*, edited by Alberic Stacpoole, 111–27. Colelgeviille: Liturgical Press, 1990.

Fiddes, Paul S. "The Status of Woman in the Thought of Karl Barth." In *After Eve: Women, Theology and the Christian Tradition*, edited by Janet Martin Soskice, 138–53. London: Marshal Pickering, 1990.

Ford, David F. *Barth and God's Story: Biblical Narrative and the Theological Method of Karl Barth in the "Church Dogmatics."* Frankfurt am Main: Verlag Peter Lang, 1985.

Ford, Joan Christine. "Toward an Anthropology of Mutuality: A Critique of Karl Barth's Doctrine of the Male-Female Order as A and B with a Comparison of the Panentheistic Theology of Jürgen Moltmann." PhD diss., Northwestern University, 1984.

Fraenkel, Peter, trans. *Natural Theology: Comprising "Nature and Grace" by Professor Dr. Emil Brunner and the Reply "No!" by Dr. Karl Barth*. Eugene, OR: Wipf & Stock, 2002.

Fraser, Elouise Renich. "Jesus' Humanity and Ours in the Theology of Karl Barth." In *Perspectives on Christology: Essays in Honor of Paul K. Jewett*, edited by Marguerite Shuster and Ricard Alfred Muller, 179–96. Grand Rapids: Zondervan, 1991.

Fraser, Elouise Renich. "Karl Barth's Doctrine of Humanity: A Reconstructive Exercise in Feminist Narrative Theology." PhD diss., Vanderbilt University, 1986. ProQuest (8616351).

Frei, Hans. "Analogy and the Spirit in the Theology of Karl Barth." Unpublished Pieces: Transcripts from the Yale Divinity School Archive. 1998–2004. http://www.library.yale.edu/div/fa/Freiindex.htm.

Frei, Hans. "The Doctrine of Revelation in the Thought of Karl Barth, 1909 to 1922: The Nature of Barth's Break with Liberalism." PhD diss., Yale University, 1956.

Frei, Hans. *The Eclipse of Biblical Narrative: A Study in Eighteenth and Nineteenth Century Hermeneutics*. New Haven: Yale University Press, 1974.

Frei, Hans. "Karl Barth: Theologian." *Reflection* 66 (May 1969): 5–9.

Frykberg, Elizabeth. *Karl Barth's Theological Anthropology: An Analogical Critique regarding Gender Relations*. Studies in Reformed Theology and History Series. Princeton: Princeton Theological Seminary, 1993.

Gockel, Matthias. *Barth and Schleiermacher on the Doctrine of Election: A Systematic Theological Comparison*. Oxford: Oxford University Press, 2006.

Gorringe, Timothy J. *Karl Barth: Against Hegemony*. Oxford: Oxford University Press, 1999.

Grant, Jacquelyn. *White Women's Christ and Black Women's Jesus: Feminist Christology and Womanist Response*. Atlanta: Scholars Press, 1989.

Green, Clifford. "Liberation Theology? Karl Barth on Women and Men." *Union Seminary Quarterly Review* 29, no. 3&4 (Spring & Summer, 1974): 221-31.

Greene-McCreight, K. E. *Ad Litteram: How Augustine, Calvin, and Barth Read the 'Plain Sense' of Genesis 1-3*. New York: Peter Lang, 1999.

Guretzki, David. "Barth, Derrida, and Différance: Is There a Difference?" *Didaskalia* 13, no. 2 (March 2002): 51-71.

Hart, John W. *Karl Barth vs. Emil Brunner: The Formation and Dissolution of a Theological Alliance, 1916-1936*. New York: Peter Lang, 2001.

Herzel, Susannah. "Correspondence between Henrietta Visser 't Hooft and Karl Barth." In *A Voice for Women: The Women's Department of the World Council of Churches*. Geneva: WCC, 1981.

Heschel, Susannah. *The Aryan Jesus: Christian Theologians and the Bible in Nazi Germany*. Princeton: Princeton University Press, 2008.

Hollywood, Amy. *Sensible Ecstasy: Mysticism, Sexual Difference and the Demands of History*. Chicago: University of Chicago Press, 2002.

Hunsinger, Deborah van Deusen. *Theology and Pastoral Counseling: A New Interdisciplinary Approach*. Grand Rapids: Eerdmans, 1995.

Hunsinger, George. *Disruptive Grace: Studies in the Theology of Karl Barth*. Grand Rapids: Eerdmans, 2000.

Hunsinger, George. *How to Read Karl Barth: The Shape of His Theology*. Oxford: Oxford University Press, 1991.

Hunsinger, George. *Reading Barth with Charity: A Hermeneutical Proposal*. Grand Rapids: Baker Academic, 2015.

Hunsinger, George. "Truth as Self-Involving: Barth and Lindbeck on the Cognitive and Performative Aspects of Truth in Theological Discourse." *JAAR* 61, no. 1 (March 1993): 41-56.

Indinopulos, Thomas A. "The Critical Weakness of Creation in Barth's Theology." *Encounter* 33 (1972): 159-69.

Irigaray, Luce. *An Ethics of Sexual Difference*. Translated by Carolyn Burke and Gillian C. Gill. Ithaca: Cornell, 1993.

Irigaray, Luce. *I Love to You: Sketch of a Possible Felicity in History*. Translated by Alison Martin. New York and London: Routledge, 1996.

Irigaray, Luce. *Sexes and Genealogies*. Translated by Gillian C. Gill. New York: Columbia, 1993.

Irigaray, Luce. *This Sex Which I Not One*. Translated by Catherine Porter. Ithaca: Cornell, 1985.

Irigaray, Luce. *Speculum of the Other Woman*. Translated by Gillian G. Gill. Ithaca: Cornell, 1985.

Janowski, C. "Zur paradigmatischen Bedeutung der Geschlechterdifferenz in Karl Barths Kirchlicher Dogmatik." In *Und drinnen waltet die zuchtige Hausfrau*, edited by H. Kuhlmann. Gütersloh: Gütersloher Verlagshaus Gerd Mohn, 1995.

Jehle, Frank. *Ever against the Stream*. Translated by Richard and Martha Burnett. Grand Rapids: Eerdmans, 2002.

Jenkins, Willis. *Ecologies of Grace: Environmental Ethics and Christian Theology*. Oxford: Oxford University Press, 2008.

Jenson, Robert W. *God after God: The God of the Past and the God of the Future, Seen in the Work of Karl Barth*. Indianapolis: Bobbs-Merrill, 1969.

Jewett, Paul K. *Man as Male and Female: A Study in Sexual Relationships from a Theological Point of View*. Grand Rapids: Eerdmans, 1975.

Johnson, Keith L. *Karl Barth and the "Analogia Entis."* London: T&T Clark, 2010.

Johnson, William Stacy. *The Mystery of God: Karl Barth and the Postmodern Foundations of Theology*. Louisville: Westminster John Knox Press, 1997.

Jones, Paul Dafydd. *The Humanity of Christ: Christology in Karl Barth's "Church Dogmatics."* London: T&T Clark, 2008.

Jones, Paul Dafydd. "Obedience, Trinity, and Election: Thinking with and beyond the *Church Dogmatics*." In *Trinity and Election in Contemporary Theology*, edited by Michael T. Dempsey, 138–61. Grand Rapids: Eerdmans, 2011.

Jones, Serene. "This God Which Is Not One: Irigaray and Barth on the Divine." In *Transfigurations: Theology and the French Feminists*, edited by C. W. Maggie Kim, Susan M. St. Ville, and Susan M. Simonaitis, 109–41. Minneapolis: Fortress, 1993.

Jónsson, Gunnlaugur A. *The Image of God: Genesis 1:26-28 in a Century of Old Testament Research*. Translated by Lorraine Svendsen. Stockholm: Almqvist & Wiksell International, 1988.

Jüngel, Eberhard. *Barth-Studien*. Zürich-Köln: Benzinger Verlag, 1982.

Jüngel, Eberhard. *God's Being Is in Becoming: The Trinitarian Being of God in the Theology of Karl Barth*. Edinburgh: T&T Clark, 2001.

Jüngel, Eberhard. *Karl Barth: A Theological Legacy*. Philadelphia: Westminster Press, 1986.

Justes, Emma J. "Theological Reflections on the Role of Women in Church and Society." *Journal of Pastoral Care* 32, no. 1 (March 1978): 42–54.

Kaplan, Marion A. "German-Jewish Feminism in the Twentieth Century." *Jewish Social Studies* (January 1976): 39–53.

Keller, Catherine. *Face of the Deep: A Theology of Becoming*. New York: Routledge, 2003.

Kelsey, David H. *The Uses of Scripture in Recent Theology*. Philadelphia: Fortress Press, 1975.

Kirschbaum, Charlotte von. *Die wirkliche Frau*. Zollikon-Zürich: Evangelischer Verlag, 1949.

Kirschbaum, Charlotte von. *The Question of Woman: The Collected Writings of Charlotte von Kirschbaum*. Translated by John Shepherd. Edited by Eleanor Jackson. Grand Rapids: Eerdmans, 1996.

Köbler, Renate. *In the Shadow of Karl Barth: Charlotte von Kirschbaum*. Translated by Keith Crim. Louisville: John Knox, 1989.

Kooi, Cornelis van der. *As in a Mirror: John Calvin and Karl Barth on Knowing God: A Diptych*. Translated by Donald Mader. Leiden: Brill, 2005.

Lindbeck, George A. "Barth and Textuality." *Theology Today* 43, no. 3 (October 1986): 361–76.

Lowe, Walter. *Theology and Difference: The Wound of Reason*. Bloomington: University Press, 1993.

Lindsay, Mark R. *Barth, Israel, and Jesus: Karl Barth's Theology of Israel*. Aldershot: Ashgate, 2007.

Louth, Andrew. *Mary and the Mystery of the Incarnation: An Essay on the Mother of God in the Theology of Karl Barth*. Fairacres: SLG Press, 1977.

Macken, John. *The Autonomy Theme in the "Church Dogmatics": Karl Barth and His Critics*. Cambridge: Cambridge University Press, 1990.

Mangina, Joseph L. *Karl Barth on the Christian Life: The Practical Knowledge of God*. New York: Peter Lang, 2001.

Marga, Amy. *Karl Barth's Dialogue with Catholicism in Göttingen and Münster: Its Significance for His Doctrine of God.* Tübingen: Mohr Siebeck, 2010.

Marquardt, Friedrich-Wilhelm. "Theological and Political Motivations of Karl Bath in the Church Struggle." In *Theological Audacities: Selected Essays*, edited by Andreas Pangritz and Paul S Chung, 190–222. Eugene, OR: Pickwick, 2010.

Matheny, Paul D. *Dogmatics and Ethics: The Theological Realism and Ethics of Karl Barth's "Church Dogmatics."* Peter Lang: Frankfurt, 1990.

McCormack, Bruce. "Beyond Nonfoundational and Postmodern Readings of Barth: Critically Realistic Dialectical Theology." *Zeitschrift für dialektische Theologie* 13 (1997): 67–95.

McCormack, Bruce. "Election and the Trinity: Theses in Response to George Hunsinger." *SJT* 63, no. 2 (2010): 203–24.

McCormack, Bruce. *Karl Barth's Critically Realistic Dialectical Theology: Its Genesis and Development, 1909-1936.* Oxford: Oxford University Press, 1995.

McCormack, Bruce. "The Ontological Presuppositions of Barth's Doctrine of the Atonement." In *The Glory of the Atonement: Biblical, Historical and Practical Perspectives: Essays in Honor of Roger R. Nicole*, edited by Charles E. Hall and Frank A James III, 346–66. Downers Grove, IL: IVP, 2004.

McCormack, Bruce. *Orthodox and Modern: Studies in the Theology of Karl Barth.* Grand Rapids: Baker, 2008.

McCormack, Bruce. "Seek God Where He May Be Found: A Response to Edwin Chr. van Driel." *SJT* 60, no.1 (2007): 62–79.

McKelway, Alexander J. "The Concept of Subordination in Barth's Special Ethics." *SJT* 32 (1979): 345–57.

McKelway, Alexander J. "Perichoretic Possibilities in Barth's Doctrine of Male and Female." *Princeton Seminary Bulletin* 7, no. 3 (January 1986): 231–43.

McKenny, Gerald P. *The Analogy of Grace: Karl Barth's Moral Theology.* Oxford: Oxford University Press, 2010.

McLean, Stuart. *Humanity in the Thought of Karl Barth.* Edinburgh: T&T Clark, 1981.

McMaken, W. Travis. *The Sign of the Gospel: Toward an Evangelical Doctrine of Infant Baptism after Karl Barth.* Minneapolis: Fortress Press, 2013.

Molnar, Paul D. "Can the Electing God Be God without Us? Some Implications of Bruce McCormack's Understanding of Barth's Doctrine of Election for the Doctrine of the Trinity." *Neue Zeitschrift für systematische Theologie und Religionsphilosophie* 49, no. 2 (January 2007): 199–222.

Molnar, Paul D. "Love of God and Love of Neighbor in the Theology of Karl Rahner and Karl Barth." *Modern Theology* 20, no. 4 (October 2004): 567–99.

Molnar, Paul D. "The Trinity, Election, and God's Ontological Freedom: A Response to Kevin W. Hector." *IJST* 8, no. 3 (2006): 294–306.

Moltmann, Jürgen. "Schöpfung, Bund und Herrlichkeit." *Evangelische Theologie* 48, no. 2 (1988): 108–27.

Moseley, Carys. *Nations and Nationalism in the Theology of Karl Barth.* Oxford: Oxford University Press, 2013.

Mueller, William A. "Karl Barth's View of the Virgin Birth." *Review and Expositor* 51, no. 4 (1954).

Muers, Rachel. "The Mute Cannot Keep Silent: Barth, von Balthasar, and Irigaray on the Construction of Women's Silence." In *Challenging Women's Orthodoxies in the Context of Faith*, edited by Susan Frank Parsons, 109–20. Aldershot: Ashgate, 2000.

Neal, Deonna D. "Be Who You Are: Karl Barth's Ethics of Creation." PhD diss., University of Notre Dame, 2010. ProQuest (3436241).

Nimmo, Paul T. *Being in Action: The Theological Shape of Barth's Ethical Vision*. London: T&T Clark, 2007.
Nimmo, Paul T. "The Orders of Creation in the Theological Ethics of Karl Barth." *SJT* 60, no. 1 (2007): 24–35.
Oakes, Kenneth. *Karl Barth on Theology and Philosophy*. Oxford: Oxford University Press, 2012.
Oh, Peter S. *Karl Barth's Trinitarian Theology: A Study in Karl Barth's Analogical Use of the Trinitarian Relation*. London: T&T Clark, 2006.
Osborn, Robert T. "Man and/or Woman According to Karl Barth." In *Theology and Corporate Conscience: Essays in Honor of Frederick Herzog*, edited by M. Douglas Meeks, Jürgen Moltmann, and Frederick R. Trost. Minneapolis: Kirk House, 1999.
Perry, Tim. "What Is Little Mary Here For?" *Pro Ecclesia* 19, no. 1 (Winter 2010): 46–68.
Prelinger, Catherine M. "Religious Dissent, Women's Rights, and the Hamburger Hochschule fuer das weibliche Geschlecht in Mid-Nineteenth-Century Germany." *Church History* (March 1976): 42–55.
Price, Daniel J. *Karl Barth's Anthropology in Light of Modern Thought*. Grand Rapids: Eerdmans, 2002.
Resch, Dustin. *A Sign of Mystery: Karl Barth's Interpretation of the Virgin Birth*. Burlington, VT: Ashgate, 2012.
Richardson, Kurt Anders. *Reading Karl Barth: New Directions for North American Theology*. Grand Rapids: Baker Academic, 2004.
Rigby, Cynthia Lynn. "The Real Word Really Became Real Flesh: Karl Barth's Contribution to a Feminist Incarnational Christology." PhD diss., Princeton Theological Seminary, 1998.
Roberts, Christopher Chenault. *Creation and Covenant: The Significance of Sexual Difference in the Moral Theology of Marriage*. London: T&T Clark, 2007.
Roberts, Richard. *A Theology on Its Way? Essays on Karl Barth*. Edinburgh: T&T Clark, 1991.
Rogers, Eugene. *Sexuality and the Christian Body: Their Way into the Triune Life*. Oxford: Blackwell, 1999.
Rogers, Eugene. "Supplementing Barth on Jews and Gender: Identifying God by Anagogy and the Spirit." *Modern Theology* 14, no. 1 (January 1998): 43–81.
Romero, Joan Arnold. "Karl Barth's Theology of the Word of God: or, How to Keep Women Silent and in Their Place." In *Women and Religion: 1972*, edited by Judith Plaskow Goldenberg, 35–48. Missoula, MT: University of Montana, 1973.
Romero, Joan Arnold. "The Protestant Principle: A Woman's-Eye View of Barth and Tillich." In *Religion and Sexism*, edited by Rosemary Ruether, 319–40. New York: Simon and Schuster, 1974.
Ruether, Rosemary Radford. "Left Hand of God in the Theology of Karl Barth: Karl Barth as a Mythopoeic Theologian." *Journal of Religious Thought* 25, no. 1 (1969): 3–26.
Ruether, Rosemary Radford. *Sexism and God-Talk: Toward a Feminist Theology*. Boston: Beacon Press, 1983.
Salomonsen, Jone. "'Love of Same, Love of Other': Reading Feminist Anthropologies with Luce Irigaray and Karl Barth." *Studia Theologica* 57, no. 2 (January 2003): 103–23.
Santmire, Paul H. "Toward a Christology of Nature: Claiming the Legacy of Joseph Sittler and Karl Barth." *Dialog* 34 (1995): 270–80.
Schreiner, Susan E. *The Theater of His Glory: Nature and the Natural Order in the Thought of John Calvin*. Durham, NC: Labyrinth, 1991.
Seban, Jean-Loup. "The Theology of Nationalism of Emanuel Hirsch." *Princeton Seminary Bulletin* 7, no. 2 (1986): 157–76.

Selinger, Suzanne, *Charlotte von Kirschbaum and Karl Barth: A Study in Biography and the History of Theology*. University Park, PA: Pennsylvania State University Press, 1998.
Sheveland, John N. *Piety and Responsibility: Patterns of Unity in Karl Rahner, Karl Barth, and Vedanta Desika*. Burlington, VT: Ashgate, 2011.
Smith, Steven G. *The Argument to the Other: Reason beyond Reason in the Thought of Karl Barth and Emmanuel Levinas*. Chico, CA: Scholars Press, 1983.
Sonderegger, Katherine. *That Jesus Christ Was Born a Jew: Karl Barth's "Doctrine of Israel."* University Park, PA: Pennsylvania State University Press, 1992.
Spencer, Archibald James. *Clearing a Space for Human Action: Ethical Ontology in the Theology of Karl Barth*. New York: Peter Lang, 2003.
Springs, Jason. "But Did It Really Happen? Frei, Henry, and Barth on Historical Reference and Critical Realism." In *Karl Barth and American Evangelicalism*, edited by Bruce McCormack and Clifford B. Anderson, 271–99. Grand Rapids: Eerdmans, 2011.
Springs, Jason. "Following at a Distance (Again): Gender, Equality, and Freedom in Karl Barth's Theological Anthropology." *Modern Theology* 28, no. 3 (July 2012): 447–77.
Stephenson, Lisa P. "Directed, Ordered and Related: The Male and Female Interpersonal Relation in Karl Barth's *Church Dogmatics*." *SJT* 61, no. 4 (2008): 435–49.
Stibbe, Matthew. "Anti-Feminism, Nationalism and the German Right, 1914–1920: A Reappraisal." *German History* (June 2002): 185–210.
Strümke, Volker. "Die Jungfrauengeburt als Geheimnis des Glaubens—ethische Annmerkungen." *Neue Zeitschrift für systematische Theologie und Religionsphilosophie* 49, no. 4 (2007): 423–41.
Tait, L. Gordon. "Karl Barth and the Virgin Mary." *Journal of Ecumenical Studies* 4 (1967): 406–25.
Thiemann, Ronald F. *Constructing a Public Theology: The Church in a Pluralistic Culture*. Louisville: WJKP, 1991.
Thiemann, Ronald F. "Response to George Lindbeck." *Theology Today* 43, no. 3 (October 1986): 377–82.
Thiemann, Ronald F. *Revelation and Theology: The Gospel as Narrated Promise*. Notre Dame: University of Notre Dame Press, 1985.
Tietz, Christiane. "Karl Barth and Charlotte von Kirschbaum." *Theology Today* 74 (July 2017): 86–111.
Torrance, Alan J. *Persons in Communion: An Essay on Trinitarian Description and Human Participation*. Edinburgh: T&T Clark, 1996.
Vischer, Wilhelm. *The Witness of the Old Testament to Christ*. Vol. 1. *The Pentateuch*, translated by A. B. Crabtree. London: Lutterworth Press, 1949.
Ward, Graham. *Barth, Derrida and the Language of Theology*. Cambridge: Cambridge University Press, 1995.
Ward, Graham. "Barth, Modernity, and Postmodernity." In *Cambridge Companion to Karl Barth*, 274–95. Cambridge: Cambridge University Press, 2000.
Ward, Graham. "The Erotics of Redemption: After Karl Barth." *Theology & Sexuality* 8 (March 1998): 52–72.
Watson, JoAnn Ford. *A Study of Karl Barth's Doctrine of Man and Woman*. New York: Vantage Press, 1995.
Webb, Stephen H. *Re-Figuring Theology: The Rhetoric of Karl Barth*. Albany: State University of New York Press, 1991.
Webster, John. *Barth's Ethics of Reconciliation*. Cambridge: Cambridge University Press, 1995.
Webster, John. *Barth's Earlier Theology: Four Studies*. New York: T&T Clark, 2005.

Webster, John. *Barth's Moral Theology: Human Action in Barth's Thought*. Edinburgh: T&T Clark, 1998.
Welker, Michael. *Creation and Reality*. Minneapolis: Fortress, 1999.
Werpehowski, William. *Karl Barth and Christian Ethics: Living in Truth*. Burlington, VT: Ashgate, 2014.
Willis, Robert. *The Ethics of Karl Barth*. Leiden: E. J. Brill, 1971.
Zerilli, Linda M.G. *Feminism and the Abyss of Freedom*. Chicago: University of Chicago Press, 2005.

INDEX

acknowledgment 27, 30, 33, 34, 99
actualism 27, 123
Adam 309
   free decision 61, 95–7, 97–101, 137
   naming of 103, 103 n. 15
   nonhuman co-workers 63 n. 2, 85 n. 3, 87–8, 92–7, 99, 100, 104, 110
   origin of 92–5, 101–3, 103 n. 15, 104, 129–30
   prefiguration of Christ 79, 83, 87, 90–2, 94–5, 102, 104, 129, 140–1
agency
   autonomy 35, 55, 129, 152
   death 91, 94–5, 97, 103–4, 110, 112
   passivity 7 n. 4, 9, 28
   receptivity 28, 122, 135
   responsibility 8, 14–15, 17, 38 n. 1, 45, 53, 59, 62, 83, 97, 98, 112–13, 134, 149, 167, 171, 178
   spontaneity 17, 117, 122–3, 129, 132 n. 13, 135, 141–2, 169 n. 16, 172
analogy 6 n. 4, 11, 41, 77, 77 n. 17, 86 n. 3, 95, 98, 103, 150 n. 2
analogy of relations 1–4, 7 n. 4, 8, 12 n. 8, 115, 116 n. 4, 125–7, 176
antisemitism 38, 38 n. 1, 39, 40–4, 57 n. 23, 57–8, 66–7, 90
   Aryan paragraph 40–2, 44
apostles 35, 55, 129, 152

baptism 41–2, 56
Barmen Declaration 42, 44 n. 15
barren 75, 92–4, 98, 100, 103–4
   sterility in Genesis 1:2 74, 75, 75 n. 16
benefactor
   Christ 124
   divine 14, 54, 95, 120, 123, 176
   Good Samaritan 50, 51, 111, 112
   human 50, 51, 60, 123, 177
beneficiary 72, 93, 104, 120, 131, 133 n. 14
benefit
   conferred by Christ 111, 122–3
   conferred by creation 91, 112
   conferred by God 62, 122–3
   conferred by neighbor 50–4, 59–60, 129, 133–4
Boddaert, Henriette Visser't Hooft 66 n. 7
body
   of Adam 97–8, 101, 103–4
   of Christ 95, 104, 165
   conception 76
   female fecundity 62, 63, 67
   female generativity 63, 81, 90, 94
   of Mary 95, 98
   maternal 16, 17, 76, 81, 93, 95
   post-menopausal 98
   soul and 2, 127 n. 12, 130, 141
Bonhoeffer, Dietrich 76 n. 17, 78 n. 19, 83 n. 1, 94
Brunner, Emil 40 n. 3, 43 n. 14, 44, 44 n. 15, 44 n. 16, 79 n. 20, 156, 156 n. 10, 166
Buber, Martin 79 n. 20, 113
Bultmann, Rudolf 43 n. 14, 44, 44 n. 15, 68 n. 10
Butler, Judith 14–15, 149 n. 1, 161 n. 12, 162 n. 13, 180

Calvin, John 69, 76 n. 17
celibacy 130, 154–5, 157, 163, 164. See under Christ; Paul
Christ (*see also* imitation of Christ)
   celibacy 12, 86 n. 3, 108, 130, 140, 150, 154–5, 177–8
   conformity to 17, 37, 47, 117, 119, 122–3, 126–7, 136, 138, 172
   disciples of 131, 132, 154, 155, 165, 178
   humanity of 2, 5, 52, 53, 55, 59, 86, 94, 95, 111, 119, 123–31, 134
   key or secret to Creation 16, 61, 71, 76, 87, 108, 115, 118, 119
   life of 24, 70, 72, 73, 90, 91, 91 n. 10, 94, 178

resurrection 65 n. 4, 91, 92, 94, 95, 103, 110
suffering and death 52, 53, 59, 91, 95, 103, 110, 111, 124, 129, 131, 133–4, 133 n. 14, 134, 136, 144, 165, 178
unmarried state 12, 13, 17, 108, 138, 140, 155, 163, 174, 177–8
church (*see also* German Church struggle)
Christ's relationship to 2, 4, 6, 12, 61, 77 n. 17, 86, 88, 92, 106–8, 110, 128 n. 11, 129, 140–1, 167, 176, 177, 179
proclamation 23–4, 26, 30–1, 32, 34, 59, 111
visible 41, 56, 60
cosmology 6, 74, 119
covenant 1, 86 n. 3, 119 (*see under* history)
between man and woman 108
creed(s) 32, 62, 67, 80
Apostle's Creed 61–3, 68, 70–2, 80, 118

Delitzsch, Franz 64 n. 3, 66
dependency
upon a network of creatures 62, 83, 87 n. 4, 92, 110
upon neighbor 14, 16, 45, 60, 110, 111, 135, 176, 178–9
upon parent 158, 168
upon the divine act 19, 27, 30, 45, 92
woman upon man 89, 168 n. 16, 169
desire
economy of 12 n. 8, 85, 85 n. 3
for God 48
between the sexes 11, 15, 87, 100, 105, 107–9, 161, 163, 169, 170, 180
dialectical relations 3 n. 2, 22, 43, 51, 93, 104, 108
gospel and law 37, 39, 45, 51, 53
veiling and unveiling 59
dialogical encounter 84, 100, 101, 108, 110, 123, 131–7, 180
dialogical personalism 4, 79 n. 20, 84
disciples 131, 132 n. 13, 152, 154–5, 165, 178. *See also* apostles
divine command
ethics of 150–5, 161
gender norms and conventions 111, 149, 157, 159, 160, 174
neighbor love 47, 53
orders of creation 44
sexual difference 149, 150, 157–8, 163
sexual reproduction 75, 78, 81, 108
Two Commandments 38 n. 1, 39, 45–55, 79, 120, 124
doubt 22, 33

ecstatic 120–1, 122, 123, 134
election
Adam and Eve 83, 99, 109, 110, 137, 141
Christ and the Church 92, 137
doctrine of 3 n. 2, 4 n. 3, 6–7, 10–11, 10 n. 6, 53 n. 21, 115–17, 115 n. 4, 117 n. 6, 118 n. 6, 120–2, 125–7, 132 n. 13
man and woman 107, 109
Yahweh and Israel 94
Ephesians 5 77 n. 17, 106, 107, 113, 129, 131, 132, 139, 140, 141
epistemic certainty 20, 21, 22, 23, 28, 59, 60, 70
epistemic vantage point 2, 15, 20–3, 23–8, 30, 63–4, 69, 71–2, 91, 97, 99, 118, 134, 163, 180
ethical deliberation 8–9, 17, 91, 99, 100, 106, 110, 151 n. 2, 152–3, 153 n. 8, 158, 167–9, 169 n. 16, 173–4, 180
ethical duty 37, 46, 47, 53, 92
ethical instruction 152 n. 5, 153 n. 8
ethical obligation 14, 17, 37, 39, 45, 46, 51–2, 57, 59–60, 61, 62, 117, 122, 128, 136, 144, 149, 167, 176, 179
of Adam 91, 93, 96, 97, 111, 113, 179
of Eve 99, 112
of men over women 171, 175
ethics (*see also* divine command; orders of creation)
boundary case 155, 157, 164
casuistry 151, 152 n. 5
imperative 134, 138, 157, 166, 180
"ought" 156–7, 160, 166, 172, 180
special ethics 1, 12 n. 8, 16, 17, 61, 100, 113, 150 n. 2, 168
theological practice 37–9, 38 n. 1, 44, 54, 57
ethnicity 43, 56, 60, 80, 112, 164, 179
Eve
Adam's naming of 17, 34, 35, 81, 83, 86 n. 3, 91, 97, 113, 141, 151

Adam's recognition of 12 n. 8, 34–5, 83, 85 n. 3, 86 n. 3, 89, 91, 97, 98, 137
completion of Adam's humanity 86, 90, 91–3, 95, 97–101, 102, 105, 112, 117 n. 5
creation of 4, 6, 84, 86–7, 95, 97–106
free decision of 98–100, 102 n. 13, 104, 108, 141
humanity of 98–9, 102, 112
as model agent 16, 35, 60, 61, 83, 100, 111–12
as neighbor 59, 79, 102, 111–12, 179
order of origination 6, 17, 95, 97–101, 103, 130
silence of 85 n. 3, 89, 92, 98–9, 100, 101–5, 106, 108–10, 142, 167, 172, 176
subordination of 77 n. 17, 88, 95, 101, 103, 104, 110, 129

fatherhood 33, 75–6, 104, 126 n. 10, 139, 167
paternity 62, 66, 75, 76, 107, 126
feeling 21, 22, 28, 52
fellowship (*see also* I and Thou)
between the sexes 61, 77 n. 17, 84, 88, 112, 114, 131, 139–44, 149, 150, 154, 163–4, 165, 167, 169, 177–80
with Christ 53, 59
Christ with others 87, 118, 131 n. 13, 155, 174, 177–9
Elizabeth and Mary 33, 111
as history 120–2, 124, 134–5
inter-human 4, 5, 11, 14, 17, 52, 53, 59, 87, 125, 128, 153, 174
same-sex 12, 85, 110, 111, 162, 163, 177
trinitarian 2, 4, 11, 70, 115, 116 n. 4, 120, 122, 125 n. 10
feminine
envy 2, 106, 107, 158, 159, 160, 166, 169, 170, 174
passivity 7, 9, 74, 75, 75 n. 16, 76, 81, 87, 142, 169 n. 16, 170, 176
restraint 2, 8, 17, 83, 92, 101, 112, 113, 137, 142, 145, 168, 171, 172–3, 176, 177
feminist critique 7, 35, 62, 75, 177, 180

feminist movement 65, 65 n. 5, 67
Barth's depiction of 2, 106, 107, 134, 152, 159–60, 170, 171
Barth's response to 35, 105–6, 126 n. 10, 137, 142, 143, 143 n. 15, 154, 159–60, 161, 172
Feuerbach, Ludwig 113
forgiveness 48, 53, 152
freedom
divine 24, 30, 56, 75, 115, 116 n. 4, 157
human 87, 88–9, 117 n. 5, 133 n. 13, 135, 139, 140, 178

Galatians 3:28 41, 142, 143, 143 n. 15
gender
Butler, Judith 14–15, 149 n. 1
conventions 32, 34, 80, 111, 139, 149, 150, 156, 158, 159, 160, 162, 173–4, 180–1
norms 14–15, 149, 150, 153, 156, 157, 159, 160–2, 164–5, 173–4, 176, 180–1
stereotypes 66 n. 5, 80, 139, 157, 166, 180
generativity
maternal 63 n. 2, 75–6, 81, 90, 94, 95
paternal 81
Genesis 1:2 74–6, 93
Genesis 3 88, 89, 89 n. 6, 109
German Church struggle 32, 37–8, 40–4, 55–8
German Christians 63, 81, 89, 89 n. 7, 90
Gogarten, Friedrich 44, 44 n. 15, 79 n. 20
Good Samaritan 16, 19, 38 n. 1, 39, 43, 49–60, 87–8, 93, 102, 110–12, 117, 120, 124–5, 127, 134, 137–8, 145, 178–9
gratitude 14, 33, 34, 61, 71, 89, 97, 100, 120–3, 156
Gunkel, Hermann 64 n. 3, 66, 74, 75, 78, 94

habits 16, 19, 20–3
Hegel, Georg Wilhelm Friedrich 20, 22, 25, 78, 88
heteronormativity 1, 2, 10, 11, 11 n. 8, 15, 17, 37, 59, 84, 87, 88, 118, 131, 132

n. 13, 145, 147, 150, 154–5, 164 n. 14, 165, 174, 175, 177–9
heterosexism 2, 10, 144, 175, 180
heterosexuality 12 n. 8, 13, 17, 87, 126, 132 n. 13, 154, 174
Hirsch, Emanuel 40
history
　biblical saga 64, 67, 71–5
　covenant history 69, 71–3, 75, 90–1, 93, 94, 106–7, 110
　creation history 71–5, 85 n. 3, 90–1, 94, 100, 102, 122–4
　Hegel 22
　intersubjective relations 120–2, 124, 134–5
　myth 64, 66, 68–9
homosexuality 11, 12 n. 8, 162–3, 164 n. 14, 165, 177, 179
hope 20, 23, 32, 33, 35, 47, 48, 54, 55, 60, 80, 90, 92, 93–5, 100, 104, 110
humility 20, 21, 23, 89, 90, 92, 144 n. 16

I and Thou 4, 5 n. 3, 12 n. 8, 19, 38 n. 1, 77 n. 17, 78–81, 84, 85 n. 3, 86, 100–1, 108, 113, 123, 125, 125 n. 10, 127 n. 11, 128–38, 159, 161–5. *See under* fellowship
imago dei 2, 5, 11, 17, 62–3, 74, 76 n. 17, 78, 78 n. 19, 79, 79 n. 20, 80, 85 n. 3, 102 n. 14, 125, 127, 132 n. 13, 146 n. 17. *See under* Christ
　divine likeness 17, 62, 63, 64, 74, 76–80, 108, 109, 127
imitation of biblical models 15, 19, 31, 35, 50–1, 54–5, 69, 80, 110, 112, 179
imitation of Christ 8, 14, 51, 59, 122–9, 131–7, 165, 176, 179. *See under* Christ
　Christ's celibacy 130, 154, 155, 178
　male prerogative 17, 112, 129, 134, 138, 175
　women 117, 141, 142, 167, 176
isolation 19, 47, 70, 110, 135, 163–4

Jews and Judaism 41, 43 n. 14, 57 n. 23, 58 n. 24, 73. *See also* antisemitism
judgment 21, 29, 31, 33, 118 n. 6, 139, 151, 152, 161

Kant, Immanuel 21, 22, 24 n. 4, 27, 68, 88, 88 n. 5, 89 n. 6
　neo-kantian 20 n. 1, 24 n. 4

limitations
　creaturely 122, 125
　epistemic 110
loveless 46, 48
love of God 39, 46, 47–9, 120–2, 124
love of neighbor 38, 39, 49–59, 74, 93, 120, 123–137, 180
Luther, Martin 25, 39, 40, 45, 57 n. 22, 71, 76 n. 17

male
　agential initiative 89, 89 n. 6, 105, 110, 141, 144 n. 16, 166, 175, 176
　agential precedence 59, 85 n. 3, 105, 108, 117, 129, 138–9, 144 n. 16, 156, 166, 168–9, 173, 175
　decision making 99–100, 105, 107
　ethical prerogative 2, 11, 14, 17, 35, 60, 83, 99, 100, 102, 105–7, 109, 111, 113, 128–9, 141–3, 145, 159, 160, 166, 170–3, 176–7
　gaze 91, 100, 170
　tyranny or abuse 110, 134, 170–3
　virility 66, 75 n. 16, 87, 89 n. 7
marital norm 1, 13, 37, 61, 86 n. 3, 87, 90–110, 113–4, 126 n. 10, 137–47, 149, 155–65, 173–4, 177–80
　Christ's relation to his fellows 12, 13, 17, 86, 106, 108, 138, 140, 154–6, 147, 163–5, 174, 177–9
　Christ's relation to the Church 12 n. 8, 106–8, 113, 129, 140, 146–7, 164–5, 177, 179
　orders of creation 37, 44
　Paul 86, 86 n. 3, 107–8, 140–4, 147, 152, 154–5, 163–4, 165, 177–8, 179
　sexual reproduction 80–1, 85 n. 3, 106–8, 140
Mary
　Elizabeth 16, 19, 20, 31, 32–4, 88, 98, 101, 110–12, 178, 179
　model agent 16, 19, 20, 31, 32–4, 87, 88, 101, 110–12, 178, 179
　virgin conception 32, 32 n. 6, 34, 95, 98

Zechariah 31, 32–4
maternity 16–17, 62–3, 64–7, 90, 107. *See also* body
   conception 32–4, 76
   maternal imagery 2, 63–4, 67, 74–6, 80–1, 87, 90, 93, 94–5
miracle 21, 27, 29, 30, 32, 34, 54, 55, 64
mirror
   Christ as 59, 119, 134, 150, 165
   Eden as 99
   Eve as 58, 85, 100, 104, 110
   neighbor as 37, 49–50, 52–3, 56, 58 n. 24, 134
   woman as 170
   of the Word 47, 94, 119
modern Protestant theology 19, 20, 20 n. 1, 29
monastic orders 138, 162, 165, 177, 179
motherhood. *See* maternity
mystery 30, 33, 56, 119, 158, 161
mythology 16, 62–9, 71–6, 81, 88–9, 93–4

National Socialism 40–3, 44 n. 15, 62–3, 63 n. 2, 76, 81, 89–90, 164 n. 15
natural theology 12 n. 8, 16–17, 37, 43 n. 14, 44–6, 62–3, 68, 77, 81, 86 n. 3, 119–20, 139, 144 n. 16, 150, 160–1, 163, 164 n. 14, 174
Nietzsche, Friedrich 133–4, 138, 165

obedience
   of Christ 32, 118 n. 6, 126 n. 10
   divine command 15, 34–5, 46, 48, 61, 62, 111, 149, 154, 155, 159, 160
   right hearing of 28, 29, 32, 33
1 Corinthians 6 140–1
1 Corinthians 7 154, 155, 163
1 Corinthians 11 101, 102, 140, 142, 143 n. 15, 159
1 Corinthians 14:34 34, 41, 101, 111, 159
order
   binaries 2–8, 12 n. 8, 14–15, 132 n. 13, 140, 160, 162, 174, 175, 180
   dyads 12, 114, 130, 131, 132 n. 13, 114, 145, 162 n. 13, 165, 175, 176–7, 179
   origination 4, 4 n. 3, 6, 7 n. 4, 95, 101–3, 129–30
   patterns of 2–8, 114, 117 n. 5, 127 n. 12, 175–6

   sequence 3 n. 2, 4, 5 n. 3, 7 n. 4, 75 n. 16, 95, 104–5, 129–30, 165–8, 171
orders of creation 16, 37–47, 57 n. 22, 65, 74, 81, 83, 164 n. 15

patriarchal 87, 90, 130
patrilineal genealogies 81, 107, 140
Paul
   on celibacy 140, 154–5, 177–8
   unmarried state of 86, 140, 155, 178
philosophy
   mythology 67–9, 68 n. 10, 88–9
   theology 20–3, 44 n. 16
prophetic witness 24, 25, 73, 90, 98, 107, 108, 109
prophets 35, 42 n. 9, 55, 107, 108

race 16, 39–42, 56, 58, 90, 164 n. 15, 180–1
reason 21–2, 27, 67, 71
relationship between the sexes 1–14, 76–80, 90–110, 137–44, 155–75, 177–80
   co-humanity 1, 12 n. 8, 132 n. 13, 157, 167 (*see under* fellowship)
   misery of 106–8, 169–71
   mutuality or reciprocity 2–4, 17, 101, 103–4, 106, 108, 110, 113–4, 117, 128, 131 n. 13, 138–9, 142–4, 176 (*see under* order)
religious experience 21, 27, 29, 30, 46
revelatory event
   acknowledgement of 27–30, 32–4, 91, 97, 99, 105
   Adam 97–9
   capacity for 9, 16, 19–20, 27–8, 32, 46, 62, 68, 75–7, 92–4, 98, 118
   confession of 32, 33, 61–2, 69, 72, 80, 89, 91, 98–9, 102–3, 106, 108, 110–11
   Elizabeth and Zechariah 32–4
   experience of 20–1, 26–30, 105
   history 20, 25–7, 27 n. 5 (*see also under* history)
   knowledge of 9, 23–30, 32, 97–8
   language 24, 77, 32, 80
   Mary 32–4
   media of 24, 33, 37, 46–7, 57–8, 61, 80, 94, 96, 137, 152–3, 160, 173
   neighbor as 51–4, 59

objectivity 20, 21, 23, 26, 28, 47
promise 25, 33–4, 48, 69, 93, 96, 103, 107, 111

sacrament 41, 52, 53, 53 n. 21, 56, 57, 73, 96
   baptism 41–2, 53 n. 21, 56
Schleiermacher, Friedrich 20–2, 26, 32 n. 6, 68, 89 n. 6
Scripture
   authorial voices 16, 20, 27, 35, 54, 55, 64, 57, 67, 69, 73, 80, 91, 109
   biblical narratives 49, 54, 64, 65 n. 4, 67, 71–4, 97, 112
   figural reading 16–17, 51, 61, 65 n. 4, 67, 73 n. 14, 88, 91–2, 94, 102–3, 106–10, 152, 154
   imagination 68, 71–2, 130
   literal meaning 64, 65 n. 4, 73
   plain sense 73 n. 13, 73 n. 14, 91, 103
   saga 67, 71–5
self-assertion 134, 136, 159, 160, 169, 172
self-awareness 21, 29, 56, 59
self-determination 27–30, 59, 93, 97, 119
self-disclosure 35, 72, 110, 124, 135, 14
self-discovery 46, 48
self-justification 45–50, 55, 56, 58 n. 23, 135
self-knowledge 22, 24, 46, 47, 48, 119
self-love 47, 62, 110, 163
self-reflection 17, 30, 46, 118, 176, 180
self-sufficiency 20, 70, 137, 163
sexism 1, 10, 126 n. 10, 144, 175–7, 180

silence 34, 41, 108, 110, 159, 172, 177. *See also* Eve; I Corinthians 14:34
Song of Songs 77 n. 17, 86, 88, 101, 106, 108–10, 113, 139, 142

theological method 19, 23, 31, 38 n. 1, 73, 130, 150–3
   christocentric 6, 7, 8, 9, 11–12, 15, 17, 23, 63, 69, 79, 88, 115, 115 n. 4, 118–20, 132 n. 13, 140, 150, 154, 155, 176, 178, 179
   doctrine of the Trinity 10–11, 115 n. 4
Trinity
   doctrine of 2–7, 10–13, 78–9, 84–5, 114 n. 3, 115–17
   incarnate Word 70, 120–2, 125–8, 132 n. 13
   mutuality or reciprocity 3–4, 3 n. 2, 13, 79, 125
   perichoresis 3–4

Vischer, Wilhelm 76 n. 17, 78 n. 19, 78 n. 20
von Kirschbaum, Charlotte 13 n. 9, 43, 66, 66 n. 5, 66 n. 7, 78 n. 20, 145 n. 17
von Rad, Gerhard 62 n. 1, 72 n. 12
vulnerability 15, 18, 100, 135, 176, 180, 181

woman. *See also* under feminine
   dignity of 3, 107, 112, 126 n. 10, 166–7
   humanity of 3, 83, 112, 145, 176

www.ingramcontent.com/pod-product-compliance
Lightning Source LLC
Chambersburg PA
CBHW052044300426
44117CB00012B/1964